GLOBAL EUROPE

GLOBAL EUROPE

The European Union in World Affairs

Christopher Piening

LYNNE
RIENNER
PUBLISHERS

BOULDER
LONDON

To Claude and Jenny

Published in the United States of America in 1997 by
Lynne Rienner Publishers, Inc.
1800 30th Street, Boulder, Colorado 80301

and in the United Kingdom by
Lynne Rienner Publishers, Inc.
3 Henrietta Street, Covent Garden, London WC2E 8LU

Library of Congress Cataloging-in-Publication Data
Piening, Christopher, 1945–
  Global Europe : the European Union in world affairs / Christopher
Piening.
    Includes bibliographical references and index.
    ISBN 1-55587-694-3 (hc : alk. paper)
    ISBN 1-55587-700-1 (pbk. : alk. paper)
    1. European Union countries—Foreign relations. 2. European
Union. I. Title.
D1058.P54   1997
327.4—dc21   97-43
                                                                        CIP

British Cataloguing in Publication Data
A Cataloguing in Publication record for this book
is available from the British Library.

Printed and bound in the United States of America

      The paper used in this publication meets the requirements
 ∞   of the American National Standard for Permanence of
      Paper for Printed Library Materials Z39.48-1984.

    5 4 3 2 1

Contents

Tables and Figures

Tables

Figures

Foreword

The European Union is the world's foremost trading power, its biggest investor, its most important donor of development and humanitarian aid. It constitutes the planet's single largest market, has a GNP larger than that of the United States, and its population—370 million people—puts it in third place after China and India. Yet the EU's image abroad does not always reflect the impact it has. Both in Europe itself and further afield, it is the individual member states that still often occupy center stage. The EU's international role and influence as an entity rather than a collection of nation-states still frequently goes unacknowledged.

Here is a book that aims to show the European Union for what it has increasingly come to be: a world power in its own right—not a superpower in the old Cold War sense of the term, but an economic power whose activities have come to have a significant effect around the globe. *Global Europe* (as the book is fittingly entitled) examines the European Union's role as partner, trader, competitor, benefactor, investor, and paradigm for countries and emerging regional groupings throughout the world. At the same time, it demystifies the mechanics of the EU's international role, in particular by shedding light on the operations of the common trade policy, development policy, and the still evolving foreign and security policy, the three central planks of the EU's external activities.

I welcome the appearance of this book, which succeeds in providing in a single volume a succinct and readable overview of the European Union's worldwide role at the end of the twentieth century. I have no doubt that it will fill a significant gap in the growing literature on the EU and its activities, not only in Europe but internationally as well.

Klaus Hänsch
President of the European Parliament, 1994–1997

Acknowledgments

I always enjoy reading the acknowledgments at the beginning of what I know is going to be a dull if worthy book. If nothing else, they give authors the chance to get personal, to prove they're real human beings who actually know other human beings, and are not just turgid specialists obsessed with Antarctic fungi or the Common Foreign and Security Policy of the European Union.

Here I offer a few acknowledgments of my own. Most of this book was written in Seattle during time I spent at the University of Washington lecturing, teaching, and researching. My first thanks must go to the many colleagues and friends in the Jackson School of International Studies, whose often unwitting support provided an environment that made writing a book seem an obvious thing to do. More generally, I would like to thank all those at the European Parliament who made it possible for me to take the time to pursue my research in Seattle as an EU Fellow.

Katherine Kittel, associate director of the Center for West European Studies, was always there to offer a laconic word of encouragement, and John Keeler, the center's director, quickly taught me that *nothing,* not even writing a book or teaching students, is as important as an afternoon in the Kingdome watching Randy Johnson, Ken Griffey Jr., Edgar Martinez, and the other Mariners greats knocking the socks off the Sox. Jim Caporaso knew a thing or two about cooking a great dinner, and Carolyn Scheve knew all about eating one. (Jim, to his credit, also knew a great publisher!) Joe Jupille knew more about the minutiae of Europe than I did, and Sheila Nair offered her insights on Asia. I can't say that any of these people (except maybe Joe, who contributed the information about the EC-U.S. beef hormone dispute) actually provided much advice on writing the book, but without them it wouldn't have been written.

I finished the book in Brussels. I must thank the numerous colleagues there who read sections of my manuscript and offered their comments and suggestions. Two who rate special mention are Alberto Rodas, whose detailed criticisms of my chapter on Latin America helped eliminate some fairly gross errors, and Mike Shackleton, who wised me up to an error of judgment that I would otherwise have persisted with and that might have landed me in some fairly deep trouble. Vera Jordan deserves an honorable mention for her help with the illustrations in the book.

But at the end of it all, what's a manuscript without a publisher? So to conclude, I'd like to say a personal and very warm thank-you to Lynne Rienner, who not only thought the project worth doing, but—through a process of subtle yet constant encouragement—kept me believing it was *me* doing *her* a favor in getting the book written.

—*C. P.*

Introduction

The purpose of this book is to show how and why the European Union (EU) has come to assume the status of an emerging global power. Its focus is on the practical, political, and economic consequences that have resulted from the EU's becoming an internationally significant actor; and if it contains a little speculation here and there, it steers well clear of the minefield of foreign policy or integration theory. Because it attempts to cover Europe's relations with the entire world in just nine chapters, it looks more at the big picture than at the minutiae of individual issues or relationships: whole volumes, after all, have been written just about the EU's relations with the United States or the developing world, and even they have not always been comprehensive. What this book seeks to do instead is substitute breadth for depth and provide an overview of the growth of the EU's external relations over the forty-odd years of the EU's existence. The aim is to show something of the complexity of the web of formal and informal ties that now link the EU with all but half a dozen of the world's countries—and to explain how and why those ties were forged.

To begin with, and to avoid confusion later, a word about terminology. In November 1993, upon the entry into force of the Maastricht Treaty, the European Community (EC) became the European Union. Since the events described in these pages cover the pre- and post-Maastricht periods, it seemed only proper in writing this book to use the term "European Community" when referring to events in the past and "European Union" in describing post-1993 occurrences or speculating about the future. Sometimes, as the reader will discover, the distinction is hard to draw, or drawing it leads to the use of both terms in a single sentence.

What I have not attempted, however, is to differentiate between "European Communities" (plural) and "European Community" (singular), unless there is some specific reason for doing so. Today "European Community" refers, strictly speaking, to what used to be the European *Economic* Community (EEC), now renamed by the Maastricht Treaty. But even

1

before the Maastricht Treaty, the trend had been to abandon the technically correct use of "communities" in describing the generic entity composed of the European Coal and Steel Community (ECSC), the EEC, and the European Atomic Energy Community (EAEC, or Euratom) in favor of the simpler "community." That is the approach I have used in this book.

The European Union of today started life in the 1950s as a series of three treaties that between 1951 and 1957 established the ECSC, the EEC, and Euratom. The treaties and the communities they created were aimed at bringing economic and political stability to a Europe that for the second time in a half-century had emerged from a ruinous war that had destroyed livelihoods, economies, political and physical infrastructures, and a great deal more besides.

The EC had no particular ambition to be or become a world power. Even its most farsighted initiators probably had little inkling that their creation might one day have an impact that went far beyond its borders. Their concern was in building a European structure that would promote peace and prosperity between and among its members. The coal and steel community brought into being by the first European treaty was conceived not least as a mechanism to make future conflict between France and Germany impossible: if these two vital resources were under joint administration, no individual member would be able to control the means to wage war. The subsequent treaties, and particularly the EEC Treaty, put in place a series of common policies whose objectives were the promotion of economic prosperity.

Anyone who in 1957 tried to envisage what the EC might be like by the end of the century would inevitably have concluded that a highly integrated Europe would indeed have implications for the rest of the world. After all, the preamble to the EEC Treaty spoke of contributing, through the Common Commercial Policy, "to the progressive abolition of restrictions on international trade" and confirmed (in rather quaint language) "the solidarity which binds Europe and the overseas countries;" and the body of the Treaty included provisions on how agreements with foreign states or international organizations should be negotiated and what form they could take (Articles 113, 228, and 238). But few of the pioneers of the 1950s were particularly prone to futurism; they had their hands full making their invention work in the present. Students of the first difficult decade of the existence of the EC will recall that those years were fraught with problems, both technical and political. French president Charles de Gaulle, with his rejection of the first enlargement attempts and his insistence on the preeminence of the national interest, brought the Community into its first major crises in the 1960s.

Nevertheless, and in some ways in spite of itself and its declared objectives, the EC would never be an inward-looking organization. Because three of its founding six members were colonial powers in the 1950s, other, non-European territories were linked to the emerging European entity from its very beginning. The EU's intricate and far-reaching development and cooperation policies of the present—especially the Lomé convention between the Union and the seventy African, Caribbean, and Pacific (ACP) states—have their origins in the earliest stages of the EU's evolution. The first development agreement between the Six and the mostly francophone ex-colonies of France, Belgium, and the Netherlands was concluded in 1963 in the form of the Yaoundé convention. In 1961 and 1963 the EC negotiated association agreements under Article 238 of the EEC Treaty with two of its Mediterranean neighbors, Greece and Turkey—and this within just five years of the Treaty's entry into force.

It was trade, however, that always made it inevitable that the EC would have an impact beyond its borders. The EEC Treaty set up a customs union among its six member states that came into full effect in 1968. All goods entering any Community country were subject to a common customs tariff (CCT), and the size of this tariff was determined in Brussels, not in the national capitals. Similarly, import quotas for certain goods were fixed jointly and applied Community-wide. Exporting countries wishing to sell to any of the EC's individual member states had to negotiate with the Commission in Brussels if they sought special conditions or preferences; they could no longer make separate deals with Paris or Rome or Bonn. With the creation of this customs union, the EC became an entity with which countries everywhere had to talk directly, and since the Community's member states provided markets for virtually every country in the world, that meant that no country was able to ignore the EC's arrival on the international scene.

In the early years, therefore, the Community was of *general* interest as a trading partner to countries everywhere and of *specific* interest to the developing and associated countries the EC had agreed to help through the conclusion of collective or individual agreements. Nevertheless, the EC's impact on the world at large was limited in the late 1950s and throughout the 1960s by the simple fact that at the time it comprised only six countries, whose combined economies, while significant, had not yet assumed the size and importance that would come later.

But as the Community grew, so did its importance and the scope of its external relations. By 1975, two years after the first enlargement, which saw the Six expand to Nine (with the accession of the United Kingdom, Denmark, and Ireland), the Community had already established formal relations with forty-six African, Caribbean, and Pacific countries under the Lomé agreement and had signed association agreements with Greece, Turkey, Malta, and Cyprus; cooperation agreements with Morocco, Tunisia, Algeria, Egypt, and Lebanon; preferential trade agreements with Spain and Israel; and free trade agreements with those European Free Trade Association (EFTA) countries (Austria, Finland, Iceland, Norway, Portugal, Sweden, and Switzerland) that had not followed Britain into the

EC. In numerical terms, the European Community was now linked to over 40 percent of the entire membership of the United Nations through association, cooperation, or trade agreements.

Thanks mainly to the addition of the United Kingdom, the Community of Nine had collectively become the world's largest trading bloc, accounting for about 20 percent of total world trade.[1] While this was indeed a collective total, it was more than just symbolic, since the common external tariff meant in a real sense that countries that wished to sell to any member state of the EC had to accept the tariffs and quotas that had been jointly agreed in Brussels. If the EC's own member states wanted exemptions (for example, a reduced quota on the import of certain products that might have upset their markets), they needed authorization from the Commission in Brussels; they could not negotiate such quotas independently with third countries.

By the mid-1970s, therefore, the EC had become an actor of some weight on the international trading scene. Since then, because of internal and external developments, that weight has continued to grow. Successive enlargements have brought the Community from nine member states in 1973 to fifteen today. The total gross national product (GNP) of today's European Union exceeds that of the United States by almost 15 percent. The Single European Act (SEA) of 1986 turned the territory of the Union into one vast internal market, as attractive to outsiders as it is to domestic producers. For the world's traders, the EU has become a land of opportunity on par with the United States or Japan, though one often easier to do business with due to the myriad bilateral agreements concluded over the years between Brussels and third countries. It has also become important as a trade negotiator, most notably in successive General Agreement on Tariffs and Trade (GATT) rounds, where the Commission negotiates on behalf of all the Union's member states. Indeed, GATT (now the World Trade Organization, or WTO) is just one of the numerous international organizations, including the UN and its agencies, in which the European Union plays a distinct role, either in place of or alongside the individual member states.

Over the years the EU's political impact has expanded, too, in part as a corollary to its growing significance as an economic and trading power, in part the result of conscious choices to add a foreign policy dimension to its activities. Since the mid-1980s the EU has been particularly active in its external relations. It has developed a new and intensified relationship with Latin America, due in part to Spanish and Portuguese accession but also to the fundamental political changes that have taken place in Central and South America. The momentous events in Central and Eastern Europe have involved the EU as never before in responding to events in its own backyard. And when other countries and regions became concerned that the EU was obsessed with its European neighbors to the exclusion of the wider world, Brussels launched a series of initiatives in 1994 and 1995 aimed at reinforcing ties with the Mediterranean and, farther afield, the Asian continent.

Many countries, as we have seen, became involved with the EC through contractual arrangements in the 1960s and 1970s. During this same period, however, numerous other countries as well had come to recognize that their interests dictated closer links to the EC. The United States, always a supporter of European integration efforts, had accredited an ambassador to the original coal and steel community as early as 1954. Although to this day the EU and the United States have no formal institutional ties, their relations have always been extremely close. The same is true of Canada, with which the Community concluded a unique framework agreement in 1976, an accord more notable for what it doesn't regulate than for what it does. Frequent if irregular meetings at the ministerial level took place between the governments of the two northern American countries and the EC, represented on the European side by both the Commission and the EC presidency. Sometimes such meetings were held to deal with specific trade disputes, but sometimes they had less formal agendas. In 1972 the U.S. House of Representatives initiated a series of interparliamentary meetings with the then still nonelected European Parliament (EP), which has continued without interruption on a twice-yearly basis ever since. The Canadian parliament established a similar relationship with the EP a year later, in 1973, inaugurating annual interparliamentary meetings. As the EC grew in importance and size in the 1980s, so transatlantic contacts intensified. Nevertheless, notwithstanding two transatlantic declarations concluded in November 1990 between the EC and the United States and Canada, no formal, legally binding global agreements regulating these relationships have been entered into. Even the New Transatlantic Agenda (NTA) and the EU-U.S. Joint Action Plan of December 1995 stop short of institutionalizing relations between the two sides.

The same nonrelationship applies to Japan, the EU's second most important overseas trading partner.[2] As commercial exchanges between the two sides grew throughout the 1970s and 1980s, and in particular as Japan's trade surplus with the EC became an increasing cause for concern, contacts became ever more frequent. These took the form of ministerial-level meetings, usually between the Japanese Ministry of International Trade and Industry (MITI) and the Commission. Over the years, numerous sectoral agreements regulating aspects of bilateral trade were concluded.[3] Bilateral (EC-Japan) diplomatic representations were set up by each side in Tokyo and Brussels. In spite of all this, no global agreement regulating bilateral relations exists. In 1991 the EC and Japan signed a declaration similar in form and content to the declarations with the United States and Canada; it provides for regular ministerial meetings and an annual encounter between the Japanese prime minister and the presidents of the Commission and Council. The Japanese Diet and the EP have held annual interparliamentary conferences since 1979.

Two other countries with no contractual links to the Community were Australia and New Zealand. Both had depended heavily on their trade with Britain (particularly their agricultural exports) and were thus significantly affected by the UK's accession to the Community in 1973. Despite a number of concessions agreed by the Six during enlargement negotiations, both countries were faced with an end to their special access to the British market. While various sectoral agreements were reached between these countries and Brussels over the years in areas ranging from quotas for New Zealand butter imports to trade in kangaroo products, there were no global accords between the two sides. Australia and New Zealand have turned increasingly to their Asian neighbors, successfully developing their product palettes to fit regional rather than European tastes—a rare example of how European integration has resulted in the weakening rather than the strengthening of a traditional relationship. It was only in 1996 that the Commission finally began to negotiate framework agreements with the two countries.

The Community has developed and intensified its relations with much of the rest of Asia, however. A global accord, in the form of a cooperation agreement, was signed in 1980 between the Nine and the Association of Southeast Asian Nations (ASEAN). The five original ASEAN members (Indonesia, Malaysia, the Philippines, Singapore, and Thailand) were then on the brink of major economic expansion and were, in the late 1970s, considering how to push forward their own plans for closer regional cooperation and integration. The cooperation agreement with the EC was both practical and political in intent, establishing rules covering trade, investment, market-opening measures, business cooperation, and regular consultations in the form of ministerial meetings. With the exception of the Yaoundé and Lomé conventions with the ACP countries, it was the first agreement the EC entered into with a group of countries rather than a single partner. In parallel with the agreement, a parliamentary dimension was added through the establishment of an institutionalized dialogue between the EP and the ASEAN Interparliamentary Organization (AIPO). The original EC-ASEAN agreement still stands: attempts in the late 1980s and early 1990s to renew and expand it fell afoul of Portuguese pressure on its EC partners to await a solution to the problem of East Timor. The unity of the Community's approach to ASEAN, involving a single agreement covering all the association's members, was undermined in 1996 by the conclusion of a bilateral cooperation agreement between the EU and ASEAN's newest member, Vietnam. Nevertheless, cooperation with the region as a whole has remained close and received new impetus in 1994 with the publication of a Commission strategy paper on relations with Asia and a Euro-Asian summit held in Bangkok in March 1996.

As for the rest of East and South Asia, only Myanmar (formerly Burma), Afghanistan, and North Korea are not linked to the EU through formal arrangements of one kind or another and are not about to be. In December 1996, the Commission concluded cooperation agreements with Cambodia and Laos. South Korea, for all its importance to the EU as a trading partner, had no formal ties with Brussels until 1996, when a cooperation agreement was finally signed. By contrast, the European Union's formal relations with China date back as far as 1978, and the trade agreement signed then was replaced by a more ambitious trade and economic cooperation accord in 1984. China has a separate mission in Brussels accredited to the European Union (many countries still use a single embassy and ambassador to handle both their bilateral relations with Belgium and their relations with the EU). China's links to the European Union have frequently been upset because of the European Parliament's repeated condemnations of Chinese policy and actions concerning human rights as well as pressure by the EP on the other EU institutions to make their dealings with Beijing contingent on Chinese concessions in human rights.

The developing countries of South and Southeast Asia, like those of Latin America, were never included in the EC's showpiece Lomé convention, which covered only the African, Caribbean, and Pacific states. Instead, the Indian subcontinent became linked to the EU through numerous individual bilateral agreements, all with emphasis on development needs, dating back in the case of India to 1973. More recently, a new generation of comprehensive cooperation, partnership, and development accords has been concluded with India, Sri Lanka, and Nepal; a similar accord with Pakistan was due to be concluded in early 1997.

The EC began concluding bilateral trade agreements of various types with several Latin American countries as long ago as 1974.[4] However, following the accession of Spain and Portugal to the Community in 1986, relations intensified and multilateral cooperation agreements between the Twelve and two Latin American regional groupings, the Andean Pact and the Central American Common Market (CACM),[5] were concluded in 1983 and 1987. On the political level, the European Union and Central and South America hold annual ministerial meetings in the framework of the San José and Rio Groups. The European Union and Mercosur[6] concluded a far-reaching interregional framework agreement in December 1995, the first such accord between two customs unions and designed to lead ultimately to a free trade arrangement between the two groups.

The Lomé convention, originally signed in 1975 between the Nine and forty-six ACP states, has since been renewed three times and by 1996 included seventy developing countries. Lomé provides virtually all products originating in the ACP countries with tariff- and quota-free entry to the EU market. But it offers more than just nonreciprocal trade concessions: it includes a substantial development aid component of ECU 12 billion[7] (U.S.$15.2 billion) for the first five years of the current convention (1990–1994) and a further ECU 14.625 billion (U.S.$18.3 billion) until the end of the twentieth century; it also establishes a unique mechanism to provide a price floor for the ACP countries' key exports regardless of fluctuations in world commodity prices (the Stabex scheme). The current fourth convention runs until the year 2000 and, while providing continuity with respect to its predecessors, places new emphasis on human rights protection, the environment, regional cooperation, and sustained development.

In some ways the most remarkable recent development, and one that could not have been foreseen in the Community's early years, has been the expansion of relations with the former Soviet Union and its Central and Eastern European satellites. Beginning with the recognition by the Council for Mutual Economic Assistance (CMEA or Comecon) of the European Community in 1988, ties have proliferated at a breathtaking pace. From virtually none[8] in 1988, there are now association (or Europe) agreements in force or signed with all the countries of Central and Eastern Europe,[9] the Baltic states, and Slovenia; and partnership and cooperation accords with Russia, Ukraine, Belarus, and all the other former Soviet republics except for Tajikistan and Turkmenistan. To the political and trade relations created by these agreements the EU has added considerable financial aid and investment through the Poland and Hungary: Aid for Reconstruction of the Economy (PHARE) and Technical Assistance to the Commonwealth of Independent States (TACIS) programs, along with a wealth of other assistance (in the form of know-how, training, transfers of technology, etc.). All the Central and Eastern European countries now want to take their relationships with the EU to their logical conclusions and have accordingly applied for membership.

The other region in the EU's immediate geographical neighborhood, the Mediterranean basin, has also developed an increasingly close relationship with the Union. The Community concluded its first agreements with the southern Mediterranean countries in the 1960s, and in the 1970s it negotiated trade and cooperation accords with all the Maghreb (western Arab) and Mashreq (eastern Arab) states. All of these included financial protocols offering loans and grants to aid development of infrastructures. Israel benefited from a trade agreement signed in 1975 allowing tariff-free entry to the EC market for its industrial products and preferential access for its agricultural exports. In the mid-1990s, Mediterranean association agreements were worked out between the EU and most of its southern and eastern Mediterranean neighbors. The 1995 Euro-Mediterranean conference in Barcelona confirmed the wish of almost every riparian state, including Israel and the new Palestinian entity, to cooperate with one another and to benefit from their proximity to the EU. These benefits are not merely economic but more and more often political in nature. For example, the EU is the major donor of aid and technical assistance to the

Palestinians, helping them to function in their first steps toward autonomy, supervising their first free elections, and mediating in their dealings with the Israelis.

The chapters that follow explore all these relationships and others, which form the basis for an intricate web of external relations the EU has built up over forty years. On the face of it, these relations are primarily economic and commercial in character. But the distinctions between external relations governed by *commercial* policy and foreign relations inspired by *foreign* policy have become increasingly fuzzy. The logic of the EU's common customs tariff implies a need to organize and regulate commercial relationships with countries outside the Union. To the extent that such relationships flow from the treaties, their conclusion as contractual links and formal agreements is more or less inevitable and is the bread and butter of the EU's external relations. Foreign policy, in contrast, involves deliberate choices usually separate from whatever legal obligations may arise out of the existence of the CCT, the internal market, or other common policies whose effects on third countries need to be confronted.

It can be argued, then, that the Community's relationship to the developing world, and particularly the ACP states, has always been a genuine act of *foreign* policy. It was a deliberate choice of the original Six to make special provisions for the possessions and colonies, former and present, of the member states, a choice confirmed after the 1973 enlargement. The inventiveness of the Yaoundé and Lomé conventions in creating a novel form of cooperation between a group of developed and developing countries bears all the hallmarks of foreign policy, not mere commercial expediency. In the same way, current EU involvement in Central and Eastern Europe and the Mediterranean entails deliberate choices. While these do contain an element of economic self-interest, there is more at stake than imports and exports. The security dimension is of key importance, as are considerations as varied as immigration, terrorism, drug smuggling, and pollution control—all the stuff of foreign policy in the real sense of the term.

It took the newly formed Community a few years before it felt the need to start tackling this dimension of its operations (development policy excepted), in part because the original treaties studiously avoided the issue of foreign policy, which was believed to be the sole responsibility of the individual member states. But external (i.e., foreign trade) relations, which the Community soon found itself involved in, quickly proved to have a political dimension. For the purposes of this book, it is an academic point whether the EC/EU's activities and impact beyond its borders should be characterized as external relations, foreign relations, or even foreign economic relations (a concept used by political theorists John Ikenberry and others).[10] In 1970 the EC itself invented a term, "European Political Cooperation" (EPC), that for the next twenty-three years was used to describe the process of diplomatic coordination and consultation between the foreign ministries of the member states aimed at arriving at common positions on foreign policy questions. EPC, informal at first, was institutionalized by the 1986 Single European Act and finally replaced in 1993 by the Common Foreign and Security Policy (CFSP) established by the Maastricht Treaty.

The mechanics of foreign policy cooperation are discussed in more depth in Chapter 2. But against the background of the structural framework of the EU's relations with the rest of the world as outlined in this introduction, it is worth recalling here some of the areas in which the Community/Union has acted or had an effect and that do not involve strictly economic or commercial criteria. The examples that could be given are many, and there is occasion enough later in these pages to discuss others and examine some in detail. They are, however, all instances of external actions of the EC that can best be defined as foreign policy rather than foreign *economic* policy, and that involved a response via the EPC or CFSP mechanisms, not the conventional Community machinery.

The Community was unanimous in condemning Turkey for its part in the invasion and occupation of Cyprus in 1974 (although it did not freeze Turkey's association agreement, as it had done with Greece after the coup that overthrew the democratic government there in 1967). During the British confrontation with Argentina over the Falkland/Malvinas Islands in 1982, the EC publicly supported the UK's position, despite the historical ties of some of its members (especially Italy) with Argentina. Later the Community adopted joint approaches in dealing with issues such as the Soviet intervention in Afghanistan, the apartheid regime in South Africa, the Middle East peace process, the Iraqi invasion of Kuwait, the Iranian *fatwa* on Salman Rushdie, and the Chinese repression of the Tiananmen Square demonstrations.

Incurring the displeasure of the European Community over such incidents means more than simply receiving a formal dressing down in a diplomatic *note verbale* or by the foreign minister or ambassador representing the EC presidency: it can lead to a disruption of economic links and cost the offending country dearly in financial terms. Israel noticed this after the EC delayed implementation of a new financial protocol in 1987 because of Israel's hindrance of Palestinian citrus exports (on this particular occasion, the EC acted at the prompting of one of its institutions, the European Parliament, which refused to ratify the protocol in question). Turkey's aspirations to move closer to the EU, and eventually to join it, have been thwarted for over two decades by the Community's dissatisfaction with Turkey's behavior toward Cyprus, its suppression of its Kurdish minority, and its human rights record in general.

Over the past decade, developments in Europe have occupied much of the Community's attention. Its responses have been shaped by a combination of economic and political considerations. The conclusion of the Single

European Act led to a decision to expand the internal market to include the EFTA states, with whom free trade already existed. This led to the creation of the European Economic Area (EEA), which added to free trade most of the other freedoms associated with the internal market: free movement of people, capital, and services. But it was the events following the end of the Communist regimes in Central and Eastern Europe and the Soviet Union that caused the Community to devise a whole raft of policies to deal with the new situation. These responses were not merely economic but eminently *political* in intent and character. Financial aid was only part of the story; help in kind and in know-how was meant to smooth the transition to democracy and market economics; humanitarian aid during the first two winters following the Soviet collapse helped provide relief for millions of people suffering from the effects of food and fuel shortages; and the PHARE and TACIS programs established a basis for longer-term planning for economic restructuring, considered a prerequisite for stability to be restored to the region. In one of the first joint actions under the new CFSP, the EU helped to organize and oversee Russia's first parliamentary elections in December 1993 (an exercise it was to repeat in South Africa six months later). Finally, the EU played a major role in the search for peace in the former Yugoslavia: if it failed in its goals, it was not through want of political investment in the cause but because of its lack of institutional machinery and physical capability to make intervention successful and because of the complexity of the situation.

The activities and events outlined in this introduction show just how wide-ranging the EU's international role has become, both geographically and substantively. The chapters that follow add flesh to the bare bones laid out here. They show that the Union's presence beyond its own borders has become ubiquitous. Although often unplanned, at least in any strategic sense, Europe's involvement in the wider world has grown at a pace that was certainly unanticipated. Indeed, the speed of that growth constitutes something of a problem for anyone attempting to chronicle or comment on the development of Europe's role in world affairs: like many books on the European Union, this one, too, is likely to find itself overtaken by events before the ink on its pages is dry.

Finally, a word on structure: this book could have been constructed in any one of several ways. Perhaps the most obvious would have been to examine the EU's external role in functional terms, looking at its activities in trade, development, foreign investment, economic cooperation, foreign policy, security, and so on. Such an approach would have permitted a comparative analysis of each field of action and made possible a comprehensive overview of the relative effects and impacts of different policies in a range of political and geographical contexts. Another method would have been to consider the EU's relationships with different *types* of partners— the G7, the developing world, the newly industrialized countries, the former

Communist states, international organizations, and so on. This would have allowed an analysis on the basis of the nature of the countries concerned, irrespective of their location.

Instead, the book offers a geopolitical world tour, looking at the European Union's role virtually continent by continent. This seems to reflect best the *regional* nature of international cooperation and the EU's own tendency to view the world in a mostly regional way.[11] It also makes clear, as no other approach could, just how comprehensive and all-embracing the EU's involvement in today's world is. But most significant, viewing Europe's role region by region serves to highlight how difficult it often is to draw truly functional distinctions between different types of policy activity, as trade, investment, security, and ultimately foreign policy interests are often inextricably linked.

Notes

1. The percentage of world trade claimed by the EC of nine and today's Union of fifteen member states has remained more or less constant at about 20 percent, the result of the growth of other trading powers, particularly Japan, whose share has risen dramatically.

2. Overall Japan is actually the EU's third most important trading partner, with Switzerland beating it to second place (after the United States).

3. These included ad hoc voluntary export restraint agreements, agreements by Japan to reduce or remove nontariff barriers, market-opening measures, export-promotion schemes, and so on.

4. The first EC–Latin American agreement was a nonpreferential trade accord with Uruguay, which came into force on 1 August 1974; an economic and trade cooperation agreement was concluded with Mexico a year later, entering into force on 1 November 1975.

5. The Andean Pact is made up of Bolivia, Colombia, Ecuador, Peru, and Venezuela. The CACM consisted of Costa Rica, El Salvador, Guatemala, Honduras, and Nicaragua (it is now called SICA).

6. The Southern Cone Common Market, comprising Argentina, Brazil, Uruguay, and Paraguay.

7. The Community's budget is calculated in European currency units (ECUs), whose value is based on a basket of EU currencies. One ECU will equal one *euro*, the EU's new single currency, which it plans to introduce in 1999. The ECU-U.S. exchange rate fluctuates; the rate used throughout this book to calculate dollar equivalents is ECU 1 = $1.25, the approximate aggregate rate in 1996.

8. The EC had concluded formal agreements prior to 1988 only with Yugoslavia (1970 and 1980) and Romania (1980).

9. Hungary, Poland, the Czech Republic, Slovakia, Romania, and Bulgaria.

10. See, for example, J. Ikenberry, D. A. Lake, and M. Mastanduno (eds.), *The State and American Foreign Economic Policy* (Ithaca, NY: Cornell University Press, 1988).

11. As exemplified in the European Commission's operational division of its external relations services into three separate directorates-general (DG I, DG IA, and DG IB), which, together with their subordinated directorates, cover just such specific geographical areas.

1

European Union, World Trader

> The Community is a large and powerful trading bloc. Its foreign trade policy affects other countries' welfare as much as, if not more than, its own. Through trade diplomacy and as a participant in GATT, the Community plays a key role in the evolution of the international trading system.[1]

The European Economic Community was created to facilitate trade between its six member states through the establishment of a common market. Within its borders, trade in goods was to be free: there would be no tariffs, no restrictions, and no quotas. Article 10 of the EEC Treaty extended this principle to goods imported from outside the Community. This required setting in place a common external frontier toward the outside world; otherwise, imports from abroad would enter through whichever member state offered the lowest tariffs and then circulate freely to the others. So goods coming into the Community were subject to a common customs tariff: U.S. machinery or Asian textiles faced import conditions that were identical in all six countries. The EEC Treaty foresaw other trade policy instruments as well. Foremost among these was the Community's ability to conclude bilateral and regional trade and cooperation agreements to regulate commerce with specific partners.

As the Community grew, so did the size of the market it represented. Soon it became the biggest market in the world. The Single European Act's 1992 program turned the EC into what amounted to a frontier-free, unified economic area, making the territory of the twelve member states virtually equivalent in trade terms to a single country. Exporters everywhere had a vital interest in the size of the customs levies and the nature of the nontariff barriers (NTBs) their goods had to face on entering the EC. Customs duties and protective NTBs (quantitative limits, safety norms, health and hygiene standards, etc.) were and are fixed by the Union as a whole, not by the individual member states.

13

That being the case, it is not the member states' governments but the Commission, on behalf of the Union, that negotiates these conditions with its trading partners, either individually or in the framework of multilateral agreements.

Because all the world wanted to do business with the Community, the Community had no choice but to talk to the world. The world might have preferred to work out a deal with London or Rome, but that was not an option, even if most of its exports were bound for the British or Italian markets, say, rather than the French. The analogy is simple enough: you want to sell to California, you're subject to the trade rules of the United States; you want to export to Britain, it's EU trade law that applies. In these circumstances, countries around the world began to queue up outside the Commission's door in Brussels seeking to conclude special trade deals. And the Community, always subject to the rules of the General Agreement on Tariffs and Trade, would often oblige, with association agreements, preferential or nonpreferential trade or cooperation accords, or any of a number of other special arrangements.

It is axiomatic to say that trade and economic relations lie at the root of all foreign policy. Most relations between one state and another are ultimately dictated by economic interests. A nation's prosperity, more so today than ever before, depends on being able to sell the goods or commodities it produces. For this, access to as wide a market as possible, and to a market that offers a minimum of restrictions, is essential.

The European Community and its member states were therefore always just as interested in being able to penetrate foreign markets as they were in providing access to their own markets for foreign exporters. This is why the EC has always played a major role in trade liberalization efforts, particularly in the framework of the GATT. Article 229 of the EC Treaty made the Commission responsible for relations with the GATT, and though the EC was never a member of the agreement in its own right, the Commission always represented the Community's member states in the various GATT rounds of negotiations (as well as in dispute settlement panels and other GATT mechanisms). The European Union is today a member in its own right of the GATT successor, the World Trade Organization—in addition to, not instead of, the fifteen member states.

For all these reasons, the Community soon discovered that its external relations were not simply a sort of extra obligation that came with the responsibilities of strength; rather, they were an integral part of what the Community was. Having defined itself internally, it found it had defined itself externally as well. Just as no sovereign nation has been able to avoid the need for establishing relations with its neighbors and the rest of the world, so the European Community, albeit as a supranational entity, found itself confronting the same necessity. Moreover, the obligation to conduct its trade policy jointly brought the EC advantages of scale. For its smaller member states, the increased bargaining power that came with being part of a larger entity that enjoyed the respect of major partners like Japan or the United States was a bonus.

EU Trade: Some Facts and Figures

Volvos to Russia, Scotch whisky to Japan, Godiva chocolates to Brazil, Chanel perfumes to Canada, Armani suits to Singapore, Braun shavers to Zimbabwe, Airbus to China. And vice versa: Hyundai cars, Toshiba computers, Delmonte pineapples, Boeing aircraft, Stellenbosch wines, Anchor butter, textiles from India and Guatemala all heading for Europe. The EU buys and sells in enormous quantities. Traders throughout their history, the 370 million people of the EU have profited from the economic success of European integration and become voracious consumers and assiduous producers. In value terms, the Fifteen's (EU-15) total trade with the rest of the world (exports and imports, excluding trade between the member states themselves) amounted to ECU 1,112.2 billion ($1,390 billion)[2] in 1995. In relative terms, this figure constituted around 20 percent of the Union's GDP (ECU 5,775 billion) for the year. As a proportion of total world trade, the EU accounted for around 20 percent of exports and 18.5 percent of imports.[3]

The EU's biggest trading partners are the United States, EFTA (Switzerland, Norway, and Iceland), Japan, China, Russia, and the countries of Central and Eastern Europe (see Table 1.1). Switzerland alone accounts for around 9 percent of the EU's exports and 8 percent of its imports. Overall, the EU ran a relatively modest trade deficit with the rest of the world from 1990 to 1992 and showed a small surplus in 1993 (ECU 1.16 billion) and 1994 (ECU 3.18 billion); in 1995 this jumped to a more substantial ECU 23.4 billion ($29.25 billion). This fairly balanced trade performance over the medium term compares favorably with the chronic and significant merchandise trade deficit of the United States or the surplus of Japan. The bulk of Europe's trade is in industrial products and manufactured goods: in the mid-1990s over 85 percent of its exports and around 65 percent of its imports fell into this category. Other exports include food and beverages, raw materials, and fuel; other imports are mainly agricultural and other primary commodities, oil and gas, and raw materials. According to European Commission estimates, 12 million people in the European Union owe their jobs directly to exports to the rest of the world.

The Legal Bases for the Union's External Relations

The key to understanding how and why the Community became an international actor lies in the 1957 Treaty of Rome, which set up the European

Table 1.1   Main Trading Partners of the EU-15, 1995 (values in ECU billions)

Rank	Trading Partners	EU Imports	EU Exports	Total Volume	% of Total EU Trade
1	United States	103.6	100.9	204.5	18.4
2	Switzerland	43.8	51.0	94.8	8.5
3	Japan	54.3	32.9	87.2	7.9
4	Norway	25.4	17.3	43.7	3.9
5	China	26.3	14.6	40.9	3.7
6	Russia	21.9	16.1	38.0	3.4
7	Poland	12.2	15.1	27.3	2.5
8	South Korea	10.9	12.3	23.2	2.1
9	Hong Kong	7.2	15.8	23.0	2.1
10	Turkey	9.2	13.4	22.6	2.1
11	Brazil	10.8	11.3	22.1	2.0
12	Taiwan	11.8	10.1	21.9	2.0
13	Canada	11.7	10.1	21.8	2.0
14	Czech Republic	9.0	11.6	20.6	1.9
15	Singapore	8.8	10.9	19.7	1.8
16	Saudi Arabia	8.7	8.6	17.3	1.6
17	India	7.8	9.4	17.2	1.6
18	Malaysia	9.1	7.9	17.0	1.6
19	Hungary	7.6	8.7	16.3	1.5
20	South Africa	7.7	8.5	16.2	1.5
21	Australia	5.0	10.5	15.5	1.4
22	Thailand	6.6	8.5	15.1	1.4
23	Israel	4.7	9.7	14.4	1.3
24	Indonesia	6.1	5.8	11.9	1.1
25	Algeria	6.0	4.7	10.7	1.0
26	Slovenia	4.2	5.2	9.4	0.9
27	Iran	5.4	3.4	8.8	0.8
28	Morocco	4.0	4.7	8.7	0.8
29	Argentina	3.7	4.5	8.2	0.7
30	Libya	5.8	2.3	8.1	0.7
(1)	NAFTA	118.5	115.5	234.0	21.0
(5)	ASEAN	36.7	34.5	71.2	6.4
(6)	CIS	25.3	20.8	46.1	4.1
(10)	ACP	19.8	17.4	37.2	3.3
(11)	Mercosur	15.0	16.6	31.6	2.8

Source: Eurostat

Economic Community. The EEC Treaty (renamed the European Community Treaty by the Maastricht Treaty in 1992 and referred to as such in these pages) laid the foundations for the "common market," which was to come into effect after a transitional period of twelve years (although a customs union was set up, a true common market, in which not only goods and agricultural produce but also people, capital, and services like banking or insurance could circulate freely, really came into being only with the advent of the 1992 single market, twenty-two years later than originally scheduled). The EC Treaty also established a Common Commercial Policy (for "commercial," read "trade"). "By establishing a customs union between themselves," the key Article 110 begins, "the Member States aim to contribute, in the common interest, to the harmonious development of world trade, the progressive abolition of restrictions on international trade and the lowering of customs barriers." Article 113 spells out how and on what basis the CCP is to be implemented, and Article 228 lays down the institutional and other details for negotiating agreements with individual states or international organizations. (The key EC Treaty articles relating to the Common Commercial Policy are reproduced in Appendix 1.)

Two more Treaty articles are important in providing legal bases for concluding agreements with other countries. The first is Article 238, which gives the Community the right to "conclude with one or more States or international organizations agreements establishing an *association* involving reciprocal rights and obligations, common action and special procedures" (emphasis added). The other is Article 235, a carte blanche that comes in useful not only in the field of external relations but in other aspects of the Community's work as well. It reads: "If action by the Community should prove necessary to attain, in the course of the operation of the common market, one of the objectives of the Community and this Treaty has not provided the necessary powers, the Council shall, acting unanimously on a proposal from the Commission and after consulting the European Parliament, take the appropriate measures."

It is on the basis of these Treaty articles that the Community entered into the numerous accords that now link it with more than 95 percent of the countries of the world. Article 113, together with Article 235, allows the conclusion of trade and cooperation agreements; Article 238 provides the basis for association agreements. Table 1.2 shows the agreements currently in force or in the process of completion or ratification.

What is the purpose of these agreements and what obligations do they impose on the signatories? Obviously, every agreement is tailored to the exigencies of the relationship between the EU and the country or group of countries with which it is concluded. Later chapters of this book look at some of the agreements in detail to see just what advantages they bring to the partners and to the EU itself: after all, the Union has never pretended that it does not also derive profit from such institutionalized relations. But broadly speaking, certain *types* of accord can be identified, although it is important to recall that there is no official nomenclature for Community agreements, and the categories listed below are only a rough guide. Ultimately, each reflects the specific political and economic requirements of a given relationship.

Association agreements are the most intimate form of relationship that a third country can have with the EU. In theory, they involve reciprocal obligations, not merely a series of concessions by the Union to the beneficiary country. At the heart of all association agreements is tariff-free entry into the EC market for most manufactured products, often after a transitional period, and thus the creation of a virtual free trade area or in some

Table 1.2   EU Agreements with Third Countries, 1997

Association Agreements (Articles 238 and 228 of the EC Treaty)
  European Economic Area (EEA): Iceland, Liechtenstein, Norway
  Central and Eastern Europe (Europe agreements): Bulgaria, Czech Republic, Estonia,
    Hungary, Latvia, Lithuania, Poland, Romania, Slovakia, Slovenia
  Mediterranean: Turkey (customs union); Cyprus, Malta (association agreements); Israel (free
    trade agreement); Egypt, Jordan, Morocco, Tunisia (Euro-Mediterranean accords); Algeria,
    Lebanon, Syria

Partnership and Cooperation Agreements (Articles 113, 228, and 235)
  Armenia, Azerbaijan, Belarus, Georgia, Kazakhstan, Kyrghyzstan, Moldova, Russia, Ukraine,
    Uzbekistan

Trade, Cooperation, and Framework Agreements (Articles 113, 228, and 235)
  Europe: Albania; Switzerland (free trade agreement)
  North and South America: Canada; Argentina, Brazil, Chile, Mexico, Paraguay, Uruguay;
    Andean Pact, Central America, Mercosur (interregional agreements)
  Middle East and Asia: Gulf Cooperation Council (interregional agreement); ASEAN (inter-
    regional agreement); China; Bangladesh, India, Nepal, Pakistan, Sri Lanka; Republic of
    Korea; Vietnam; Cambodia, Laos; Australia, New Zealand (pending)
  An agreement with South Africa is likely to be concluded in 1997.

Lomé convention (Article 131)
  Seventy African, Caribbean, and Pacific states (ACP)[a]

Notes: Some of these agreements were still awaiting ratification at the beginning of 1997.
a. For complete list, see Table 8.1.

cases even a customs union. The early association agreements offered the
EC's partners the eventual option of joining the Community. Although an
association agreement did not guarantee future membership, there was a
clear understanding (actually spelled out in the case of Greece and Turkey)
that the ultimate goal of the association was full membership. Any agreement based on Article 238 counts as an association agreement, though
some (like those concluded with the Maghreb and Mashreq states) were
not called association agreements and no future membership was implied.
(The EU Treaty limits membership of the Community to democratic *European* countries; non-European states are disqualified a priori, though this
did not stop Morocco from applying to join in 1987 and being duly rejected.) Like the others, however, these agreements provided for a regular
institutionalized dialogue at the political level in addition to trade and economic concessions and access to grants and loans under special financial
protocols. The recent Europe agreements with the countries of Central and
Eastern Europe are also true association accords. Though they contain no
specific pledges on membership, they are seen as a first step toward eventual accession of these countries and refer to this aim in their preambles.
The partnership agreements concluded between the EC and its member
states and the successor states of the Soviet Union are hybrid arrangements,

sharing features of more traditional cooperation accords and the Europe agreements.

The seventy developing countries of Africa, the Caribbean, and the Pacific linked to the EU under the Lomé convention enjoy a special kind of association derived from Part Four of the EC Treaty (Articles 131 to 136), which provided for largely duty-free access to the Community market for products originating in the overseas colonies and dependencies of the member states. The Part Four arrangements were carried over into the Yaoundé and Lomé conventions, which provided special benefits (trade concessions but also a package of aid and other measures) to these territories after they had achieved their independence. (The Lomé relationship is dealt with in detail in Chapter 8.)

Trade and cooperation agreements tend to be more restrictive in scope, involving tariff reductions but not tariff elimination in the initial phases, though they can eventually lead to complete abolition of customs duties. Agreements of this type are aimed at less-developed countries (LDCs). It is important in this context to understand what is meant by "cooperation." "Economic cooperation" is Commission jargon for a new type of development aid for more advanced developing countries that are not reliant exclusively on financial or humanitarian aid in the traditional sense. This aid is designed to help improve the macroeconomic and business infrastructures of the countries concerned. It does so in a variety of ways that benefit both the recipients and the EU itself; these include schemes and projects designed to encourage trade and investment and to bolster the competitiveness of local businesses, especially small and medium-sized enterprises (SMEs), through such measures as management training and information. Examples include the ECIP (European Community Investment Partners) scheme, BC-NET (Business Cooperation Network), and the European Business Information Centres (EBICs).

Preferential trade agreements offer preferential access to EC markets over and above what a country would be entitled to under the Community's generalized system of preferences (GSP).[4] The GSP, a complex scheme initiated in 1971, provides duty-free access mainly for industrial products; it applies to some 130 less-developed countries in the world. Preferential agreements can be concluded with countries that would not otherwise be eligible for GSP, as was the case with Israel. Usually, though, they are applied to developing countries. Framework agreements, such as those with Canada, Australia, and New Zealand,[5] are designed to provide an institutional structure without implying the need for specific trade or economic concessions by either side; they exist only with developed countries. As a new agreement between the European Union and a partner succeeds an older one, it is described as belonging to a new generation: a third-generation partnership and cooperation agreement was concluded with India in 1994, replacing the second- and first-generation agreements of 1982 and 1973.

The EU and GATT

Under Article 229 of the EC Treaty, the Commission is responsible for relations with "the organs" of the GATT. The Commission was never a member of the organization in its own right but was always intimately involved in negotiations, speaking on behalf of the Community as a whole. GATT rules dating from 1947, when the agreement was concluded, require non-discrimination between trading entities and introduce the notion of the most-favored nation (MFN), a yardstick against which any country can measure the treatment it receives from any other; the use of customs tariffs alone to protect national industries, with the tariffs to be "bound" in tariff schedules; compensation to trading partners if these tariffs are increased; consultation and dispute settlement procedures; and a ban on quantitative restrictions.

Successive rounds of GATT negotiations have reduced customs tariffs on industrial and agricultural products until today they represent on average only about 5 percent of product value. Antidumping procedures were introduced, NTBs and technical barriers to trade codified, and rules introduced to cover matters such as government procurement, import licensing, and customs valuation. In 1974 the GATT Multifiber Arrangement (MFA) was agreed, regulating international trade in textiles, a particularly sensitive area that was not covered under GATT rules proper. Different treatment was accorded to different suppliers under the MFA. As the world's biggest market for textiles, the EC always had a particular interest in regulating this trade, and the Commission negotiated bilateral MFA agreements with textile-producing countries around the world. Now, however, the MFA rules have been incorporated into the results of the Uruguay Round agreement that set up the WTO.

The EC's role in the protracted Uruguay Round negotiations (1986–1993) was significant, with the Commission coordinating the member states' positions in a range of sensitive areas, among them the inclusion into the new agreement of services, intellectual property rights, agriculture, and textiles. The final sticking points in the negotiations were between the EC and the United States, particularly with regard to farm trade and aircraft. The ultimately successful conclusion of the round demonstrated clearly that without the agreement of the EC as the world's biggest trading entity, no global arrangement was possible. During the closing months of the talks, most of the GATT members were obliged to sit on the sidelines as the big players, Europe and the United States, fought out the final battles together. The history of the GATT is as clear an example as any of the

EU's power to affect the international structures on which countries around the world depend for their prosperity.

The Common Agricultural Policy and International Trade

The EU's Common Agricultural Policy (CAP) has had a significant impact on exporters of farm products around the world. Later chapters dealing with the Union's relations with individual countries and regions look at specific examples in more depth.

The CAP itself was created as a corollary to the common market in industrial products. In some senses it was the price that Germany had to pay for gaining a huge market for its manufactured goods and the compensation that allowed France and Italy to keep their farmers employed at the expense of Germany and, later, Britain. The purpose of the policy spelled out in Article 39 of the EC Treaty was honorable enough: to increase agricultural productivity and ensure self-sufficiency in key areas, to keep farmers on the land by protecting their incomes, to ensure reliability and regularity of food supplies, to stabilize markets, and to ensure fair prices for the consumer. To achieve these aims, the CAP guaranteed farmers minimum income levels by creating "common organizations" of the markets for certain products (cereals, meat, olive oil, etc.). Under this system minimum guaranteed prices were set for the products in question, which farmers received as intervention payments even if there was no market demand. Farmers were thus encouraged to overproduce, knowing that whatever they could not sell at market would be bought by the intervention agency.

To ensure that imports of a given product from abroad at lower world market prices did not undercut the EC's prices, such imports were subject to levies to bring them up to the European price level. Conversely, European farmers wishing to export their produce to third countries were entitled to receive restitution payments (subsidies) equal to the difference between the guaranteed Community price for that product and the world market price at which the goods were actually sold.

Non-EU countries, not surprisingly, have always been bitterly opposed to the CAP. It means that the cost of selling to the EU is artificially high because of the import levies. It means that thanks to the restitution payments they receive, European farmers are able to export their expensive produce and thus capture market share from other exporting countries whose farmers are not so generously treated. And in more general terms, it means that production levels in the EU are much higher than they would otherwise be, thanks to the price guarantees that encourage farmers to produce more, and opportunities are therefore lost to would-be foreign exporters. (It is worth noting here that in spite of the negative effects of the CAP on other agricultural powers in the world, the EU remains a major importer of farm products.

It currently buys around 22 percent of world agricultural exports and runs a deficit in this sector of over ECU 20 billion.)

The EU has long been conscious of the ire the CAP provokes abroad. But it has also been aware of the enormous cost of the policy to its own budget. In the late 1970s and early 1980s, over two-thirds of the entire Community budget was being spent by the European Agricultural Guidance and Guarantee Fund (EAGGF), largely on farm support through intervention payments. The policy had become a thing of public ridicule as Europeans, already paying high prices in the markets for many basic foodstuffs, watched the intervention warehouses filling with unwanted products—the famous mountains of butter and grain and lakes of wine and milk.

The first steps toward reforming the CAP were decided on in the mid-1980s.[6] Involving quotas and other limitations on the production of certain farm produce, together with sociostructural measures to reduce the impact of the restrictions on farmers, these reforms turned out to have only marginal impact. In 1988 a more dramatic raft of measures was introduced.[7] These included a retreat from the old CAP principle of unlimited support for production, with a system of maximum guaranteed quantities instead placing an effective ceiling on production in most sectors. This was accompanied by a "set-aside" scheme, which compensated farmers who took at least 20 percent of their land out of cultivation for at least five years and gave financial encouragement to those who wished to leave the land or take early retirement. Finally, a transitional system of income support for farmers affected by these measures was introduced.

While these reforms went some way toward addressing the concerns of the EU's trading partners by encouraging a reduction in overall EU farm output, they did not tackle a central problem, that of export subsidies and import levies. With agriculture already proving to be a major sticking point in the Uruguay Round of GATT negotiations, the EU embarked on further reform of the CAP in 1991, the Commission again submitting a series of proposals.[8] The Council reached a political agreement on this newest reform in May 1992, and the first of the new regulations came into effect shortly afterward.

The central plank of the new reform went to the heart of the CAP by reducing the minimum guaranteed prices (the guide price) for certain key products, cereals in particular. At the end of a three-year transitional period, EU guaranteed prices were to fall by almost 30 percent to bring them largely in line with world market prices. Oilseeds, beef, and dairy products would also attract lower prices and be subject to new quotas. Farmers would be compensated by direct aid of various kinds, which meant the overall cost of the CAP to the EU's budget would not sink much, at least in the medium term. Lower prices at the farm gate should mean lower consumer prices, but the taxpayer would be paying more to finance the cost of income support and other measures to help farmers.

For the EU's trading partners, particularly the United States, this reform was good news, even if they felt it did not go far enough and was to be phased in too slowly. The reduction in the guide price for cereals meant that export subsidies could be reduced by a parallel amount. Moreover, the EU agreed to change its system of variable levies on imported agricultural goods (the difference between the prevailing world price and the EU price) to one of fixed customs duties. Along with other concessions by Brussels, including a 21 percent reduction in subsidized grain exports by century's end, this reform was sufficient to enable the Uruguay Round of GATT negotiations to come to a successful conclusion in 1993 and to be signed in Marrakech in 1994. However, agricultural policy is likely to remain a problem for the European Union and to complicate its relations with its partners for a long time to come.

Management of EU Trade: Role of the Institutions

When the world deals with the European Union on matters of trade, it talks first and foremost to the Commission, which has, in most areas, exclusive competence in this field under Articles 113–114 and 228 of the EC Treaty. A non-EU country has two immediate channels to the Commission. The first is the Commission's own representation in the country or region concerned. Usually known as the Commission's delegation, it is headed by a senior official who generally has the rank of ambassador. The second is via the country's own diplomatic representation in Brussels. Known as a mission to the European Union, it, too, is headed by an ambassador, accredited directly to the Commission and Council. Once the specifics of a trade relationship get beyond what can be done at the diplomatic level, talks move on to the level of direct contacts between officials of the Commission on the one hand and the relevant government department of the country concerned on the other. On important issues or at the conclusion of negotiations, meetings may be held between the commissioner responsible for trade and the partner country's trade minister. There would not normally be any formal contact with the EU's Council of Ministers.

It may or may not be coincidental that out of the twenty-four directorates-general (DGs) that make up the Commission, the first on the list, DG I, is responsible for external economic relations, that is, international trade. DG I has a complex structure. Since 1995 it has in fact been split into three separate but linked directorates-general, in many ways resembling (as do other Commission DGs) a ministry or department in a national government. Its three constituent parts (DG I, DG IA, and DG IB) are further divided into numerous directorates and units, or desks, each in charge of regions or individual countries or specific aspects of trade policy or program-related activities (see Table 1.3 for a breakdown of responsibilities).

Table 1.3   DG I, DG IA, DG IB: Structure and Responsibilities

DG I

External Relations: Commercial policy and relations with North America, the Far East, Australia, and New Zealand

Personnel, budget, administration, data processing, and external missions

Analysis and policy planning

Information and relations with the European Parliament

Directorate B
Relations with North America, Australia, New Zealand, NAFTA, and APEC

Directorate C
Antidumping strategy: dumping aspects (policy, investigations, and measures)

Directorate D
Sectoral commercial questions

Directorate E
Antidumping strategy: injury and Community interest aspects (policy, investigations, and measures); other instruments of external economic policy and general questions

Directorate F
Relations with Far Eastern countries

Directorate G
WTO, OECD, commercial questions with respect to agriculture and fisheries; export credit policy and export promotion

Directorate M
Services and external dimension of the Union; external relations in the research, science, nuclear energy, and environment fields

DG IA

External relations: Europe and the Newly Independent States, Common Foreign and Security Policy, and external missions

Protocol

Administration, personnel, data processing, and coordination

Relations with the European Parliament

External policy: European correspondent

Inspection of delegations

Information

Directorate A
Multilateral relations

Directorate B
Relations with Central Europe

Directorate C
Relations with the Newly Independent States and Mongolia

Directorate D
Relations with other European countries

Directorate E
Management of external missions

DG IB

External relations: Southern Mediterranean, Middle East, Latin America, South and Southeast Asia, and North-South Cooperation

Management audit and relations with the Court of Auditors

Relations with other institutions and information

Group of advisers (analyses and political matters)

Directorate A
Southern Mediterranean and Middle East

Directorate B
Latin America

Directorate C
South and Southeast Asia

Directorate D
North-South relations

Directorate E
Finance and resources

Obviously, while the three DG Is are the frontline directorates-general in the Commission on trade matters, the very nature of the EU's external commercial relations means that a great many other DGs are also involved. DG IV (Agriculture), DG VIII (Development), and DG XIV (Fisheries) are the most obvious of these, but many others (e.g., those dealing with transport, telecommunications, environment, R&D, or audiovisual media) will have input into trade issues. Moreover, the commissioners responsible for the different external relations DGs[9] and their cabinets, or private offices, will also want to play a role in overseeing the work of those parts of DG I concerned with their areas of competence.

A word about the Commission's delegations: there are around 120 of these (a partial list of them appears in Appendix 6), ranging from modest one- or two-person representations in some of the smaller ACP countries to what amount to full-fledged embassies with a range of departments in the EU's major trading partners, such as the United States and Japan. The larger delegations, headed by a senior Commission civil servant[10] holding the rank of ambassador, will include not only trade but also political, agricultural, and other departments that reflect the nature of the Union's relationship with the host country. There will also be a press and public affairs section, which may include a library or documentation center open to researchers and other interested members of the public. The different departments will be headed and in part staffed by Commission officials from the relevant directorates-general in Brussels, though usually local staff are employed too, particularly in fields where a good knowledge of local affairs is essential or where fluency in the country's language is needed. These delegations report to DG IA.

Foreign missions in Brussels accredited to the EU have also proliferated over the past few years. In many cases the job is done by ambassadors and their staffs who serve as their country's envoys not only to the EU but also to Belgium, NATO, and in some cases to one or more other European countries. But the majority of the bigger countries, for whom the EU represents a significant commercial and even political partner in its own right, maintain separate missions, staffed by diplomats whose sole job is relations with the Union. For many countries, including the United States, Japan, Russia, and China, an ambassadorship to the EU ranks as one of the more prestigious foreign postings in their diplomatic services.

The role of Commission officials serving abroad (and no doubt that of their foreign counterparts on post in Brussels, too) is more than merely engaging in negotiations or overseeing the day-to-day management of trade agreements, financial protocols, or cooperation projects. It has developed a genuinely diplomatic reach; Commission delegations abroad report back not just on trade-related issues but also on the whole range of internal economic and political matters that may affect a country's relations with the EU. Whether forthcoming elections, the banking or fiscal climate, or human rights violations in a partner country, the Commission delegation's ability to observe and interpret situations and events is of growing importance in the framework of relationships that increasingly must meet a host of political as well as economic conditions. As described below, the European Parliament has come to play a key role in this respect in recent years, and its influence cannot be disregarded.

The power of the Commission in regulating the EU's foreign trade is extensive without being all-embracing.[11] The Commission is the negotiator for the Union in reaching trade agreements, of whatever sort, with third countries. Article 113 gives it the independent right to make recommendations to the Council on the agreements it believes to be necessary, but before it can act it needs the Council's go-ahead in the form of a negotiating directive. Usually known as the Council's mandate, this spells out in some detail the framework of an agreement, including its objectives and the areas it is to cover. In fact, the mandate may itself be based on the Commission's initial recommendations, usually contained in a communication addressed to the Council and European Parliament. When negotiations are complete, the Commission can initial the agreement, but the Council concludes it on the basis of a majority vote (or in the case of Article 238 association agreements, by unanimity). Even during the negotiations themselves, the Commission is overseen by a "113 Committee" of top trade officials from the member states. Although only consultative in nature, the committee provides policy guidance and recommendations, ensuring that the Commission's negotiations are in line with member states' thinking and acceptable to them. Because of the Commission's prerogatives in the trade field and the role of the 113 Committee, the trade ministers of the member states never meet as a council; if there is ever disagreement or deadlock in the 113 Committee on how to advise the Commission to proceed, the problem is referred to Coreper, the Committee of Permanent Representatives of the member states,[12] or the General Affairs Council (i.e., the foreign ministers).

In the case of enlargement, that is, applications by third countries to join the EU, the Commission is required to give an opinion, but it is again the Council that gives the green light for the accession negotiations to begin and that must approve the outcome. In this case and in the case of most types of agreement with third countries, the assent of the European Parliament is required before the process can conclude.

It is beyond the scope of this chapter to go into the intricacies of the honorable part the Commission has played over several decades as the Union's representative and negotiator in the GATT, of which it is not even a member in its own right. Others have written at length on the subject.[13] What is worth mentioning here is the persistence of a degree of shared or mixed responsibility between the Commission, as negotiator for the Union, and the member states, as the actual representatives of the Union on the GATT. Indeed the Commission has frequently found itself negotiating not only *on behalf* of the EU's members but also *between* them, proposing compromises when their positions differ. (A similar situation applies, incidentally, in the Organization for Economic Cooperation and Development [OECD], where the Commission also speaks on behalf of the EU even though the Union is not a member in its own right.) The Commission also represents the Union in a range of other contexts, such as working groups, panels, committees, and the like in the framework of organizations such as the Lomé convention, the UN Conference on Trade and Development (UNCTAD), the European Economic Area, and the G7 group of industrialized countries, in which it participates as a sort of eighth member representing the EU as a whole (and thus, indirectly, those member states that are not themselves present in the G7). The Commission maintains a delegation in New York accredited to the United Nations, in which the EU has observer status, and another in Geneva accredited to the various international organizations based there.

The European Parliament enjoys a number of powers that give it considerable weight in the area of external relations. The assent procedure is chief among these. It applies in the cases of association agreements (Article 238), as well as "other agreements establishing a specific institutional framework by organizing cooperation procedures, agreements having important budgetary implications for the Community and agreements entailing amendment of an act adopted under the [co-decision procedure]" (Article 228). This is the bulk of agreements entered into by the EU today, and the EP is called upon to ratify them in much the same way that the U.S. Senate must ratify foreign treaties entered into by the United States. Recently, the EU has started to conclude "mixed agreements," which involve the EU and its member states; these agreements—examples are the Europe agreements with the countries of Central and Eastern Europe—require not only the EP's assent but also that of the member states' own parliaments. Parliament's assent is also required before new members can join the Union.

Assent is the end of a long process throughout which the EP is involved. The EP is consulted at the outset of an initiative intended to lead to the adoption of an international agreement under Article 238 of the EC Treaty or to the admission of new members to the Union. Indeed, since the 1983 Stuttgart "Solemn Declaration,"[14] Parliament has been consulted on all important international agreements, regardless of the legal basis on which they are to be concluded. It is also kept informed by the Commission and Council, both before and during the negotiations, under the so-called Luns-Westerterp procedure.[15] Assent to an international agreement requires a simple majority vote in Parliament (though an absolute majority is needed in the case of an accession treaty).

The assent procedure has given the EP new muscle in influencing the EU's external relations. By announcing early on in the process that it is not satisfied with the terms or conditions of a proposed accord and will not give its assent unless its views are taken into account and reflected in the Commission's negotiating stance, it can substantively alter the content of agreements. The now systematic inclusion of human rights clauses in the EU's agreements with third countries, under which the terms of any accord are subject to respect for human rights by the contracting parties and may be rescinded in the event of noncompliance, is an example of EP pressure. In 1996, when Cuba declined to pursue negotiations on a cooperation agreement with the EU because of demands that it introduce political reforms (including the release from jail of members of the political opposition), the Commission made no concessions, clearly understanding that an accord without such guarantees would be unacceptable to Parliament. In March 1995 the EU-Turkey Association Council agreed to implement the customs union that was scheduled to come into effect between the European Union and Turkey in 1996. This date had been fixed by a 1973 "additional protocol" to the original EC-Turkey association agreement. Although the customs union was not legally subject to any conditions (the human rights clause did not exist in 1964 when the association agreement was signed), the European Parliament agreed to endorse it in December 1995 only after Turkey had made a series of concessions—including a constitutional change—in regard to its laws on the detention of Kurds and others deemed to be hostile to the state and had released a number of prisoners from jail.

But even before it gained the power of assent, the EP had felt impelled to play as strong a role as it could, using whatever powers and influence it possessed. The conventions of Yaoundé and Lomé have always had a parliamentary dimension in the shape of the Joint Assembly, which brings together a representative of each of the ACP states and an equivalent number of members of the European Parliament (MEPs) in meetings twice a year to review the workings of the convention and cooperation in general. Beyond the ACP, Parliament has also set up a network of interparliamentary links with the majority of countries around the world, managed by standing interparliamentary delegations. The delegations give MEPs the opportunity to talk to parliamentarians (and, often enough, members of government) from the countries with which the EU does business, hear about their needs, investigate problems, assess the usefulness of EU-financed projects, and so on.

In the case of certain countries with which the EU has association or partnership agreements involving an institutionalized structure, special joint parliamentary committees have been set up to review the working of the agreements and identify problems. Finally, Parliament's budgetary powers give it the ability to influence the conduct of certain types of programs that involve EU expenditure, for example, the PHARE and TACIS schemes aimed at helping the countries of Central and Eastern Europe and the Commonwealth of Independent States (CIS) (see Chapter 3).

To the extent that the European Union's external economic relations result in legal acts' being adopted on the basis of the relevant treaty articles (e.g., establishing a trade agreement with a third country or committing the EU to a particular course of action in the framework of some larger agreement, like the GATT), they are not so very different in terms of institutional mechanics from other EU legislative activity. The Commission proposes. The Council, with the European Parliament, disposes. What is different is the Commission's role as negotiator and spokesperson for the Union as a whole. While the Council's ultimate power to accept or reject an agreement is no less than its power to accept or reject any other legislative act that is subject to co-decision with the Parliament (i.e., that needs the latter's *approval* rather than just its *opinion*), its level of involvement in reaching the agreement is a great deal smaller than the Commission's. The European Union's trade and economic relations with the wider world are therefore a good example of its ability to present a single face to its partners and to act with a degree of coherence reminiscent of that of a nation-state. This is less the case with regard to the other aspect of the Union's external relations, its Common Foreign and Security Policy, as the next chapter makes clear.

Notes

1. Dermot McAleese, "External Trade Policy of the European Community," in D. McAleese et al., *Africa and the European Community After 1992* (Washington, DC: Economic Development Institute, 1993), p. 19.

2. These and other trade figures quoted in this book are taken from various 1996 issues of Eurostat's *External Trade* series (monthly statistics), unless otherwise indicated.

3. These figures all concern trade in *goods*. Trade in *services*—transport, tourism, insurance, and so on—now accounts for around 60 percent of the value of the EU's total foreign exchange receipts and expenditures.

4. For a fuller discussion of GSP, see Chapter 8.

5. At the beginning of 1997, the framework agreements with Australia and New Zealand were still pending.

6. On the basis of the 1983 Commission document COM(83) 500 and the subsequent 1985 Commission green paper, COM(85) 333.

7. On the basis of two further Commission proposals, COM(87) 410 and 512.

8. A Commission reflection paper in February 1991 entitled "The Development and Future of the CAP," COM(91) 100, was followed by a second communication, COM(91) 258, in July 1991 and a series of specific proposals.

9. For the Commission's 1995–1999 term of office, the external affairs portfolios are divided among four commissioners: Sir Leon Brittan (DG I: industrialized countries, China, and other parts of Asia; the common trade policy; and the WTO and OECD), Hans van den Broek (DG IA: Central and Eastern Europe; the CIS; Cyprus, Malta and Turkey; and the CFSP), Manuel Marin (DG IB: southern

Mediterranean, the Middle East, Latin America, and parts of Asia), and João de Deus Pinheiro (DG VIII: the ACP and South Africa).

10. Individuals have occasionally been recruited from outside the Commission to fill the post of head of delegation, particularly in some of the ACP countries. One noteworthy if exceptional case was that of former Dutch prime minister Andreas van Agt (now retired), who served successively as EU ambassador in Tokyo and Washington in the 1980s and 1990s.

11. For an account of the Commission's role in the EU's external relations, see Michael Smith, "The Commission and External Relations," in Geoffrey Edwards and David Spence (eds.), *The European Commission* (Harlow: Longman, 1994).

12. The permanent representations are the "embassies" of the member states accredited to the European Community. They are headed by a permanent representative, invariably a senior diplomat of ambassadorial rank.

13. See, for example, Hugo Paemen and Alexandra Bensch, *GATT to WTO: The European Community in the Uruguay Round* (Leuven, Belgium: Leuven University Press, 1995).

14. *Bulletin of the European Communities* (hereafter *Bulletin*), 7/8–1983.

15. Joseph Luns and Tjerk Westerterp were presidents of the Council (in 1964 and 1973, respectively) who agreed to grant the European Parliament this right.

2

Toward a Common
Foreign Policy

There is a distinction to be drawn between external relations and foreign policy, though it is not always as clear-cut as it may seem. Chapter 1 made the point that most relations between states are ultimately based on economic considerations, and to that extent the EU, as an international trading power, was always actively engaged in external relations. Perhaps it would be true to say that since its earliest days the European Community was an actor in the field of external relations *by default*, but it *chose* to move toward developing a common foreign policy that would be distinct from what it was already doing in its (trading) relationships with the rest of the world. Political theorists have been arguing for years about the whys and wherefores of the EC's growing tendency to seek foreign policy consensus and pursue joint actions. Explanations range from neofunctionalist "spillover" theory, which suggests that action in one area may lead the actors concerned to collaborate in a related sector,[1] to interdependence theory, which posits that the EC is forced to react as an entity when its constituent members lack the individual muscle (or unity of purpose) to do so.[2] There is also a link between foreign *economic* policy and foreign policy as such.[3] Indeed some political scientists believe that certain European Community member states were anxious to create an artificial distinction between external (economic) relations and foreign policy, when in fact such distinctions were illusory.[4] What is clear is that the protection of its worldwide interests—whether in the domain of energy resources, commodity prices, investment security, or whatever—has always compelled the EU to take a proactive role in international affairs. But it has had to do so using the weapons of commerce and diplomacy, not military power. And it is possession of a realistic defense (and offense) capability that distinguishes foreign policy actors from onlookers. The EU, like Japan, has often been described as an economic giant but a political pygmy.

Nevertheless, the European Community began harboring notions of developing its own foreign policy as far back as 1969 and took its first tentative steps toward this goal in the form of "political cooperation."

Twenty-five years later the Maastricht Treaty created the European Union on the basis of three pillars, one of which was the Common Foreign and Security Policy.[5] This chapter examines the evolution of the foreign policy dimension of the EC and considers the impact of today's CFSP and its likely future course.

The Beginnings of European Political Cooperation

If things had turned out differently, the six original members of the European Coal and Steel Community, the forerunner of the EEC and the European Community as it came to be, might have found themselves having to invent a common foreign policy as early as the mid-1950s. The vehicle for this policy would have been the European Defence Community (EDC), which was drafted and signed by the Six in May 1952 but, as the result of changing international and national political circumstances, never ratified because the French National Assembly voted against it in 1954. The EDC included the blueprint for a "political community," and certainly the creation of the joint European military structure proposed by the draft treaty would have had major repercussions in the foreign policy domain, forcing the Community to confront the issue of how to manage its external relations in a completely different way. The stillborn Defence Community thus remains the first key event in the development of a common foreign policy for the EC (see Table 2.1).

But the EDC's failure led to the establishment of an alternative, economic route toward European integration: the EEC and the project for a common market. That in turn, as Chapter 1 has shown, created the need for the Community to develop an external identity as a corollary to the customs union that was taking shape within its borders. But the setting up of the EEC did not prevent one more French-inspired effort to give the Community more of a political character. The so-called Fouchet Plan[6] negotiations from 1960 to 1962 were based on President de Gaulle's preference for an intergovernmental rather than a supranational approach to European cooperation. While the goal was to add a political dimension (which would have included foreign policy) to the more economic and trade-oriented approach of the EEC, the excessively intergovernmental character of the proposal led to its being rejected in 1962. All of the Six except France were concerned that the Fouchet Plan would turn the Community into "une Europe des patries," a Europe of nations.

But with de Gaulle's political demise, the same change in climate that led to French acceptance of the British application for EC membership put the question of political union back on the table. The final communiqué of the 1969 Hague summit of the six EC leaders stated that the beginning of the final stage of creating the common market meant "paving the way

Table 2.1 Landmarks in the Development of a European Common Foreign Policy

1952	European Defence Community (EDC) signed by Six	The EDC, which never entered into force because of the failure of the French National Assembly to ratify it, would have set up a common defense system backed by foreign policy coordination among the Six.
1962	Fouchet Plan	An "intergovernmental committee on political union," chaired by French diplomat Christian Fouchet, draws up a draft statute for a European Union of States, which includes plans for foreign policy and security cooperation; the plan is rejected by most member states on the grounds that it is too intergovernmental in nature.
1969	The Hague Summit	Leaders of the Six call for a "United Europe capable of assuming its responsibilities in the world of tomorrow."
1970	Luxembourg Report	Foreign ministers create intergovernmental machinery for "political cooperation" designed to foster a joint approach to foreign policy.
1973	Copenhagen Report	Foreign ministers of the Nine review workings of European Political Cooperation (EPC) and establish principle of consultation among member states before taking foreign policy decisions.
1981	London Report	Foreign ministers agree to associate Commission with EPC process "at all levels." Joint action replaces cooperation as main EPC goal.
1986	Single European Act	EPC institutionalized. "High Contracting Parties" undertake to pursue joint formulation and implementation of foreign policy. European Parliament "associated" with the process.
1992	Maastricht Treaty (Treaty on European Union)	Common Foreign and Security Policy (CFSP) established as intergovernmental second pillar of new treaty. Security included formally as area for cooperation. Foreign policy now part of European Union activities, though not subject to the "Community method."

for a United Europe capable of assuming its responsibilities in the world of tomorrow and of making a contribution commensurate with its traditions and mission."[7] In response to this vision, the foreign ministers in 1970 drew up what came to be called the Luxembourg Report.[8] This created intergovernmental machinery—regular meetings of the foreign ministers and a Political Committee of senior diplomats—designed to foster cooperation in the field of foreign policy between the member states. In deference to French wishes, this "political cooperation" was purely intergovernmental in character, did not involve the Commission or other EC institutions, and was not subject to the jurisdiction of the European Court of

Justice. The Commission, according to the Luxembourg Report, would be "consulted" if the discussions of the foreign ministers related in any way to the work of the EC.

When the initial experiences of European political cooperation came to be reviewed in 1973, this time by the foreign ministers of the Nine rather than the Six, it had become clear that the role of the member states could not always be divorced entirely from that of the Community as a whole. A grudging reference in the foreign ministers' September 1973 Copenhagen Report[9] (which established the principle of consultation among the member states when taking important foreign policy decisions) acknowledged the Commission's participation in the discussions on the Conference on Security and Cooperation in Europe (CSCE), which had been going on since 1970. The Commission had expertise in the economic area, and the CSCE involved, inter alia, economic cooperation. So did relations with the Mediterranean countries: thus, when the Euro-Arab Dialogue was launched at the end of 1973 after the Arab-Israeli war, it became more and more unrealistic to exclude the Commission from the deliberations of the foreign ministers. For the rest of the 1970s, the Commission's role in EPC gradually grew in a pragmatic rather than formal manner: the strictly intergovernmental approach remained the order of the day, still largely at the insistence of France.

The change in the French presidency in 1981 led to a new approach. Claude Cheysson, President François Mitterrand's new foreign minister, had himself been a member of the Commission during the 1970s and knew firsthand what the arm's-length attitude of EPC to the EC's institutions meant. With the active support of the French, the foreign ministers in their London Report[10] of October 1981 for the first time formally associated the Commission with the EPC process "at all levels." More than that, the foreign ministers declared the main aim of political cooperation to be "joint action" rather than the mere cooperation or coordination of policies that had characterized EPC until then. The political aspects of security were also brought under the political cooperation umbrella. The ministers agreed, furthermore, to strengthen the consultation machinery between their respective ministries, to cooperate through their embassies abroad, and to allow direct contacts between EPC and third countries, using the troika of the current Council president and the latter's predecessor and successor.[11]

The EPC's tentative moves toward joint foreign policy making had not yielded any spectacular results during the 1970s. While expansion from six to nine members had vastly increased the impact of the EC as an actor in the international trading arena, it remained unimpressive in terms of its political visibility. However, the changes to EPC methods introduced by the London Report in 1981 were rapidly followed by two events that gave the Community the opportunity to show that it was capable of acting in a unified fashion in reaction to significant international events. The first was the imposition of martial law in Poland in 1982 following the Solidarity strikes that led to the fall of Party Secretary Edward Gierek and his replacement by the Soviet-backed hard-liner Wojciech Jaruzelski. The Community reacted by imposing a series of sanctions on the Soviet Union, the first time that such a measure targeting a third country had been taken jointly by member states. The second event occurred later the same year, when Argentina invaded the Falkland/Malvinas Islands; once again the Community reacted as one, declaring its solidarity with the United Kingdom and imposing economic and trade sanctions against the Buenos Aires government.

The early 1980s saw an intensification of debate within the institutions of the Community and in its member states about the future direction of the European integration process and, not least, the political role that the EC should assume. The Genscher-Colombo Plan of 1981 (named after the foreign ministers of Germany and Italy) made a series of proposals designed to widen the scope of EC responsibilities and improve the decision-making structures; among other ideas EPC would get its own secretariat, thus partly removing it from the strictly intergovernmental mold in which it had been operating. The plan was not warmly endorsed by the member states, resulting only in the Stuttgart "Solemn Declaration" of June 1983, which was little more than a reaffirmation of principles and intentions and did not expand the EC's foreign policy role or power. It did, however, further strengthen the role of the Council presidency in EPC, specifically its "powers of initiative, of coordination and of representation in relations with third countries."[12]

The European Parliament, meanwhile, had drawn up a Draft Treaty on European Union,[13] which was a radical if premature attempt to reshape the entire Community—reorganizing it into a "union"—and to provide it with institutional structures better adapted to its growing role. The Draft Treaty spelled out the aims of the Union's foreign policy and proposed that it should be subject to the same institutional rules as other aspects of the Union's activities. The Draft Treaty was too ambitious for the times, but it had an impact on the other institutions and on the member states' governments, who, meeting in the European Council in Fontainebleau in June 1984, commissioned a report to be drawn up by an ad hoc committee under the chairmanship of Irish senator James Dooge. The Dooge Report[14] referred to the EP's Draft Treaty only in passing but adopted some of its ideas. It proposed completing the internal market and expanding foreign policy activities and adding security to the issues on the EPC's agenda.

The Institutionalization of EU Foreign Policy Making

The breakthrough for the Community's foreign policy cooperation efforts in fact came soon afterward, in December 1985, with the agreement on the

Single European Act. The SEA is remembered today principally for launching the "1992 process," which was to lead to the creation of a border-free internal (or single) market (and which, as we have seen and will see in later chapters, had repercussions for trading countries around the world). But the "single" in Single European Act has nothing to do with the single market. It refers to the fact that one and the same agreement contained the changes to the EC treaties necessary to establish the internal market *and* an intergovernmental accord on EPC. Title III of the act ("Treaty provisions on European Cooperation in the sphere of foreign policy") establishes, for the first time, a legal basis for EPC. Article 30 (see Appendix 2) of the SEA provides that the member states (referred to throughout as the "High Contracting Parties" to underline the intergovernmental nature of the agreement) will undertake to pursue the joint formulation and implementation of a European foreign policy. The Commission remains associated with the policymaking process and (along with the EC presidency) is given the job of ensuring that there are no inconsistencies between EPC policies and existing Community policies in external affairs. The European Parliament is also associated, though in a purely consultative role. But the willingness of EPC at least to listen to the EP's views was a recognition that intergovernmental though it may have been, political cooperation in foreign affairs was assuming more of a Community dimension.

The machinery of political cooperation remained, nonetheless strictly intergovernmental in structure. This machinery is worth describing, because most of the mechanisms and working methods of EPC remain intact under the Common Foreign and Security Policy later created by the Maastricht Treaty. At the top of the EPC pyramid was the European Council, the twice-yearly meeting of the heads of state and government of the member states. The European Council is not a Community institution as such[15] but a self-defined political directorate whose role is to provide guidance (if not inspiration) for the actual institutions and, in the case of EPC, for foreign policy initiatives. The "foreign ministers meeting in the framework of political cooperation" was the unwieldy description applied to the Council when its members gathered to discuss foreign policy as opposed to Community business. This body would meet at least six times a year (sometimes directly before or after a regular meeting of the Council), and more often if necessary. It would act on decisions of the European Council and, through its president (i.e., the foreign minister of the country holding the presidency at a given moment), would be the "face" of European foreign policy to the outside world.

The foreign ministers were assisted by the Political Committee, comprising senior foreign ministry officials (the "political directors") from the member states, whose job was to prepare the meetings of the ministers but, more important, to maintain a continuity of contact and remain up-to-date with current events. The Political Committee established working groups to monitor and report on specific areas of interest. Abroad, the diplomatic representations of the member states worked together closely, with the ambassador of the country that held the presidency chairing agreed meetings and contacts and, if necessary, representing EPC in contacts with the foreign ministry of the host country. While the Commission was always present at EPC meetings and at meetings of the Political Committee and its working groups, its role (like that of Coreper) was confined to those aspects of EPC discussions with a Community dimension. However, this was—and is—most of them.

The practical application of EPC was set out by the foreign ministers themselves in a decision[16] they adopted on the occasion of the signing of the SEA in February 1986. This decision included details on how the European Parliament was to be associated: the president of the foreign ministers[17] was to make an annual statement to the Parliament on past activities and future plans of EPC and take part in a plenary debate. The EP would be kept informed of current EPC activities through quarterly "colloquies" between the presidency and members of the Parliament's Political Affairs Committee, which was responsible for foreign policy questions. EPC's aim was to ensure that the member states were able to use their joint influence in the most effective way possible: to this end, they were to cooperate in international organizations, and their respective ambassadors abroad (including the head of the Commission's delegation) were to meet regularly to coordinate their views and prepare joint reports. Areas to be covered by this cooperation included political and economic information sharing, helping one another in practical and material ways, communications, acting together in the event of local crises, consular matters, health and medical facilities, schooling, information and cultural affairs, and development aid. Finally, the foreign ministers defined the role of the newly created EPC Secretariat, which had been set up under Article 30 and for the first time provided a degree of independent administrative support separate from that of the Council Secretariat.

From EPC to the CFSP

In the early and mid-1980s, when thought was being given to strengthening political cooperation and indeed establishing the basis for an eventual common foreign policy for the European Community, there were as yet few signs that profound changes in the international landscape lay just over the horizon. The world was still the bipolar place that it had been ever since the EC was set up. Mikhail Gorbachev and perestroika had not yet arrived, the Soviet Union was still at war in Afghanistan, South Africa was firmly in the grip of apartheid, the majority of countries in Latin America were still ruled by dictators, and the problems of the Middle East looked

as intractable as ever. It was therefore to the credit of Europe's leaders that
they recognized that the growing importance of the EC merited a more coherent approach to foreign policy issues even though there was no immediate crisis or threat that might have served as a catalyst. Working together
to adopt joint positions in international organizations like the United Nations and the OECD, entering into political as well as economic dialogue
with third countries and regional groupings, pressing for the restoration of
democracy and human rights in places where they were missing—these
were laudable goals inspired by more than mere expediency.

By the time the Single European Act came into force in July 1987,[18]
however, the world had started to alter. Not only was the Cold War drawing to a close, its front line was crumbling in the heart of Europe itself.
The disintegration of the Communist bloc on the Community's own
doorstep was to have immense repercussions for the future of the European integration process in general and for a common strategy toward foreign policy in particular. There could be no question of exclusively bilateral foreign policy approaches by the EC's individual member states to the
countries of Eastern and Central Europe, not least because it was immediately clear that the thrust of policy toward the new democracies would
have to be in the economic field. A series of first-generation trade and cooperation agreements, beginning with Hungary in 1988, was negotiated by
the Community and signed with nearly all the former East bloc countries,[19] and nearly all of these have since been succeeded by second-generation association agreements. These latter agreements in particular are
highly political in their aims and a perfect example of how fine the line is
between foreign policy and external relations, not least as far as the Community and its member states are concerned. The events in Central and
Eastern Europe, and the role the European Union has come to play in
them, are discussed in detail in Chapter 3.

In 1989 the European Council decided to hold a new intergovernmental conference (IGC) to consider amending the EC treaties with a view to
creating an Economic and Monetary Union (EMU). Pressure immediately
developed, initially in the European Parliament, for the scope of the conference to be extended to embrace political union as well. Political union
was a vaguely defined concept but certainly included a thorough reform of
the Community's institutional structures (considered essential if EMU was
to be a success), an expansion of the Community's competencies into new
areas, and the "communitarization" of foreign policy. There was a widespread belief, as expressed in the EP's reports on the planned IGC, that
Economic and Monetary Union without flanking policies in other areas
(social, regional, communications, the environment, etc.) and an accompa-
nying reinforcement of democracy and the rights of citizens would render
EMU unworkable.

In mid-1990 the decision was taken to expand the IGC on Economic and Monetary Union to include political union as well (in fact, formally there were two conferences, one on EMU, the other on political union). The Maastricht Treaty, which emerged from the deliberations of the governments, is a marvel of complexity born of the need to compromise. It turns the Community into a Union built on three pillars, the central one of which comprises the existing Community treaties amended to include a commitment to EMU and a number of new policies and institutional adjustments. The second pillar, Title V of the Treaty, (see Appendix 3) is a rewritten version of EPC, renamed the Common Foreign and Security Policy but still based on intergovernmental principles. The third pillar, also intergovernmental in nature, involves cooperation in the field of justice and home affairs, including such matters as illegal immigration, police cooperation, combating narcotics trafficking, and so on.

Though still intergovernmental, the CFSP does represent a further step toward making foreign policy a genuine common endeavor. The very nature of the Maastricht Treaty—whose official title is the Treaty on European Union and which entered into force only in November 1993[20]—brings to Community affairs a new dichotomy: that between Union and Community. The Union embraces the activities of the Community, as defined in the EC treaties, plus those of the two intergovernmental pillars. The Common Foreign and Security Policy is thus a Union activity but not a Community one. But the very fact that the activities of the member states, acting together, and those of the Community, acting on behalf of the member states, have been assembled under the single umbrella of the Union is a step forward in terms of clarity and intent. Gone are the terminological somersaults needed to explain European foreign policy making. The Maastricht Treaty replaces the ambiguous "European Political Cooperation," a term that carefully avoids use of the actual words "foreign policy," with "Common Foreign and Security Policy," which could hardly be more explicit. The latter is an activity of the "Union and its Member States" (Article J.1.1).

Most important is the end to the fiction that it is the "foreign ministers meeting in political cooperation" who deal with foreign policy rather than the Council, an institution of the Community. The CFSP places the Council at the heart of the process. The Union is represented in foreign affairs by the presidency (Article J.5), the same presidency that deals with all other Community business. The Commission is "fully associated with the work carried out in the common foreign and security policy field" (Article J.9). The European Parliament is consulted on "the main aspects and the basic choices" of the CFSP, and the presidency is to take its views "into consideration"; the EP is also to be kept "regularly informed" by the presidency and the Commission and can ask questions and make

recommendations (Article J.7). The "principles . . . and general guidelines" for the CFSP are defined by the European Council (Article J.8).

All this is a long way from the tortuous inception of Europe's foreign
policy efforts, disingenuously presented as no more than loose cooperation
among the foreign ministries of countries that also happened to belong to
the European Community. While the CFSP is not a *common* policy in the
sense that the Common Agricultural Policy or the Common Commercial
Policy are, it has the potential to produce results that properly reflect the
Union's priorities and concerns. It is not fully covered by the Community's
institutional structures, nor does it operate in complete isolation from
them. The Commission shares the right of initiative with the member
states (in the Community context, this right is *exclusive*), Parliament plays
an active role,[21] and the CFSP relies for its operating and administrative
expenses (and sometimes for the cost of implementing policies, too) on the
Community budget (Article J.11). It is worth noting here that after the
entry into force of the Maastricht Treaty and the creation of the CFSP, the
European Parliament changed the name of its Political Affairs Committee
to "Committee on Foreign Affairs, Security, and Defence Policy." For its
part, the European Commission divided DG I, which formerly covered external relations on its own, into DG I and DG IA; the latter took over responsibility for foreign policy issues.

Objectives and Scope of the CFSP

Article J.1 of Title V of the Maastricht Treaty defines the goals of the
CFSP as follows:

- to safeguard the common values, fundamental interests and independence of the Union;
- to strengthen the security of the Union and its Member States in all
  ways;
- to preserve peace and strengthen international security, in accordance
  with the principles of the United Nations Charter as well as the principles of the Helsinki Final Act and the objectives of the Paris Charter;
- to promote international cooperation;
- to develop and consolidate democracy and the rule of law, and respect
  for human rights and fundamental freedoms.

These objectives are to be pursued by the *Union* (Article J.1.3)
through the establishment of "systematic cooperation between Member
States" and through the gradual implementation of joint action in areas
where the member states share important interests. Joint actions, at least in
a formal sense, are a novelty that did not exist under EPC. The first joint
action the Union carried out under the terms of the CFSP (in this case, its

provision on supporting the consolidation of democracy) was in connection with the Russian parliamentary elections of December 1993, the Union and its member states providing technical and logistical support and playing a central part in the international election observation effort. Joint actions (see Table 2.2) are decided on in principle by the Council (according to Article J.3 of the Treaty, "on the basis of general guidelines from the European Council"), and the details are subject to qualified majority voting rather than unanimity. Once a joint action has been agreed, the Union's member states are bound by it and have to ensure that their own policies accord with it.

A special meeting of the European Council in October 1993 designated five areas for joint action:

1. promotion of peace and stability in Europe
2. support for the Middle East peace process
3. cooperation with a democratic South Africa
4. settlement of the conflict in the former Yugoslavia
5. support for the democratic process in Russia

The Russian elections joint action was a good example of the genuinely "Union" dimension of a foreign policy activity. The Commission's delegation in Moscow played the central role in coordinating the Community's own contribution (in human resources, money, and equipment) and the contributions of the individual member states and acted as the nerve center

Table 2.2   Examples of Joint Actions Under the CFSP, 1993–1996

Support for the convoying of humanitarian aid in Bosnia-Herzegovina (Decision of 8 November 1993)

Dispatch of a team of observers for the parliamentary elections in the Russian Federation (Decision of 9 November 1993)

Support for the transition toward a democratic and multiracial South Africa (Decision of 6 December 1993)

Support for the Middle East peace process (Decision of 19 April 1994)

Preparation for the 1995 conference on the nonproliferation of nuclear weapons (Decision of 25 July 1994)

Support for European Union administration of the town of Mostar, Bosnia-Herzegovina (Decision of 12 December 1994)

Observation of elections to the Palestinian Council and the coordination of the international operation for observing the elections (Decision of 25 September 1995)

Participation of the European Union in the Korean Peninsular Energy Development Organization (KEDO) (Decision of 5 March 1996)

Nomination of an EU Special Envoy for the African Great Lakes Region (Rwanda and Burundi) (Decision of 25 March 1996)

during the deployment of EU observers to electoral districts around the country, working with the various member states' embassies to ensure that national teams were integrated into the overall Union effort. Meanwhile, the Belgian embassy (Belgium being the country holding the presidency at the time) cooperated with its troika partners in arranging political briefings for all the incoming teams of observers.

The CFSP is, of course, mainly about foreign policy. But what makes it fundamentally different from pre-Maastricht political cooperation is that for the first time since the demise of the European Defence Community of the early 1950s, *security* is brought into the Union domain. As cited above, one of the objectives of the Common Foreign and Security Policy is "to strengthen the security of the Union and its Member States in all ways." The first paragraph of Article J.4 spells out in surprisingly unambiguous language just what this could lead to: the CFSP, it says, "shall include all questions related to the security of the Union, *including the eventual framing of a common defence policy, which might in time lead to a common defence*" (emphasis added).

In fact, this rather startling possibility is rapidly put into perspective by the small print of Article J.4, which hands over to the Western European Union (WEU)[22] the role of elaborating and implementing decisions and actions of the Union that have defense implications. In a declaration by the WEU member states annexed to the Maastricht Treaty, the practical arrangements for accomplishing this aim are set out; these include the transfer of the organization's secretariat to Brussels (from London) and the establishment of "close cooperation" and sharing of information between the WEU and the EU's institutions. Moreover, the WEU as the Union's defense arm, is not to prejudice the prerogatives of individual member states either within the North Atlantic Treaty Organization (NATO) or in cooperating with one another on a bilateral basis.

It remains to be seen how effective the security aspect of the CFSP will be. Until now there have been no practical examples of the policy's actually being applied (with the possible exception of the role of the WEU in helping to enforce sanctions during the Bosnian war; see Chapter 3). But regardless of the immediate impact of security policy on the defense capabilities of the European Union, that this issue—so long taboo even in the framework of EPC—should now have assumed a kind of respectability is significant in more than just a symbolic way. The prospect of an eventual "common defence" held out in Article J.4 undoubtedly remains a long way off. Nevertheless, that it is now a matter for contemplation is a first sign that the European Union's days as a political pygmy may be drawing to a close. A single market, an Economic and Monetary Union, and a joint foreign policy are three significant components of a federal entity; a common defense may come to be seen as the final element in creating unity out of union.

Europe's Foreign Policy: The Issues

Before concluding this chapter, which has looked largely at the development and modalities of foreign policy making in the EC from its beginnings until the present, it is worth considering some of the major issues that have been and are likely to be the focus of this policy. In the past, political cooperation has tended to be used predominantly though not exclusively in response to crises. Thus the Community reacted with economic sanctions to the Argentinean invasion of the Falkland/Malvinas Islands, to the Iraqi invasion of Kuwait, and to the Iranian *fatwa* against Salman Rushdie; it responded to the war in the former Yugoslavia by supporting humanitarian aid efforts, deploying EU monitors, and appointing a mediator; it reacted to the Russian intervention in Chechnya by postponing the conclusion of the partnership agreement that had just been negotiated. These and many other examples characterize the fire-fighting quality of EPC and CFSP actions and responses.

Particularly since the mid-1980s, however, the Community has also begun to look at the broader picture, and this may well start to become the norm. In 1986, for example, a working party on human rights was set up under EPC following a declaration by the Twelve about the importance they attached to this question. Since then, the Community, and now the Union, regularly issues statements or declarations whenever it becomes aware of human rights abuses anywhere in the world, and brings these directly to the attention of the government concerned. It has intervened on behalf of individuals who may be imprisoned or facing the death penalty and made formal protests to the authorities involved. The European Parliament is especially active in this field, having passed hundreds of resolutions condemning human rights violations. Armed now with the power to withhold its assent to agreements between the EU and third countries, the Parliament has gained considerable leverage and is perceived by many countries as unreasonably meddling in this respect.

There are numerous other areas, too, where the EU continues to play a quiet and more long-term foreign policy role. It has long been involved in the CSCE (now the Organization for Security and Cooperation in Europe [OSCE]) process and works as well in other international fora, not least in the United Nations and its agencies. Over the years it has played an active role as an accredited observer in bodies such as UNCTAD, the Food and Agriculture Organization (FAO), the International Monetary Fund (IMF), the International Labour Organisation (ILO), the Rio Conference on the environment, and the UN women's conferences, to name but a few. The EC is a signatory to the Convention on the Law of the Sea, even though not all of its member states have yet signed, and party to a host of international environmental agreements, ranging from the Barcelona convention for the protection of the Mediterranean Sea against pollution to the

Canberra convention on the conservation of Antarctic marine living resources.

These are all activities in which the EU has been involved with little fanfare but that nevertheless constitute the bread and butter of international relations. While they may not always count strictly as *foreign policy,* and Community involvement has often been the result of its legal obligations under articles of the treaties rather than because of EPC or CFSP initiatives, such activities have served to give the institutions, and particularly the Commission, the experience of being an international player. At the same time, they have heightened awareness in the member states' capitals that it has become virtually impossible to pursue national policy without taking full account of the Community dimension.

That said, the CFSP has not so far produced any spectacular results that might differentiate it from political cooperation in its earlier forms. The danger was always that the new, more grandiose title conferred on EPC by the Maastricht Treaty would raise expectations beyond what was achievable in the short term. The new name and the revised procedures embodied in the CFSP have not in themselves been able to make the member states any more likely to agree on appropriate action in a given situation than they were in the past. As before, a common foreign policy, to say nothing of a common security policy, remains an elusive goal. It has worked best so far in cases where a long-standing identity of opinion has existed (such as on South Africa) or where the novelty of a situation has not yet resulted in a wide range of differing national positions or interests that might have overshadowed a successful common approach (such as toward Central and Eastern Europe and Russia). Granted, arriving at a common approach to foreign policy is not an easy thing for fifteen still sovereign states to do, especially when the machinery for cooperation leaves each participant with the right to undermine the plans of the others. But as later chapters of this book argue, what have sometimes been perceived as failures of the CFSP (such as the EU's role in Bosnia) are not necessarily a reflection on the policymaking apparatus itself but rather on the intrinsic difficulties in finding solutions to complex problems. After all, it is not as if the finely tuned foreign policy machines of Foggy Bottom, the Quai d'Orsay, or Whitehall have proved any more adept at dealing with issues like Bosnia, Rwanda/Burundi, or Iraq.

It seems apparent that much of what the EU *has* achieved internationally has been the result not of deliberate foreign policy choices but of hybrid policymaking based more on the traditional Community method than on intergovernmental cooperation under EPC or the CFSP. The genealogy of the November 1995 Euro-Mediterranean conference and the Barcelona Declaration, for example, can be traced back to the global Mediterranean policy initiated by the European Community at the beginning of the 1970s and reinforced regularly since then. The signature of the New Transatlantic

Agenda between the EU and the United States—an eminently political action—was not based on any CFSP decision but emerged from years of close contacts spanning decades of cooperation (and sometimes argument) in almost every conceivable field. The first Euro-Asian summit, which took place in March 1996 in Bangkok, was as much the culmination of a series of Commission-inspired initiatives designed to reinvigorate ties with the countries and regions of Asia (and a response to an Asian invitation) as the result of any deliberate foreign policy worked out at the intergovernmental level. All these events and contacts and many others besides are part of an evolving pattern of EU external relations, economic as well as "political," which together form the stuff of foreign policy in the wider sense. The coming chapters attempt to situate these activities in a geopolitical context and to assess them in terms of their effect and impact, irrespective of their genesis as either Community or intergovernmental initiatives.

Notes

1. The spillover concept was elaborated by Ernst Haas. See, for example, E. B. Haas, *The Uniting of Europe* (Stanford, CA: Stanford University Press, 1958). See also Philippe Schmitter, "Three Neofunctional Hypotheses About International Integration," *International Organizations* 23, no. 1 (1969), pp. 161–166.

2. See Carole Webb, "Introduction: Variations on a Theoretical Theme," in Helen Wallace, William Wallace, and Carole Webb (eds.), *Policy-making in the European Communities* (New York: Praeger, 1981).

3. See J. Ikenberry, D. A. Lake, and M. Mastanduno (eds.), *The State and American Foreign Economic Policy* (Ithaca, NY: Cornell University Press, 1988).

4. See Roy H. Ginsberg, *Foreign Policy Actions of the European Community: The Politics of Scale* (Boulder, CO: Lynne Rienner, 1989), p. 45.

5. The Treaty on European Union (the Maastricht Treaty) consists of three pillars: the Community pillar, comprising the three original EC treaties; the CFSP pillar; and the justice and home affairs pillar. The latter two pillars are based on intergovernmental cooperation and are therefore outside the Community structure.

6. Christian Fouchet was the French diplomat who chaired the negotiating committee set up to draft proposals for a political union.

7. *Bulletin*, 1–1970, p. 12.

8. Ibid., 11–1970, pp. 9–14.

9. Ibid., 9–1973, pp. 14–21.

10. Ibid., 11–1981, and supplement, 3–1981.

11. The troika system, involving the country holding the presidency, plus the previous and next holders, was designed to ensure a measure of continuity and also to help smaller member states during their tenures as Council president by giving them the support of two other states, at least one of which would likely be a larger one. This makes it possible for countries like Luxembourg, Greece, or Ireland, say, to function in the presidency in spite of being diplomatically present in only a limited number of foreign capitals or having foreign ministries that dispose of only limited staff and other resources.

12. *Bulletin*, 6–1983, p. 26.

13. "Resolution on the Draft Treaty Establishing the European Union," *Official Journal* C 77, 19 March 1984, p. 33.

14. "Report of the Adhoc Committee on Institutional Matters," in *A New Phase in European Union* (Luxembourg: European Parliament, 1985).

15. The appellation "European Council" was adopted by the heads of state and government at their Paris meeting in December 1974; these meetings had previously been known simply as "summits." Article 2 of the Single European Act gave the European Council formal status by describing its role and stipulating that it should meet at least twice annually. Article D of the Treaty on European Union specified that the role of the European Council was to "provide the Union with the necessary impetus for its development and [to] define the general political guidelines thereof."

16. *Bulletin*, 2–1986, p. 115.

17. It is important to recall the distinction between the "foreign ministers meeting in political cooperation" and the foreign ministers sitting in the Council. Although they were of course precisely the same people, they met as the "Council" only when discussing *Community* business. Since EPC took place on the intergovernmental level, the foreign ministers met as representatives of their respective countries, not as members of the Council, when discussing foreign policy. The presidency of the foreign ministers was held by the same country that held the presidency of the Council (which rotates from member state to member state on a quasi-alphabetical basis every six months).

18. Although the SEA had been agreed at the end of 1985 and signed in February 1986, delays in national ratification procedures meant that almost eighteen months elapsed before it finally entered into force on 1 July 1987.

19. These entered into force as follows: Hungary, 1 December 1988; Poland, 1 December 1989; Czechoslovakia and Bulgaria, 1 November 1990; Romania, 1 May 1991; Albania, 1 December 1992; Estonia, 1 March 1993; Latvia and Lithuania, 1 February 1993; Slovenia, 5 April 1993.

20. As was the case with the Single European Act, problems ratifying the Treaty on European Union at the national level led to a delay of almost two years between its conclusion and signature and its actual entry into force.

21 The European Parliament has always proved well able to use its often limited powers to great effect in many areas. The CFSP is likely to be no exception to this rule. Already the EP has successfully lobbied the Council and Commission on a range of foreign policy issues, including human rights, relations with South Africa, and EU policy on the Middle East.

22. The WEU is a military alliance set up in 1954 among the six original EC member states plus the United Kingdom. Spain, Portugal, and Greece have since joined, and the remaining EU states have observer status in the organization.

3

The EU's Near Abroad:
The European Neighbors

The European Community was never coy about its title. It unashamedly appropriated the name of the entire European continent in describing itself and its institutions. It apparently occurred to none of the EC's founders in the early 1950s that their new enterprise might better be called the *Western* European Community. Indeed, when it began life, the "European" Community consisted of only six out of a total of some thirty European countries, not counting the Soviet Union. At least the Strasbourg-based Council of Europe, set up in 1949, could claim the membership of every European state west of the iron curtain, as well as Turkey. But the EC, having already established the *European* Coal and Steel Community, went blithely on to set up the *European* Economic Community and the *European* Atomic Energy Community. The "*European* Assembly" (later the European Parliament) was the name given to the consultative body of parliamentarians who were supposed to (and subsequently did) inject some semblance of democracy into the "European" endeavor. Later the "European Council" was the name given to the summit meetings of the heads of state and government of what by then were nine countries. As recently as 1994, the Commission of the European Communities, as it had been more or less accurately called, changed its official appellation to "European Commission." By that time there were over forty European countries, only twelve of which were members of the European Union.

Though its name was appropriated by a group of countries in its midst, the bulk of Europe remained independent of the Community, though certainly not unaffected by it. In its early days, the EC had no formal ties with the Soviet Union and its East bloc satellites, nor with their economic organization, the CMEA. But the EC quickly concluded agreements with its western neighbors, signing association agreements with Greece and Turkey (in 1961 and 1963, respectively) and with Malta and Cyprus (in 1970 and 1972). In the early 1970s, immediately following British, Danish, and Irish accession to the EC, the Community entered into free trade agreements with the remaining EFTA countries (Austria, Iceland, Norway, Portugal, Sweden, and Switzerland). These countries collectively formed the EC's most important trading partner, accounting for a greater two-way flow of commerce than with the United States and Japan combined. The free trade relationship was upgraded in the early 1990s to a novel arrangement known as the European Economic Area. Under the terms of the agreements, the EFTA states subscribed to virtually all of the economic and commercial aspects of the single European market; the EEA thus constituted an internal market of eighteen countries, twelve in the EC and six in EFTA (Switzerland's electorate refused to ratify the treaty in a referendum and the country did not accede to the EEA). In the event, the significance of the EEA dwindled following the accession of three of the EFTA states, Austria, Finland, and Sweden to the EU in 1995, leaving only Iceland, Liechtenstein, and Norway as non-EU members of the EEA.

The EU's relations with its Central and Eastern European neighbors have only recently become important. Until 1988 the Soviet Union and the other state trading countries of Eastern Europe did not even accord the European Community diplomatic recognition. But the momentous events of the late 1980s not only changed all that, they made the EC's relations with its eastern neighbors a matter of the highest political priority. In just a few short years, starting with the establishment of formal ties between the EC and Comecon in 1988, an institutionalized relationship has been developed between West and East whose political and economic ramifications are, to say the least, profound.

This chapter examines the development of the EU's relations with its European neighbors and considers the prospects for a European Union that truly embraces the entire continent.

EFTA, the EEA, and Enlargement

The European Union's relations with its immediate neighbors have always been close. The Community treaties made it clear from the outset that membership was open to all European countries. However, in the early 1950s Britain showed considerable hesitancy about the part it should play in the emerging supranational structures; although at least five of the six founding members of the ECSC, as well as the United States, urged Britain to abandon its misgivings, it decided against joining. It also spurned the next stage in the integration process, the establishment of the EEC; and because Britain held back, its closest European trading partners—Ireland, Denmark, and Norway—had no option but to do the same. Spain and Portugal were both nondemocratic, and therefore excluded themselves automatically. Neutral Sweden and Switzerland wanted nothing to do with the construction of a Western European bloc, and Austria and Finland were prevented from even applying because of the terms of their postwar agreements with the Soviet Union. In 1959 Britain led six of its non-EC neighbors[1] in creating the European Free Trade Association, an intergovernmental arrangement designed to provide a larger, tariff-free market for those European countries that had decided to remain outside the Community.

But Britain soon changed its mind and made its first application to join the Community in 1961, just three years after the EEC Treaty had entered into force. Its application was rejected because of opposition from France, and a similar rejection followed a renewed bid in 1967. When the United Kingdom did finally succeed in becoming a member in 1973, twenty-one years had elapsed since the European Coal and Steel Community had begun operations. The story of British indecision on Europe and its gradual conversion to the political and economic necessity of membership as the incipient Community grew and progressed is a good example of the attraction that the EC has always exerted on nonmember European countries. Britain believed it had a world role to play and could best do so independently; it also continued to believe that the Commonwealth could provide an economic and trading partnership in which the UK could have a dominant role. But the reality of the EC, along with changing realities elsewhere in the world, soon made it clear that Europe offered greater opportunities than any nostalgic adherence to a disintegrating empire and an increasingly disparate Commonwealth. The encouragement of the United States, moreover, helped persuade Britain that its destiny lay in Europe: for President John F. Kennedy in particular, the place for the United States' oldest ally was within the new European enterprise, not at arm's length from it.

A fundamental reality of the EC was that the decisions it took regarding its own internal rules had an inevitable effect on all other countries that wished to do business with it. Community regulations have thus often led to trade and other disagreements with the EC's partners, whether over agricultural preferences or export subsidies or the application of rules on matters as diverse as environmental standards or food additives. The greater the volume of trade a country conducted with the EC, the more it found itself subject to rules and regulations it had not helped formulate but with which it nevertheless had to comply. In these circumstances, would it not be better to be *part* of the Community, contributing to and influencing its decisionmaking processes from within, than merely to observe the process from the outside but have to accept the results anyway? The urge to be part of the EC was therefore always strong among many European countries that had not joined in the early years.

For Britain, the choice was truly a complex one, involving as it did the recognition that to cast its lot with its European neighbors was, to some extent at least, to turn its back on its imperial history and its Commonwealth connections and even, despite U.S. encouragement, on the special relationship it continued to enjoy with the United States. But the logic of belonging won the day: ultimately, it would be easier to safeguard Commonwealth interests if Britain, economically strong, were inside the Community than if, weakened, it were to remain outside. British membership would also help to ensure that the EC retained its transatlantic vocation, counterbalancing French reticence toward an overly close relationship with the United States. (It was this reticence that contributed to de Gaulle's hostility to UK membership throughout the 1960s: if Britain joined, the president declared at a press conference on 14 January 1963, the Community "would not endure for long . . . [but] instead would become a colossal Atlantic community under American domination and direction."[2])

For most of the other European states that joined the Community in the 1970s, 1980s, and 1990s, the choice was simpler and less fraught with political overtones. The governments of Denmark, Ireland, and Norway chose to apply for EC membership primarily because of their extremely close economic and trading ties with the UK: they simply could not afford to remain outside the Community if Britain were in it. Ireland additionally saw its own membership in the EC as an opportunity to loosen its extreme dependency on the UK, with which it had a virtual economic and monetary union (Ireland had not become a member of EFTA, not least because of the customs union it enjoyed with Britain). As a poorer country, Ireland also stood to gain directly in economic terms through the CAP and the mooted ERDF, the European Regional Development Fund.[3] Denmark and Norway were not overly enthusiastic about acceding to the Community but believed it was in their best economic interests to do so, given the volume of their trade with Britain (it was by no means certain before the entry negotiations that the enlarged Community would be prepared to conclude free trade agreements with all the EFTA countries). In the event, the Norwegian people rejected membership in a referendum held after their government had already signed the accession treaty in 1972, and the country did not form part of the 1973 enlargement.

Once the Community included the United Kingdom, the organization's size and its economic and political importance immediately and dramatically increased. If the Community of the Six had been worth aspiring to join, it had become even more attractive once it was the Community of the Nine. But in 1973 there were no other potential applicants. Switzerland, whose long tradition of neutrality had kept it from joining even the United Nations, did not consider EC membership (moreover, its complex system of direct democracy, which leaves it with an extraordinarily weak central government, would make it technically impossible for the Swiss confederation to join without first undertaking major constitutional reforms). Austria and Finland were constrained by the legacy of Soviet influence that condemned both to a peripheral political position in Western Europe, and Iceland was economically too dependent on its fishery to countenance membership in a Community with a common fisheries policy. Sweden had decided on political grounds (because of its neutrality) not to apply along with Denmark and Norway, who were both members of NATO. Moreover, all these countries, former partners of Britain and Denmark in EFTA, quickly negotiated free trade agreements with the Nine, thus not only keeping their privileged access to the important UK market but gaining tariff-free entry for their nonagricultural products to the wider EC market as well.

Of the non-EFTA countries, Greece was in the grip of a military dictatorship and its association agreement with the EC (which foresaw eventual accession) was frozen pending a return to democracy. Turkey, which also had an association agreement with the Community and aspired to eventual membership, was still far too backward economically to be considered for accession and in 1974 caused considerable upset by invading Cyprus and occupying the island's northern part. Spain and Portugal, the two Iberian dictatorships, qualified on neither political nor economic criteria for membership, and Portugal negotiated a free trade agreement with the Nine along with its fellow EFTA members. The only other possible applicants, Cyprus and Malta—both of which, as former British colonies, had had privileged access to the UK market—were granted associate status in 1974.

But while many Western European countries still stood aloof from the Community in the 1970s, six of them would join by the 1990s. The first to do so was Greece. Its association agreement with the Community had specifically envisaged eventual membership. Following its return to democracy after military rule that lasted from 1967 to 1974, Athens applied for accession. For the new Greek government, the Community held out the hope of economic support and a stable political environment. The Commission gave a negative opinion on the application, primarily on economic grounds. But the Council put political considerations first and opened negotiations with the government of President Constantine Karamanlis in 1976. A year later, newly democratic Portugal applied to join the Community and was followed by Spain in 1978. The three former dictatorships of southern Europe were about to shift the EC's geographical center of gravity toward the Mediterranean.

Greek membership took effect on 1 January 1981. The negotiations with the Iberian countries were more prolonged. Spain had a large population and was economically backward but with a huge agricultural sector whose products competed with many of those of France and Italy. Accommodating its fishery into the Community framework also presented a complex problem. Portugal caused less trouble; though it was extremely poor, it was also small enough for its economic problems to be absorbed more easily by existing Community structures. Indeed the EC provided a generous package of financial and other aid to Portugal during the pre-accession period designed to facilitate its transition into the Community environment. While all the existing member states fully recognized the political imperative of Spanish and Portuguese membership, not least in order to consolidate the relatively recent transition to democracy by both countries, they were well aware of the costs that the accession would bring. Unlike in the case of the previous enlargement in 1973, which resulted overall in a net gain in budgetary terms for the existing members,[4] the southern expansion involved taking on board three countries that would be net beneficiaries from the EC's budget. Wealthier member states would have to foot the bill, since none of the poorer members were willing to see their receipts from the Community reduced.

In spite of the difficulties, however, terms were finally agreed in March 1985 and the two countries became the eleventh and twelfth members of the EC on 1 January 1986. The Community had proved once again that it was capable of change and adaptation. But it had also demonstrated to aspiring new members that joining was not easy: Spain in particular was not let off the fundamental requirement of accepting the *acquis communautaire,* the almost sacrosanct body of existing Community rules and legislation that any new member is obliged to adopt on entry. Its misgivings about introducing a value-added tax and ending protectionism in a number of areas led to one of a number of crises during the negotiations, but Spain had to back down. Clearly, as the field of the Community's activities and the corpus of its law continued to expand, there would be an ever greater *acquis* that potential future applicants would need to accept.

Spanish and Portuguese accession coincided with the decision to move the entire Community forward through the overdue creation of a genuine internal market, the "1992 project." The Single European Act, signed in February 1986, provided the blueprint and the institutional structures for establishing an economic area in which the borders between the EC's member states would effectively cease to exist. Between and among the twelve Community countries, goods, capital, services, and people would be free to move without restriction. For the EFTA countries, the vast majority of whose trade was with their Community neighbors, this was a cause for some concern. They could not afford to find themselves facing barriers to the sale of their products on the huge EC market resulting from the introduction of a host of new rules and regulations. Like other countries around the world, they feared the emergence of a "Fortress Europe" of which they would not be part. They would need to adapt rapidly to meet the challenge of changes over which they had no influence.

As early as 1984, the EFTA states had sought to intensify their relations with the EC; in April of that year the two sides signed a joint declaration in Luxembourg aimed at setting up an *espace économique européenne,* a European Economic Space, or EES. A "high-level contact group" was created, and two EC-EFTA conventions on trade and transport were concluded in 1987. But as the EC's internal market preparations gathered speed, the EFTA states became increasingly worried that they would be marginalized by the new developments. Most of them began introducing copycat legislation to ensure that their own rules and regulations matched those of the internal market.[5] Some began for the first time to think seriously about joining the Community. This was something that Brussels was less than keen on: the EC had just been through years of difficult enlargement talks and was now engaged in extremely complex internal reforms to meet the 1992 deadline. Another enlargement was the last thing it needed.

It was against this background that Commission president Jacques Delors in January 1989 proposed building on the EES idea and creating an association between the Twelve and the seven EFTA states.[6] Stopping short of actual membership, it would give the EFTA countries a say in the decisionmaking process in the areas covered by the association, namely, all internal market activities and a number of flanking policies such as research and development, consumer and social policy, transport, and the environment. The EFTA states welcomed the proposal, and negotiations began in mid-1990 to create a European Economic Area (revising the rather contrived English translation of *espace économique*).

The agreement, signed in May 1992, was far-reaching. Although it did not extend to a formal customs union, it turned the nineteen countries of the EC and EFTA into a single market. The EFTA states had to accept not only the free movement of goods but also the other freedoms: of services, capital, and persons. The last of these meant that immigration controls between the two groups would disappear, with EC citizens given the right to live and work in EFTA countries and vice versa. For EFTA, the agreement meant accepting vast parts of the *acquis communautaire*. While many sectors remained outside the terms of the EEA (e.g., the Common Agricultural Policy, the common trade policy, taxation and financial matters, etc.), the agreement was a genuine halfway house toward actual membership and for the first time gave non-EC countries a say (albeit limited) in policy formulation and decisionmaking in matters relating to the internal market (at least to the extent that they concerned the EEA). The EEA is overseen by a council (consisting of members of the EC Council and Commission and one member of each EFTA government) and administered by a joint committee of senior officials from the two sides. Disputes are settled by an EFTA Court of Justice working with the EC's Court, and surveillance bodies are set up by the two sides to ensure that the agreement is being properly implemented and respected. There is even a measure of parliamentary control, exercised by a joint parliamentary committee of members of the European Parliament and the national EFTA parliaments.

A unique example of cooperation between separate regional groupings, the EEA agreement demonstrates the imaginative lengths to which the Community is willing to go to accommodate the interests of third countries.

The full potential of the agreement, however, was never realized. In the first place, the Swiss electorate voted against ratification of the agreement, so that when the EEA came into force, on 1 July 1993, it did so without the most powerful of the EFTA economies. But more important, the long drawn out negotiations on the EEA, which lasted over two years, had occurred at a time of major political change in Europe. Between the beginning and end of the EEA talks, the Soviet Union had collapsed and the EC's own IGCs on political and economic union had begun and been concluded with the signature of the Maastricht Treaty on European Union. The Community had also concluded the first of a number of association agreements with the countries of Central and Eastern Europe and started preparations for the negotiation of partnership agreements with several of the successor states of the former Soviet Union. In these circumstances, many of the EFTA states had come to see the EEA as no more than a step on the way to full EC membership. Indeed Austria, having received a green light from Moscow, had already put in an application for full EC membership in July 1989, before the EEA talks had even started. Sweden, its vaunted neutrality no longer an issue in the post–Cold War era, applied in June 1991, Finland in March 1992, Switzerland in May 1992 and Norway in November of that year. Of the EFTA countries, all except Iceland (still concerned about the impact membership would have on its fishery) and tiny Liechtenstein[7] had sought accession to the EU even before the entry into force of the EEA agreement.

Switzerland's government decided not to pursue its application following rejection by the Swiss people in a referendum on the country's EEA membership. Austria, Finland, and Sweden negotiated entry terms that were approved in referenda in 1994, allowing them to take their places in the European Union on 1 January 1995. The long and complex negotiations that led to the novel EEA agreement were thus ultimately in vain; the EEA now extends beyond the fifteen member states of the EU to encompass only Iceland, Norway, and Liechtenstein. These three, together with Switzerland,[8] are now the last remaining states of Western Europe not to form part of the Union.

Central and Eastern Europe

If the Community certainly always saw its western neighbors as potential applicants and eventual members, it had never really imagined that it might one day have to expand its vision of Europe to include the lost states beyond its *eastern* frontier. While it would be an exaggeration to say that the original Community was born out of the postwar division of Europe, it is true that its expansion and growth were strongly conditioned by the existence of two distinct blocs in Europe. In strategic terms, the presence of a strong economically and if possible politically integrated Western

Europe was in the overriding security interest of the West as a whole. Had the Soviet-dominated East collapsed sooner, it is doubtful whether the same impetus would have existed that spurred the Community on during the 1970s and especially the 1980s. Nor would the United States have backed the EC so wholeheartedly.

For the Soviet Union and its client states in Central and Eastern Europe, the EC served as a constant reminder of what market-driven economies, working together, could achieve. The USSR-led CMEA (Comecon) failed to achieve any real measure of economic or structural integration among its members, none of which recovered the economic strength they had enjoyed before the war. Efforts by the Community in the early 1970s to cooperate with the CMEA came to nothing: while the Soviet Union was prepared to see the creation of strictly bilateral EC-CMEA links, the Community rejected this as unworkable in the absence of any genuine supranational structure within Comecon. Brussels wanted bilateral agreements with individual CMEA member states, not with the organization per se, which lacked the institutional machinery to act on behalf of its members. In 1974 the Community offered to conclude a series of trade agreements with individual Comecon states. Only Romania responded, and the EC signed a general agreement on trade in industrial products with Bucharest in 1980 (the Community's only other formal agreement with a European Communist country was with Yugoslavia, an associate member of Comecon: a first accord had been concluded in 1970 and was upgraded to a preferential trade and cooperation agreement in 1980).

The emergence of Mikhail Gorbachev as Soviet leader in 1985 changed everything. Within two years the CMEA had accepted the Community's original proposal, which was for formal contacts between the two organizations, with specific trade agreements to be negotiated bilaterally between the EC and those individual Comecon states that were interested. It was on this basis that the EC and the CMEA signed a joint declaration of mutual recognition on 25 June 1988; the two sides would cooperate in areas where they were competent but leave individual agreements to be worked out separately. There was no lack of interest. A series of first-generation agreements was quickly concluded between the Community and Hungary (September 1988), Czechoslovakia (December 1988), Poland (September 1989), the Soviet Union (December 1989), and the GDR and Bulgaria (May 1990).

As far as Comecon itself was concerned, its belated acceptance of the inevitable turned out to be no more than a final gesture. Three years after the joint declaration, in 1991, the Council for Mutual Economic Assistance quietly wound up its affairs and ceased to exist. The Soviet Union was on the point of collapse, and with it the Soviet bloc. For the countries that now emerged, independent but bruised, their economies in a state of shock, their environments dangerously damaged, their politicians discredited, and their internal stability at risk, the European Community appeared over the western horizon as their only sure anchorage.

The first-generation agreements—agreements on trade and commercial and economic cooperation—were all country-specific. The trade provisions included most-favored nation treatment, mutual trade concessions, and an end to EC import quotas; they also held out the prospect of eventual trade liberalization in the form of tariff cuts. Commercial cooperation involved exchange of trade and economic information and statistics, contacts between business and professional associations, cooperation between customs authorities, and investment promotion. The targets of economic cooperation were industry, mining, energy and technological research, the environment, financial services, training, standards, and so on. Unlike similar agreements between the Community and various other areas of the world (e.g., the Mediterranean countries), these accords contained no financial protocols or other forms of direct aid.

In parallel with the conclusion of the series of first-generation agreements, the Community and its Western partners were actively engaged in confronting the wider consequences posed by the collapse of the state-trading economies of the East. There was a clear recognition that the changed circumstances involved risks but also offered opportunities. An unstable, economically depressed region in Europe's eastern half could lead quickly to catastrophic repercussions for the Community. A massive influx of economic refugees was the last thing the countries of the EC needed, as they were already suffering from record levels of unemployment. But instability could have more dire consequences, including the possibility of civil strife and the reemergence of authoritarian regimes. Successful reform, on the contrary, would in time provide the Community (and the West in general) with huge new markets and offer exporters and investors alike the chance to cash in on transforming an economic disaster area into a series of modern, consumer-oriented market economies. More than that, political stability would allow Western Europe and NATO to realize huge military savings once they could relax their defensive postures, so long geared to the possibility of attack from the East.

The first discussion about how to respond to the new situation took place at the European Council meeting in Rhodes in December 1988. At the G7 summit in Paris in July 1989, participants (including the United States, Canada, and Japan) agreed to give the EC's Commission the lead role as coordinator of Western aid to Poland and Hungary, the first two of the Central European states to embark on political and economic reform. The aid itself was to come from a group of twenty-four countries (the G-24) consisting of the EC and EFTA states plus Australia, Canada, Japan, New Zealand, Turkey, and the United States (the member countries of the OECD). In December 1989 the European Council decided on the creation of the European Bank for Reconstruction and Development (EBRD) to provide loans to the countries of Central and Eastern Europe, and a meeting of the G-24 convened in Brussels to discuss the aid program for Poland and Hungary (by then named PHARE). They agreed the program would be extended to other countries in the area once these countries had embarked on the necessary economic and political reforms.

The PHARE program was indeed extended. In May 1990 Bulgaria, Czechoslovakia, the GDR, and Yugoslavia became beneficiaries of the scheme (though the GDR was reunited with the Federal Republic later that year, and after the breakup of Yugoslavia only Slovenia continued to receive PHARE funding). Eventually, all other Central and Eastern European countries (including Albania and the Baltic republics of Estonia, Latvia, and Lithuania) also became beneficiaries. The amounts involved were considerable: from $640 million in 1990, annual allocations have risen every year to almost $1.3 billion in 1996. Funding is supplied in the form of nonreimbursable grants and is intended primarily to help create the conditions for a market-oriented economy based on private ownership. Priority areas are agreed with each recipient country on an annual basis; these may include agriculture, industry, investment, energy, training, safeguarding the environment, trade and services, and so on. The PHARE budget is also used to finance a number of other programs, such as the PHARE Democracy Program, intended to strengthen social and democratic institutions in the recipient countries; TEMPUS, the Trans-European Mobility Program for University Studies; COST, or Cooperation in Science and Technology; Jopp, the joint venture support program; and Overture, a program to encourage East-West cooperation in local government.

In 1992 a separate program with similar aims was set up to help the newly independent countries of the former Soviet Union. Known as Technical Assistance to the CIS, the scheme is designed to help build the structures necessary for economic reform, at both the administrative and technical levels. TACIS funding until 1996 averaged around $600 million per year. To parallel these institutionalized assistance programs, the European Union also provided extensive emergency and humanitarian aid in cash and in kind. Particularly during the first two years following the collapse of the Soviet Union, substantial quantities of emergency food aid, along with medicine, fuel, and other urgently needed supplies, were dispatched to Russia and other former Soviet republics. While countries from around the world (as well as international agencies such as the World Bank) have joined in the efforts to provide funding to Central and Eastern Europe and the CIS, the European Union has been by far the most significant overall contributor and has had the biggest involvement on the ground in channeling the international aid effort.

The Europe Agreements

But the countries of the region looked to the Community to do more than just provide aid. They wanted above all closer contractual ties to the EC and the commitment to their development that that would bring. The first generation of trade and cooperation agreements was thus in the view of both the EC itself and the partner countries just a stepping stone toward something more. That something was to be a series of association agreements (known as Europe agreements) with the Central and Eastern European countries and partnership agreements with Russia and other member nations of the CIS. The Europe agreements were the first of their kind because they were negotiated by the Commission on behalf of the Community *and* the individual EC member states. Known as "mixed agreements," they covered areas that lay within the competence of both the Community (e.g., trade and economic cooperation) and the member states (e.g., political and cultural cooperation[9]). The first three agreements of this kind were negotiated in 1991 with Poland, Hungary, and Czechoslovakia (the latter agreement had to be renegotiated after Czechoslovakia split into the Czech Republic and Slovakia in 1993). The Polish and Hungarian accords came into force on 1 February 1994, and those with the Czech Republic and Slovakia, as well as two others that had since been concluded with Bulgaria and Romania, a year later, on 1 February 1995. Europe agreements have since been negotiated with the three Baltic republics and Slovenia and are likely to come into force in 1997.

What do these agreements offer? The preamble of each recognizes that the final objective of the country concerned is to become a member of the European Union and that in the meantime it seeks full integration into the political, economic, and security order of a new Europe. The agreements regulate the whole range of economic and trade relations between the parties. The EU moves unilaterally and rapidly toward reducing its tariffs and import restrictions, while its partners do so more gradually. The associated countries are to adapt their legislation in all relevant areas, including the field of competition law, to match that of the EC. Discrimination against workers or businesses of an associated country established in the Union is banned. The agreements set up institutional frameworks for political dialogue and institute cultural cooperation, designed to help make up for generations of separation between Western and Central and Eastern European countries and their peoples. And in each case the entire bilateral relationship is institutionalized through the establishment of an association council (comprising the EC's Council on the one hand and members of the partner country's government on the other) and, at the parliamentary level, an association parliamentary committee of members of the European Parliament and the national parliament concerned.

All the agreements contain specific reference to respect for human rights, the Helsinki Final Act, and the Paris Charter; and (except in the cases of Poland and Hungary) suspension clauses allow the agreements to be rescinded in the event of violation of these principles. The accords fail to address, however, the question of freedom of movement of people. Poland in particular had pressed for free entry to the European Union of its citizens by the end of the agreement's transitional period; without it, Poland argued, there would likely be an upsurge in the number of Poles living and working illegally in the EC.[10] The issue would need to be confronted later, once negotiations on enlargement with Poland and the other Central and Eastern European countries began. But the Community was unwilling to grasp this particular nettle at the time of negotiating the Europe agreements, fearing that existing xenophobic tendencies in many EC countries would only be exacerbated. Germany was particularly reluctant, since it would be the principal destination for most migrants. Having just had to absorb massive population shifts following reunification as well as the influx of large numbers of ethnic Germans from elsewhere in Eastern Europe and the former Soviet Union, Germany was not ready to open the floodgates still wider.

Nonetheless, these agreements clearly represent a milestone in relations between Western and Eastern Europe. Together with the comprehensive aid programs already established, they offer a clear signal not only to the associated countries themselves but also to interested parties such as Russia that the European Union is committed to their economic and political integration. But for almost all of the new democracies, this remains an interim stage. Their final goal is full membership in the EU as soon as possible, and all the associated countries have now formally applied for accession. The EU accepted the principle of membership as early as June 1993, when the European Council meeting in Copenhagen declared formally that "the associated countries of Central and Eastern Europe that so desire shall become members of the European Union."[11] Accession would assume, however, that the applicants were stable democracies, had functioning market economies, were able to cope with the competitive pressures within the Union, and were willing to accept the *acquis communautaire*, including political and Economic and Monetary Union. The Union, for its part, would need to show the necessary capacity to absorb new members while, in the words of the European Council's final declaration, "maintaining the momentum of European integration."[12]

The option of widening without deepening the Union was thus ruled out, a position that was confirmed at subsequent meetings of the European Council (notably at Corfu in June 1994 and at Essen in December 1994). For the EU, this will mean considerable internal adjustment. With the present fifteen member states, the institutional structures of the Union, designed for a Community of six, can barely cope. The survival of the national veto right in the Council on a wide range of issues means that decisionmaking can be blocked by just one state. The present membership of the Commission, the EU's executive body, is twenty, a figure already widely held to be excessive. The European Parliament currently has 626 MEPs; a Union of twenty-five[13] states or more, with a population of almost 500 million, risks becoming bogged down in its own bureaucratic organization if the machinery is not streamlined. The 1996 intergovernmental conference, called to review the workings of the Maastricht Treaty, has already begun to address these questions.

Meanwhile, the applicant states have much to do: in June 1995 the Commission published a white paper[14] setting out its thoughts on the first stage of the Essen European Council's pre-accession strategy and providing advice on how the associated countries could align their national legislation with that of the EU's internal market as an essential prerequisite to ultimate membership. While the eventual incorporation of the Central and Eastern European countries into the Union is politically inevitable, the speed of their accession will depend on their economic progress and the concessions they are willing to make to achieve it—for example, agreeing to lengthy transition periods perhaps involving initial exclusion from certain common policies. The question also remains whether the applicant countries will join en bloc or whether entry negotiations, and eventual accession, will be staggered, allowing the economically more advanced countries to join first. It seems likely at present that Poland, Hungary, the Czech Republic, and perhaps Slovenia may well be admitted first, with most or all of the other applicants having to wait, perhaps for a good number of years. In any event, the next enlargement is unlikely to take place before the year 2001 or 2002. (The question of the accession of Cyprus and Malta, with whom entry negotiations were scheduled to begin six months after the conclusion of the 1996 IGC, is discussed in the next chapter.)

Yugoslavia and Albania

The war in the former Yugoslavia began in June 1991 after Slovenia and Croatia declared their independence from the Socialist Federated Republic of Yugoslavia. Belgrade had been one Communist capital with which the EC had always enjoyed relatively easy relations; only an associate member of Comecon and outside the Soviet orbit, Marshall Tito's Yugoslavia had concluded a trade agreement with the Community in 1970, followed by a preferential trade and cooperation accord in 1980. It was natural for the Community to want to intercede diplomatically after the Yugoslav federal army invaded Slovenia two days after the latter had declared independence from Yugoslavia, and it appeared that a lightning visit to Belgrade the same day by the troika of EC foreign ministers contributed to a rapid cessation of hostilities in the newly independent republic. A team of EC peacekeepers was dispatched to the area, and the blue and gold European flag on uniforms and vehicles began to appear on TV screens around the world. This auspicious start to EC involvement was short-lived.

In July 1991 the conflict spread to Croatia, with Serbian forces, backed by the Yugoslav army, pledged to protect the Serbian minority (which, according to prewar figures, accounted for only around 12 percent of Croatia's population). At the European Community's insistence, an international peace conference was convened in The Hague in September 1991; Lord Carrington was appointed the EC's mediator, with Cyrus Vance assuming the same role on behalf of the United Nations. These efforts notwithstanding, the war in Croatia raged on, with Serbian troops laying siege to Zadar, Dubrovnik, and Vukovar, and Zagreb being bombed by the Yugoslav air force. In January 1992 the Community accorded diplomatic recognition to Slovenia and Croatia. This move, taken largely at the insistence of Germany, was privately opposed by many member states (particularly in the case of Croatia), but the overriding concern was to present a united front to uphold EC credibility. In the event, the Serbs lost all confidence in the Community as a neutral arbitrator.

Although an EC-mediated cease-fire was agreed in Croatia in January 1992 between the Zagreb government and the Serb-held Krajina region, to be policed by UN peacekeepers, a new conflict was developing in Bosnia-Herzegovina. Here, too, the Serbs (31.5 percent of the population) were pitted against the non-Serbs (Muslims, 43.8 percent, and Croats, 17.3 percent). An EC-inspired referendum on independence took place in Bosnia during the final days of February 1992. Largely boycotted by the Serbs, it came out clearly in favor of secession from Yugoslavia. The Community (and most other countries, including the United States) recognized the new Republic of Bosnia-Herzegovina. Unwilling to accept the decision to separate from Serbia, the Bosnian Serb population formed an army (initially assisted by the Yugoslav federal army) and began its program of "ethnically cleansing" its strongholds throughout the country. By the end of 1992, the Bosnian Serbs had seized 70 percent of Bosnian territory and effectively blockaded the capital, Sarajevo. To complicate matters, Bosnian Muslims and Croats began to clash in areas where the two groups shared territory, most memorably in the southwestern town of Mostar. After the creation of the Muslim-Croat federation, Mostar was placed under EU administration, with the agreement of the town's Muslim and Croat inhabitants. Under the authority first of Hans Koschnik, former mayor of Bremen, and then (from April 1996) Ricardo Perez Casado, former mayor of Valencia, and (from July 1996) Sir Martin Garrod, a former British army general, a team of EU officials and 140 police officers began helping rebuild the town's shattered physical, political, and social structures.

While all this was going on, a further diplomatic problem was brewing. The same EC-sponsored commission[15] that had recommended recognition of Slovenia and Croatia had also supported recognizing the independence of Macedonia. Greece, however, objected on the grounds that this former Yugoslav republic had appropriated the name and symbols of the similarly named Greek province and even had designs on Greek territory. While this struck most of Athens' EC partners as manifestly absurd, it was a major political issue in Greece, and the governments of Constantine

Mitsotakis (and subsequently Andreas Papandreou) refused to allow Community recognition of Macedonia until the latter renounced its name. Out of reluctant solidarity with Greece, all twelve member states and the EC itself initially withheld recognition of what became known as FYROM, the Former Yugoslav Republic of Macedonia. Indeed, it was under this name that independent Macedonia was admitted to the United Nations in April 1993. Greece maintained a blockade of Macedonia until the government in Skopje made a number of concessions in the autumn of 1995, including amending its constitution to make it clear that it had no designs on Greek territory and changing its flag.

A joint EC-UN-sponsored conference on Bosnia, held in London in August 1992, was attended by the leaders of all the Yugoslav successor states. The conference was followed by five months of talks in Geneva. In January 1993 Lord Owen (Lord Carrington had resigned as EC mediator out of frustration over what he considered to be persistent Serbian deception) and Cyrus Vance produced a peace plan partitioning Bosnia into three areas that would together form a single state. This proved unacceptable to the parties, and the war raged on. In August 1993 Owen and Cyrus Vance's successor as UN mediator, Thorwald Stoltenberg, proposed a new plan that awarded 52 percent of Bosnian territory to the Serbs, 30 percent to the Muslims, and 18 percent to the Croats. The warring sides rejected this, too. Although the final peace agreement reached at Dayton, Ohio, in November 1995 changed these percentages slightly (with the Serbs receiving around 49 percent of the territory, and the new Muslim-Croat Federation taking the rest), the difference was not significant. Rather, war-weariness and the increasing hopelessness of either side in achieving a military victory led to its unenthusiastic acceptance.

For the European Community (by war's end, the European Union), the Yugoslav experience was an honest attempt at providing mediation in a conflict in its own backyard. Its lack of obvious success was due to numerous factors, all of which demonstrated the limits of joint action in foreign policy under EPC and the CFSP as presently constituted.[16] The need for unanimity obliged the Community to take decisions (such as those on Croatia and Macedonia) that may not have been the most appropriate: for example, the fear of a split in ranks, threatened by German and Greek plans to act unilaterally if there was no consensus, forced the majority to acquiesce. Other unilateral moves, such as President Mitterrand's unannounced visit to Sarajevo in June 1991 in an unsuccessful one-man attempt to break the Serbian siege, undermined the agreement made at the Lisbon European Council meeting that same month to coordinate policies more closely. But above all, it was simply the EC's inability to take effective (i.e., military) action that brought its efforts to nothing. Although it was able to impose economic sanctions on Serbia, that was all the muscle it possessed. With no military capability of its own and member states unable or unwilling to intervene militarily themselves, its options were limited. As the events of summer and autumn 1995 proved, once there was a clear show of force, with NATO bombing Serb positions to force a withdrawal and an end to the siege of Sarajevo, a solution became possible.

Nevertheless, while the Yugoslav conflict showed the limits to joint European foreign policy making (or to be more precise, showed what was and was not possible at the current stage of integration), the particular circumstances were unusual and unlikely to have been susceptible to a rapid solution even had there been more concerted outside intervention. Similar conflicts elsewhere have not proved easy to resolve. The U.S. experience in Central America in the 1980s showed that even attempts by a world superpower to deal with local wars do not necessarily yield quick results. It is only partly true to suggest that an end to the Bosnian war had to wait until the United States was ready to intervene. During the war's early stages, U.S. politicians and military strategists debating U.S. involvement clearly recognized that imposing a peace on the warring factions in a country with the complex geography and topography of Bosnia would not only not be easy but could prove impossible. Finally, it can be argued, the war had to run itself out before the parties could be brought to the negotiating table, and nothing the European Community did or could have done would have expedited the end.

If the peace in Bosnia holds, the European Union will be called on to make a major contribution toward reconstructing the country. This is likely to take many forms: in the short term, massive quantities of emergency aid will be channeled into the country (as it has been, in lesser quantities, over the past few years, to the extent that roads have been open and the Sarajevo airport able to receive transport aircraft); in the medium term, a comprehensive assistance and reconstruction package will be implemented, covering infrastructure, democratization, administration, industrialization, training, and the like. In parallel with this practical help, the EU is likely to conclude second-generation agreements with all the Yugoslav successor states, similar to those already in force with Slovenia and the Central and Eastern European countries. Ultimately, there is no reason to suppose that some or all of these countries will not eventually become members of the European Union.

The same is true of the other Adriatic state, Albania. Always the most closed of the Communist states, Albania had no links of any kind to the EC prior to 1990. Since the collapse of the old regime, however, Albania has been the beneficiary of substantial amounts of Community aid, and the EC has concluded a trade and cooperation agreement with Tirana. The country's extreme degree of underdevelopment means that it will take some time before it is ready for a second-generation association agreement. But the country's relatively small economy could well respond quickly to the economic reforms now under way and could be attractive to investors. Albania, too, will undoubtedly be a candidate for accession to the EU in the foreseeable future.

Russia and the Newly Independent States (NIS)

The Soviet Union always dealt with the European Community on a pragmatic basis. Like any other country, it was not able to deny the existence of the EC entirely, since trade matters had to be negotiated directly with Brussels under the terms of the Common Commercial Policy, and the common customs tariff was a fact of life that the USSR could not ignore. Nevertheless, Moscow always refused to accord diplomatic recognition to the EC and had no ambassador in Brussels accredited to the Community (though for a number of years staff at the Soviet embassies in Brussels and Luxembourg had informal contacts with the Commission and the European Parliament). Nor did it conclude any trade agreement with the EC. It always insisted that Comecon should be the natural (and equal) partner for the EC, a notion that the Community rejected on the practical grounds that the CMEA lacked the supranational institutions that might allow the two bodies to do business with one another. The Community, as an earlier section of this chapter has described, offered to conclude bilateral agreements with the Soviet Union and any other CMEA state that wished them, a proposal that was consistently rejected until 1988, when the EC and the CMEA signed the Luxembourg joint declaration establishing mutual relations.

A little over a year later, at the end of 1989, the Community and the USSR signed a trade and cooperation agreement similar in content to the first-generation agreements concluded with the Central and Eastern European countries. This was a modest first step, designed not least to reassure the Soviet leadership that the Community regarded the USSR as an integral part of the new European architecture. But there was also plenty of room for an expansion of EC-USSR trade, which in 1990 amounted to a total volume of only ECU 5.8 billion ($7.4 billion), equivalent to about half of total EC trade with Singapore at the time. In 1991 the Soviet Union sent an ambassador to Brussels and the EC opened a delegation office in Moscow, with Michael Emerson as the first ambassador. For the first time since the creation of the European Community, its relations with the Soviet Union were on the same footing as those with almost every other important state in the world.

But the situation in the USSR in 1991 was deteriorating rapidly. Food shortages led to massive disruptions that winter and again in 1992, particularly in the major cities of Russia, and the Community launched an emergency food aid operation. At the same time, it protested about Soviet repression in the Baltic republics, which had declared their independence (Lithuania in 1990, Estonia and Latvia in 1991). In August 1991 President

Gorbachev was forced from office by a coup and was succeeded by Boris Yeltsin. By December of that year the situation in the Soviet Union had become untenable, and the USSR was formally dissolved. For the member states of the EC, which had just signed the Maastricht Treaty and negotiated a series of association agreements with Poland, Hungary, and Czechoslovakia, the collapse of the Soviet Union—and, more to the point, the arrival on the international scene of twelve newly independent states on the territory of the former USSR—meant new challenges.

On the basis of a series of guidelines adopted by its foreign ministers in December 1991, the Community decided to recognize all the Soviet successor states, provided they respected human rights and the rule of law and subscribed to the Helsinki accords and the Paris Charter. Despite the creation of the Commonwealth of Independent States, to which Georgia initially did not subscribe, there was no centralized authority, and new relationships had to be forged bilaterally with all twelve countries. In January 1992 the Commission proposed a new type of mixed agreement to regulate relations between the EC and the new states similar to but not as far-reaching as the Europe agreements with the Central and Eastern European countries.

The partnership and cooperation agreements (PCAs), as they were called, involved both the EC as such and its member states, just as in the case of the Europe association agreements. Each was to be designed to fit the particular conditions of the partner country concerned. Although they are not aimed at integrating the partners into the internal market and therefore do not include the "four freedoms"—freedom of movement for goods, capital, services, and persons—the agreements do provide for a substantial degree of economic cooperation and trade liberalization, including improved access for NIS exports to the EU's market and the prospect of eventual free trade. Unlike the Europe agreements, the PCAs do not hold out the possibility of ultimate EU membership. The first partnership agreements were signed with Russia and Ukraine (in June 1994), followed by Moldova (November 1994), and Belarus (March 1995). Similar but less exhaustive agreements were concluded with Kazakhstan and Kyrghyzstan at the beginning of 1995. During the remainder of that year, the Commission negotiated PCAs with Armenia, Azerbaijan, Georgia, and Uzbekistan; at the end of 1996 ten of the twelve non-Baltic successor states to the Soviet Union had thus concluded agreements with the EU, leaving only Tajikistan and Turkmenistan with no formal links to the Union. There is every reason to suppose that they, too, will conclude PCAs with the EU in due course (though the lack of democratic reform in both countries and the ongoing civil conflict and reported human rights abuses in Tajikistan may mean a considerable delay).

In parallel with the conclusion of these agreements, the Community has played an ongoing part in the political and economic development of Russia and the other NIS. It has provided advice and practical help with

the organization and observation of the first free elections in many of the
countries; arranged visits to the Commission and European Parliament for
NIS civil servants and politicians to study administrative and democratic
structures and processes; sponsored seminars and courses for businesspeople; and above all, through the TACIS and other programs, created a
stream of financial and practical aid designed to encourage economic development. When necessary, it has also given emergency aid, especially
medical and food supplies, to help alleviate some of the worst effects of
the difficult reform process, in particular where it has been exacerbated by
conflicts such as those in the Caucasus and Armenia.

The future of the European Union's relationship with Russia, Ukraine,
Belarus, and the other NIS is unclear. There is no doubt that these countries will become major trading partners for the EU. By 1995 Russia alone
already ranked fifth overall as a destination for the Fifteen's exports; its
total trade with the Union, at ECU 38 billion ($47.5 billion), represented
an almost sevenfold increase over the figure for EU trade *with the entire
Soviet Union* just six years previously. The CIS as a whole ranked fourth,
after Japan, as an EU trading partner, with business worth ECU 46 billion
($57.5 billion) in 1995. Given the enormous growth potential of these
countries, the region seems certain to become even more important both as
market and supplier for the European Union in the coming years.

Accession by any of these countries to the EU is unlikely, however,
certainly in the medium term. Most do not qualify as "European" countries. Russia itself, because of its size, could not conceivably become an
integral part of the European Union in its present form. Ukraine and Belarus, whose size and economic strength would not exclude them a priori,
are more likely to remain part of a Slavic economic area dominated by
Russia. Romanian-speaking Moldova, in contrast, may seek to join the EU,
particularly if Romania accedes. But all this is mere speculation. All that
is clear at present is that the NIS and the EU will continue to strengthen
their ties. Geography, economics, and historical links make the two European regions natural partners.

Notes

1. Austria, Denmark, Norway, Portugal, Sweden, and Switzerland. Finland became an associate member in 1961 and a full member in 1986. Iceland joined in
1970 and Liechtenstein in 1991.

2. Frances Nicholson and Roger East, *From the Six to the Twelve: The Enlargement of the European Communities* (Harlow: Longman, 1987), pp. 30–32.

3. The possibility of setting up a regional fund had been discussed during the
accession negotiations and became Community policy after the Paris summit of
October 1972, but the ERDF was not in fact set up until 1976.

4. The nature and structure of the British economy (in particular its small but
highly efficient agricultural sector) meant that the UK was eligible for only limited

payments from the EC budget under the CAP's Guarantee Fund; it thus joined Germany as the second largest net contributor to the Community. Although Ireland and Denmark were both net beneficiaries, overall the EC profited from the 1973 enlargement.

5. The internal market project involved the adoption by the EC of almost 300 pieces of legislation designed primarily to bring national provisions into line with one another: there could be totally free movement of goods, services, capital, and people only if everyone observed the same set of rules.

6. In 1989 comprising Austria, Finland, Iceland, Liechtenstein, Norway, Sweden, and Switzerland.

7. Liechtenstein, with a population of 30,000 and a GDP of $630 million, has a customs union with Switzerland.

8. After the negative vote in its referendum on EEA membership, Switzerland decided not to pursue its application for membership in the EU; however, the application has not been officially withdrawn.

9. Since European Political Cooperation and later the Common Foreign and Security Policy were intergovernmental rather than Community issues, cooperation on political matters (described as "political dialogue" in the Europe agreements) with third countries had to involve the individual member states: hence the need for them to be party to the agreements in their own right. The same applied technically to some aspects of cultural cooperation, an area in which the Community had only limited responsibilities.

10. See John Pinder, *The European Community and Eastern Europe* (New York: Council on Foreign Relations Press, 1991), pp. 67–69.

11. *Bulletin*, 6–1993, p. 13.

12. Ibid., p. 13.

13. Current applicants from Central and Eastern Europe include Bulgaria, the Czech Republic, Estonia, Hungary, Latvia, Lithuania, Poland, Romania, Slovakia, and Slovenia. Further applications can be expected in due course from Albania, Croatia, and, in the longer term, from the other former republics of Yugoslavia.

14. Commission, *Preparation of the Associated Countries of Central and Eastern Europe for Integration into the Internal Market of the Union*, COM(95) 163 final, 3 May 1995.

15. Set up in December 1991 by the EC foreign ministers to report on requests for recognition by former Yugoslav republics, the commission was headed by Judge Robert Badinter.

16. See, for instance, Simon Nuttall, "Yugoslavia: Deus ex Machina, or Machina sine Deo?" *The European Union 1993: Annual Review of Activities* (Oxford: Blackwell, 1994), p. 11.

4

The EU's Near Abroad: The Mediterranean and the Middle East

The European Union's partnership with many of its closest European neighbors is a recent development, as the previous chapter has shown. The collapse of the rigid structures of Soviet-dominated Europe dates back only to the late 1980s. In the course of a few short years, the EU's relationship to its former ideological enemies has been turned on its head. From virtually no relations at all, the Europe agreements with the Central and Eastern European countries and the partnership agreements with Russia, Ukraine, and the other former Soviet republics have turned the continent into something not so far removed from Gorbachev's vision of a "Common European Home." The pace of the events that created this new situation and the rapidity of the European Union's response to it meant that the EU-Europe relationship dominated Brussels' external affairs agenda for a number of years. As later chapters of this book show, this preoccupation with events in Europe led to the conviction in various parts of the world that the EU was somehow neglecting its wider international responsibilities. This feeling was compounded by the profound institutional changes set in motion by the Single European Act and, later, the conclusion of the Maastricht Treaty. The former, with its overtones implying establishment of a "Fortress Europe," led to concern in much of the international community about access to the new single market; and the implications of the latter, which changed the European Community into a "Union" replete with common foreign policy and a potential single currency, were simply not understood.

Of all the regions of the world to have suffered a period of perceived if not actual neglect by Brussels, none was more important to the EU's own security than its other "near abroad," the southern shore of the Mediterranean and the Middle East. For thousands of years, the Mediterranean was the cultural and economic heart not only of Europe but of the world. The peoples and civilizations that flourished on its shores and islands, together with the three great monotheistic religions that it spawned, provided the foundations for Western civilization as a whole. In modern times the region has maintained much of its importance, politically, economically, and strategically. Much of North Africa and the Middle East was under direct European colonial rule or mandate until after World War II, with the last of the formerly French colonies not gaining independence until well after the European Community was set up. The creation of Israel led to decades of conflict between the Jewish state and its Arab neighbors. Oil from the Persian Gulf states became essential for Europe's postwar economic recovery and for the growth and prosperity of the Community. Out of the struggle of the Palestinians and the rise of Islamic fundamentalism emerged terrorism and hostage-taking, with Europe and Europeans often the principal non-Israeli targets (though the United States has borne its fair share of attacks and abductions). Economic (and political) migrants, especially from North Africa, sought a better life in the European Community. And at the same time, countries like Morocco, Tunisia, Egypt, and Israel became major tourist destinations for sun- and culture-hungry Europeans.

Europe not only bought oil from the Arabs; it also became the major market for the subtropical agricultural produce of many of the southern and eastern Mediterranean states, and increasingly for their industrial products and textile exports as well. In return, Europe supplied most of the latter's needs for manufactured goods and technology (as well as arms). Leaving oil and gas out of the equation, the EU has substantial trade surpluses with most countries in the region (see Figure 4.1). It has also been the major supplier of development aid. With the exception of the oil-rich states of the Arabian peninsula, many of the countries of North Africa and the Middle East are poor and in need of European aid and cooperation as well as trade. Measured in gross domestic product (GDP), the current wealth gap between the EU and the Maghreb and Mashreq states of the southern and eastern Mediterranean stands at around ten to one. The failure of pan-Arabism as a vehicle for mutual support and the absence of prosperous markets among the southern and eastern Mediterranean countries themselves mean that the poorer states in the region have nowhere else to turn but Europe.

At the same time, however, the end of the Cold War has lessened the strategic importance of the Mediterranean. Until the mid-1980s, there was intense competition between the superpowers for influence in the Middle East and North Africa, with both sides providing their "clients" with everything from direct financial support to arms. This interest has largely dissipated. In parallel to the diminishing significance of the Mediterranean area in terms of its place in the East-West conflict, both Europe and the United States are no longer as dependent as they once were on Middle East oil supplies. The 1973 oil shock led to a concentrated and prolonged European effort to diversify its energy requirements and sourcing. While

Figure 4.1   EU-15–Mediterranean Trade, 1995 (in ECU billions)

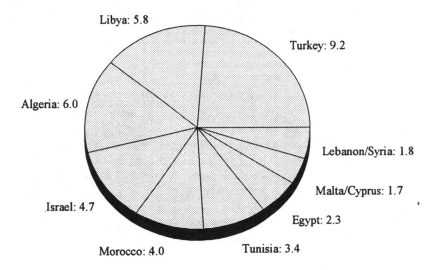

EU Imports

Libya: 5.8

Turkey: 9.2

Algeria: 6.0

Lebanon/Syria: 1.8

Malta/Cyprus: 1.7

Israel: 4.7

Egypt: 2.3

Morocco: 4.0   Tunisia: 3.4

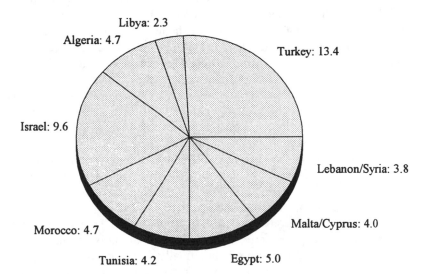

EU Exports

Libya: 2.3

Algeria: 4.7

Turkey: 13.4

Israel: 9.6

Lebanon/Syria: 3.8

Malta/Cyprus: 4.0

Morocco: 4.7

Tunisia: 4.2   Egypt: 5.0

Source: Eurostat

petroleum supplies from the Persian Gulf remain important, they no longer play the role they once did. Because of the development of North Sea oil and gas, the increased contribution of nuclear power (especially in France and Belgium), and the availability of oil and gas from Russia and other sources in the former Soviet Union and elsewhere, Europe is less at the mercy of Middle Eastern suppliers. The progress in the search for an end to the Arab-Israeli conflict has also served to lessen tensions in the area and thus the likelihood of any repeat of the events of the 1970s.

So in these circumstances, what are the parameters of Europe's links to its Mediterranean and Middle Eastern neighbors today? This chapter examines the development of the EU's relations with the Mediterranean and looks at the situation in the aftermath of the Barcelona conference of November 1995 and the latest series of agreements with the riparian states of the southern and eastern Mediterranean and the Persian Gulf. It also considers the position of the two Mediterranean islands, Cyprus and Malta. Finally, it examines the status of Europe's long-standing relationship with Turkey. Associated with the EC since 1963, and with a customs union in place since the beginning of 1996, Ankara has always been kept at arm's length by Brussels, needed and spurned in equal measure.

The "Global Mediterranean Policy" and the Euro-Arab Dialogue

The European Community launched its "global Mediterranean policy" at the Paris summit of October 1972. Designed to establish a "global approach in all the Community's relations with the Mediterranean countries,"[1] the policy sought to bring into a single and coordinated framework the multiplicity of bilateral relations and agreements that existed between the EC and various southern and eastern Mediterranean states individually. The earliest of these were with Lebanon and Israel, with which the Community signed preferential trade agreements in 1964. These were followed by first-generation association agreements with Tunisia and Morocco in 1969 and a trade agreement with Egypt in 1972. By the early 1970s, the Commission's aim was to conclude cooperation agreements with all interested countries on the Mediterranean's southern and eastern shores. The result was the signature of accords with the three Maghreb states of Morocco, Tunisia, and Algeria in 1976 and the Mashreq states of Egypt, Jordan, and Syria in 1977 and Lebanon in 1978.

Concluded on the basis of Article 238 of the EC Treaty, the accords were known as "cooperation agreements." The Commission had claimed that each one would be tailored specifically to the needs of the partner country concerned,[2] but with minor differences they all shared the same characteristics. The agreements offered:

- Trade preferences, opening EC markets to all industrial products with the exception of certain "sensitive" products (such as textiles and refined petroleum) and offering considerable concessions on agricultural produce (the specific items varying from country to country). In return, the partners gave most-favored-nation treatment to Community exports (association agreements are supposed to be based on reciprocity, but the Mediterranean accords were only nominally reciprocal).
- Financial and technical cooperation (aid). Each agreement had a financial protocol annexed to it, laying down the total amount to be made available by the Community in the form of loans and grants from the EC's budget, and the amount that would be lent by the European Investment Bank (EIB). The protocols have been renewed at intervals of five years. Between the conclusion of the agreements and the end of 1996, four financial protocols had been implemented, worth a total (in grants and loans) of ECU 2.69 billion ($3.36 billion) to the Maghreb and ECU 2.33 billion ($2.9 billion) to the Mashreq countries (Syria was excluded from the third and fourth protocols on political grounds).[3]
- Common institutions in the form of a council of ministers, which holds an annual meeting. This is backed up by a committee at the ambassadorial level to assist the council. The Commission has opened permanent delegations in each of the Maghreb and Mashreq countries.
- In the case of the Maghreb partners, migrant workers residing in European Union countries are given privileged status, particularly with regard to eligibility for social security benefits.

In parallel with the negotiation of new agreements with the Arab states of the region, the EC also updated its 1964 preferential trade accord with Israel. In 1975 Brussels signed a free trade agreement with Tel Aviv, which covered not only industrial goods but also made available tariff concessions for much of the country's agricultural produce. Later, in 1995, this was replaced by a Mediterranean association agreement, a far-reaching accord that reinforced trade and political links. Similar third-generation agreements have also been negotiated with Morocco, Tunisia, Jordan, and Egypt, and the Commission plans to update the EU's existing accords with the remaining southern and eastern Mediterranean countries as soon as political and economic circumstances permit.

The institutionalization of relations between the EC and the Maghreb and Mashreq countries began before and continued through and beyond the events of 1973. To that extent, the Community's "global Mediterranean policy" cannot be seen as a reaction to the possibility of an interruption of oil flows from the Middle East. Its motivation was primarily economic in nature, an attempt to regulate relations with close neighbors with a view to the eventual creation of a Mediterranean free trade area. It was the 1973 October War between Israel and its Arab neighbors—and the resulting Arab oil embargo of states perceived to be supporters of Israel (in Europe, principally the Netherlands)—that caused the European Community to rethink its *political* as well as economic relationship to the Arab world. The EC's foreign ministers issued a declaration in November 1973 urging the Israelis to withdraw from the occupied territories of Gaza and the West Bank and acknowledging the legitimate rights of the Palestinian people. Later that month, a meeting of Arab heads of state in Algiers welcomed the EC's position (which in fact went no further than UN Security Council Resolution 242, which the EC's member states had already backed) and effectively launched the idea of a European-Arab dialogue by noting that "Europe is linked to the Arab world through the Mediterranean by profound affinities of civilization and by vital interests which can only be developed within the framework of confidence and mutually advantageous cooperation."[4]

The Euro-Arab Dialogue, as it became known, officially came into being on 31 July 1974 at a meeting between the president and secretary-general of the Arab League and the presidents of the Commission and Council. An agreement was reached to establish an institutional structure (based on a general commission and a series of specialized working parties[5]) for ongoing discussions on a range of economic, technological, social, and cultural issues.[6] The agreement followed French-inspired moves at the EC summit in Copenhagen in December 1973, which was attended by five Arab foreign ministers, and a series of further consultations, including a March 1974 meeting of Community foreign ministers and a meeting of the Arab League in Tunis later that same month.

Almost two years passed before the first meeting of the general commission took place in Luxembourg in May 1976. The delay was due in part to the EC's refusal to accept the formal presence of a distinct Palestine Liberation Organization (PLO) delegation on the Arab side and in part to the question of the political dimension to be accorded to the dialogue. The problem of Palestinian representation was resolved by constituting a unified Arab delegation, whose composition was a matter for the Arabs themselves to determine. The more general question of the nature of the dialogue itself—was it to be primarily political, as the Arabs wished, or economic and technical, as the Europeans preferred?—resulted in a compromise, with practical issues dominating the work of the specialized groups and a more political agenda forming the basis for the general commission meetings. In the four general commission meetings held between 1976 and 1978, the final communiqués reflected this dichotomy, dealing both with political matters (the role of the PLO, Israeli policy, the situation in Lebanon) and the more technical issues that had been discussed by the working groups.[7]

The March 1979 Camp David peace accord between Egypt and Israel caused a deep rift in the Arab world and led to the subsequent suspension of Egypt from the Arab League. The European Community, too, was suspicious of the agreement, considering it to be a step away from its own preferred option of a global settlement of the Middle East conflict. In the EC's view, the partial settlement represented by Camp David did nothing to address the central problem of finding a homeland for the Palestinian people. The Community's concern found expression in its Venice Declaration[8] of 13 June 1980. Repeating their call for a "comprehensive solution" to the Israeli-Arab conflict and committing the EC to work "in a more concrete way" toward peace, the leaders of the nine member states spelled out the two principles that would in future form the basis of Community policy: the right to existence and security for all states in the region, including Israel, and recognition of the "legitimate rights of the Palestinian people."

Under the first of these principles, the declaration stressed that every country was "entitled to live in peace within secure, recognized and guaranteed borders," and under the second that the Palestinian people "must be placed in a position . . . to exercise fully their right to self-determination." The principles applied to all the parties concerned, including the PLO, which would "have to be associated with the negotiations." The Nine would not accept "any unilateral initiative designed to change the status of Jerusalem" and stressed the "need for Israel to put an end to the territorial occupation" that it had imposed; they considered that the Jewish settlements on Palestinian land were a "serious obstacle to peace." The Venice Declaration concluded by calling for a renunciation of the use of force by all the parties and pledged the Community to intervene actively at the diplomatic level with all the parties concerned.

The Venice Declaration was in some senses merely a codification of policies that had been emerging for some time. It served notice on the Arabs that the EC considered Israel's borders inviolable, and on Israel that it considered the occupied territories and the settlements to be an impediment to peace. In spite of some prevarication in the early 1980s, the declaration has remained the cornerstone of EU policy on the Arab-Israeli conflict ever since. The policy has been successful to the extent that both sides have moved toward accepting the principles it contains—Israel through handing over occupied territory to the Palestinian Authority, the Palestinians by renouncing the PLO's long-standing pledge to seek the destruction of the Israeli state.

But if Camp David and the Venice Declaration may with hindsight be seen to have marked the fragile beginnings of a gradual Arab-Israeli rapprochement, the situation in the region deteriorated throughout much of the 1980s before showing signs of improvement. The Euro-Arab Dialogue reflected this. The Iran-Iraq war; the assassination of Egyptian president

Anwar Sadat; the escalating civil war in Lebanon and the Israeli invasion of 1982; the growth of terrorism in the form of hijackings, bombings, and hostage-taking; the branding of Syria and Libya as "terrorist states"—all this served to make political dialogue with the Arab world as a whole difficult. The failure to agree on a final communiqué at the fifth meeting of the Euro-Arab Dialogue's general commission in Athens in December 1983[9] led to the effective end of multilateral EC-Arab political dialogue for the remainder of the decade.

Relations with the Gulf States

The August 1990 invasion of Kuwait by Saddam Hussein's Iraq coincided with the end of the Cold War and the European Community's first steps toward developing a coherent policy for dealing with its Central and Eastern European neighbors. Unlike the peaceful breakup of the former Soviet bloc, however, which required (and got) a coordinated economic response, the Gulf crisis was of the sort that the EC was least able to deal with. The Community's foreign ministers, meeting in EPC, immediately condemned the Iraqi move and imposed economic sanctions. But the Twelve were completely unable to fashion an effective and concerted reaction. Within two weeks of the invasion, a group of MEPs had left for a five-day visit to the region, meeting kings and presidents in Alexandria, Riyadh, Damascus, Amman, and Tunis (and bumping into the odd EC foreign affairs minister on the way[10]). But the Community proved to be powerless in diplomacy. The Western response was global, with individual European Community countries committing forces (or, in Germany's case, money) to the successful U.S.-led bid to evict Saddam's troops from Kuwait. Only after the war was Brussels able to provide a degree of coordinated help in the form of emergency and other aid to the worst-hit states, such as Jordan.

The states most directly threatened by the Iraqi invasion were the members of the Gulf Cooperation Council (GCC), a regional organization set up in 1981. Comprising all the states of the Arabian peninsula except for North and South Yemen (Saudi Arabia, Kuwait, Bahrain, Qatar, Oman, and the United Arab Emirates), it was created as a response to the instability in the region occasioned by the Iran-Iraq war[11] and brought together a group of oil-producing countries with shared economic interests. The GCC was of immediate interest to the European Community. Here was a group of countries on which the EC had come to depend for a significant (if diminishing) proportion of its energy needs (23.7 percent of oil imports in 1994) and that was at the same time at one remove from the frontline Arab states involved in the conflict with Israel. Moreover, the Community always welcomed the opportunity of dealing with coherent regional groupings of states, such as EFTA or ASEAN; the GCC offered just such an opportunity and was all the more attractive as a potential partner in light of the fragmentation and ineffectiveness displayed by the Arab League in the wake of the Camp David accords. The secretary-general of the GCC visited the Commission in Brussels in 1982, and a Commission delegation went to Riyadh, seat of the Gulf Cooperation Council's secretariat, in 1984 to discuss the possibility of formalizing the relationship between the two regions. The following year, GCC and European Community ministers met in Luxembourg and agreed to work toward a comprehensive trade and cooperation agreement.

It took until mid-1988 for an agreement to be finalized, and it was the beginning of 1990 before it entered into force. The agreement, a framework cooperation accord along the lines of that between the EC and the ASEAN countries, stresses economic cooperation and institutionalizes dialogue through a joint council, which meets yearly. Cooperation covers economics, agriculture, fisheries, industry, energy, science and technology, investment, the environment, and trade. The last of these is particularly important given the nature and scale of the trading relationship: some 85 percent of EU imports from GCC countries are petroleum and petroleum products, while most of the Union's exports are manufactured goods and food products (in 1995 and preceding years, the Gulf states constituted the EU's fifth largest export market). A key theme for discussion under this heading is trade diversification.

Not surprisingly, there was pressure from the outset, especially from the GCC side, to develop the initial agreement into a full-fledged trade accord and indeed to transform the EC-Gulf relationship into a free trade area. Negotiations to this end started in 1990 but made little progress. One of the major sticking points concerned the difficulties involved in allowing unhindered access to the European market of GCC exports of refined and transformed petroleum products, which would compete directly with the EU's own petrochemical industry. This would not be offset by the quid pro quo of duty-free access of European goods to the Gulf markets, since the existing import duties could be replaced by internal sales taxes,[12] effectively discouraging additional sales to the region. The European Union would also prefer to see the Gulf states themselves form a customs union, something they have so far failed to do. However, with plans now in place to create a Euro-Mediterranean free trade zone by 2010 (see the following section), excluding the Gulf region indefinitely would be politically as well as economically questionable; it is thus more likely than not that in spite of the failure to make much further headway during meetings between the two sides in 1996, the existing cooperation accord with the GCC will be upgraded in the near future.

The EU's relations with the other two major powers in the Gulf region, Iraq and Iran, remain minimal. The UN embargo on trade with Iraq, imposed in the wake of its invasion of Kuwait, has reduced economic relations to practically zero. There is also considerable concern at Baghdad's continued human rights abuses, in particular against its own Kurdish minority. Ties with Iran are also cool, not least because of the continuing refusal of the Teheran regime to lift the *fatwa* against Salman Rushdie, an EU citizen, and because of its alleged support for terrorism in the Middle East. Contacts over the past few years have been increasing gradually, however, as the Iranians have sought to adopt a more moderate position internationally. Nevertheless, Iran and Iraq remain two of just a tiny handful of countries with which the European Union has no formal relationships or agreements (the others are Afghanistan, Libya, Myanmar, and North Korea).

The New Mediterranean Policy of the 1990s

In spite of the 1972 launch of a "global Mediterranean policy" and the attempt at making a success of the Euro-Arab Dialogue, the European Community's relations with most of the region remained largely bilateral in character throughout the 1970s and 1980s. The cooperation agreements with the Maghreb and Mashreq countries remained in force and were updated in 1987 to take account of the recent accession of Spain and Portugal. The Euro-Arab Dialogue did not succeed in any serious way in its original goal of creating an overarching political relationship, and a number of Arab countries (notably Libya, Syria, and Iraq) effectively excluded themselves from the EC's efforts to cultivate closer bilateral relations with them. Only the Gulf Cooperation Council provided a working regional partnership with which the EC could do business on a multilateral basis; the principal pan-Arab organization, the Arab League, has always been too disunited to serve as a credible partner.

Among the best examples of the Arabs' frustration with their own inability to find common ground must be Morocco's application in July 1987 to join the European Community (it was rejected in short order on the grounds that Morocco was not a European country). EC diplomacy in the region, such as it was, tended to be reactive rather than proactive, confronting each new twist in the complex series of events (the Iran-Iraq war, the Lebanese civil war, the Israel-Lebanon and Israel-Syria conflicts, the imprisonment of EC nationals as hostages, etc.) as it arose.

The beginning of a real reassessment of Community policy toward the Mediterranean came in 1990 with the first of a series of Commission policy papers in the form of communications to the Council and European Parliament. Entitled *Redirecting the Community's Mediterranean Policy,* it stressed the importance of the social and economic development of the region for the Community's security "in the broadest sense."[13] It proposed a greater emphasis on horizontal rather than strictly bilateral cooperation; such cooperation would include transport, energy, and telecommunications.

The 1990 "redirection" seems to have been devised primarily with a view to providing a new basis on which to renew the financial protocols attached to the various cooperation agreements (the third in the series of five-year protocols was on the point of expiring).

A second Commission communication on the future of relations between the Community and the Maghreb countries followed in 1992.[14] It proposed that on expiration of the latest financial protocols in 1996, a new regional framework with the Maghreb countries should be set up, leading to a "Euro-Maghreb partnership" and a free trade area. The Commission's ideas were endorsed at the June 1992 meeting of the European Council in Lisbon: the Maghreb was declared to be a geographical area of common interest under the new Common Foreign and Security Policy. Although limited to the Maghreb countries, the proposals for a partnership were extendable, and in 1993 the Middle East was dealt with in two further Commission papers. The first of these, on future relations and cooperation between the Community and the Middle East, envisaged the goal of regional cooperation, possibly "along the lines of the OECD," and a regional free trade area.[15] The second concerned support for the Middle East peace process and attempted to situate the EU's role in the multilateral efforts then under way.[16]

In retrospect, all these initiatives can now be seen as steps in a process that culminated in yet another Commission policy paper in 1994 and, beyond that, in the Euro-Mediterranean conference in Barcelona in November 1995. In part, the step-by-step approach until then had reflected the Commission's caution and its desire to move ahead first in those areas where success seemed most likely; but it had to do as well with the evolving situation in the Mediterranean region as a whole, and in particular with the progress in the Middle East peace process. In 1990 and 1992, an approach embracing the entire Mediterranean basin seemed doomed to failure and was therefore not contemplated as an immediate option. By 1994, however, the situation was showing dramatic changes as Israel and the PLO seemed poised to translate their Washington accord into a workable peace. Moreover, the EU's experience with its policies toward Central and Eastern Europe, not least in the use of its PHARE program, gave it added reason to believe that a similar all-encompassing strategy would be the most appropriate way to strengthen ties with the Mediterranean.

The 1994 Commission communication was entitled *Strengthening the Mediterranean Policy of the European Union: Establishing a Euro-Mediterranean Partnership*. The Mediterranean basin, it said, constituted "an area of strategic importance for the Community." It continued:

> The peace and stability of the region are of the highest priority to Europe.
> To consolidate that peace and stability in the region, a number of challenges have to be faced, notably:

- to support political reform, respect for human rights and freedom of expression as a means to contain extremism;
- to promote economic reform, leading to sustained growth and improved living standards, a consequent diminution of violence and an easing of migratory pressures.[17]

Accordingly, the Commission suggested setting up a Euro-Mediterranean zone of peace and stability, complete with a "code of conduct" for the solution of disputes among Mediterranean countries and confidence-building measures to be developed in liaison with the WEU and "transatlantic partners." It believed the European Union should develop its political dialogue with its Mediterranean partners, placing special emphasis on human rights and the principles of democracy and good governance, and expand the dialogue to include security issues.

With the southern and eastern Mediterranean already identified by the European Council as a priority area for joint action,[18] the Commission saw the region as highly susceptible to a common EU approach under its new Common Foreign and Security Policy. Alongside the political and security dimension, a massive effort needed to be made to help reduce the economic gap between Europe and its southern neighbors. It would have to be on a similar scale as that already in place for the Central and Eastern European countries: the Commission proposed establishing a MED (Mediterranean) program, modeled on the PHARE program, with an initial endowment of ECU 5.5 billion ($6.9 billion) over a five-year period, renewable for a further five years. Identifying the environment, energy, migration, trade, and investment as the principal areas of Euro-Mediterranean "interdependence," the Commission's policy paper proposed using the MED funding

- to promote the socioeconomic development of the Mediterranean countries;
- to support modernization and economic restructuring with a view to the progressive establishment of a free trade area;
- to promote direct investment in the area via joint ventures;
- to encourage job creation;
- to promote regional cooperation, including in the environmental field; and
- to support the Middle East peace process.

The Barcelona Euro-Mediterranean Conference

The Commission's communication proposed that a Euro-Mediterranean conference be held in 1995 to "reach agreement on a series of economic and political guidelines for Euro-Mediterranean policy into the next

century, which could be set out in a new Charter."[19] The idea for a conference was endorsed by the European Council at its December 1994 meeting
in Essen, and it was duly convened in Barcelona in November 1995. It
brought together the foreign ministers of the fifteen EU member states and
all the Mediterranean states except Libya, plus Jordan; Yasser Arafat represented the Palestinian Authority. The conference concluded by agreeing
an ambitious new framework of relations, articulated in the Barcelona
Declaration[20] and accompanied by a detailed work program designed to
give practical effect to the objectives set out in the body of the declaration.
While it is too early to assess the impact of the new Euro-Mediterranean
partnership that was formally established by the Barcelona Declaration,
the blueprint it offers for the future relationship between the EU and the
Mediterranean is worth describing in some detail. Not only is it historic in
terms of its goals and scope, particularly coming as it does at a period of
détente in the region unparalleled since the inception of the European
Community, it is also interesting seen in terms of its complementarity vis-
à-vis the EU's policy toward its other near abroad, the countries of Central
and Eastern Europe.

The declaration establishes a comprehensive partnership among the
participants (the "Euro-Mediterranean partnership") on the basis of three
pillars: a strengthened and regular political dialogue; the development of
economic and financial cooperation; and greater emphasis on the social,
cultural, and human dimension.

The political dialogue is aimed at establishing a political and security
partnership based on a common area of peace and stability. In a "declaration of principles,"[21] the signatories—and they include the Turks and the
Cypriots, the Syrians and the Israelis, as well as every other EU and
Mediterranean state with the exception of Libya—undertake a number of
commitments that seem extraordinarily far-reaching. If implemented, they
would totally banish conflict and human rights abuses from the Mediterranean basin. The signatories pledge to honor the United Nations Charter
and the Universal Declaration of Human Rights and to respect "human
rights and fundamental freedoms and guarantee the effective legitimate exercise of such rights and freedoms." They promise to develop the rule of
law and democracy in their political systems and to ensure respect for diversity and pluralism in their societies by combating "manifestations of in-
tolerance, racism and xenophobia." Each will respect the territorial integrity and unity of the other partners, and disputes will be settled by
peaceful means without "recourse to the threat or use of force against the
territorial integrity of another participant," including the acquisition of territory by force. They pledge to cooperate in preventing and combating terrorism and "fight together against the expansion and diversification of organized crime and combat the drugs problem in all its aspects." The parties
also undertake to pursue a verifiable "Middle East Zone free of weapons

of mass destruction, nuclear, chemical and biological" and to consider practical steps to prevent the proliferation of such weapons. They will refrain from developing military capacity "beyond their legitimate defence requirements." Finally, the signatories are to consider what confidence- and security-building measures they might take with a view to "the creation of an 'area of peace and stability in the Mediterranean', including the long term possibility of establishing a Euro-Mediterranean pact to that end."

The second pillar of the Barcelona Declaration is designed to create an area of shared prosperity through economic and financial partnership. Taking as its long-term objectives the acceleration of the pace of socioeconomic development, improving the living conditions of the region's people and increasing their employment opportunities, reducing the wealth gap between North and South, and encouraging regional cooperation and integration, this aspect of the partnership is to be based on three approaches:

- the progressive establishment of a free trade area;
- economic cooperation and "concerted action";
- an increase in EU aid to its partners.

The free trade area is to be phased in gradually over a fifteen-year period, with 2010 set as the target date. The signatories agree to eliminate tariff and nontariff barriers to trade in manufactured goods on the basis of timetables to be negotiated. Trade in farm products will be liberalized "as far as the various agricultural policies allow and with due respect to the results achieved within the GATT negotiations." Trade in services, including right of establishment, is also to be liberalized "progressively." To help this process along, the participants decide to adopt a series of technical measures (on rules of origin, certification, competition, etc.), to pursue policies based on market economics, and to modernize their economic and social structures. To mitigate possible social consequences resulting from these changes, they are to promote programs "for the benefit of the neediest populations."

Economic cooperation and concerted action cover a range of fields and are predicated not least on a recognition that regional cooperation among the non-EU countries of the Mediterranean is central to the success of a free trade area that will link not only the richer European countries and their Mediterranean neighbors but also the North African and Middle Eastern countries. To make this happen, the signatories agree, investment needs to be encouraged, both internally and in the form of foreign direct investment (FDI), and joint ventures and cooperation between enterprises have to be supported. The environment is singled out as being a key area for cooperation, and although the Mediterranean Sea features prominently here, issues such as combating desertification and avoiding the environmental consequences of industrialization are also referred to specifically. The role of women in development is highlighted, and the signatories undertake "to promote [women's] active participation in economic and social life and in the creation of employment." Fish conservation, the energy sector, water supply and management, and the restructuring of agriculture are also listed as priority sectors for cooperation. Other areas in which there is agreement to cooperate include transport and telecommunications, maritime law and services, science and technology, and exchange of statistics; local authorities are to be encouraged to work together in support of regional planning.

A final aspect of economic and financial partnership is aid. This, the signatories acknowledge, is a prerequisite to progress in the other areas of agreed action. In fact the amount involved—ECU 4.685 billion ($5.85 billion) in the form of grants from the Community's budget over the period 1995–1999, plus increased loans from the European Investment Bank— had already been agreed at the Cannes European Council meeting in June 1995 and is less than the ECU 5.5 billion proposed by the Commission. Nevertheless, it is a significant contribution, corresponding as it does to the total amount made available over the previous twenty years of financial protocols; moreover, it is in addition to other official development assistance (ODA) funds from individual EU member states, and it puts the Mediterranean region on a similar footing to the Central and Eastern European countries in terms of direct Community aid.

The third pillar, partnership in social, cultural, and human affairs—is a recognition that trade, investment, economic cooperation, and FDI are only part of a wider process that must include the human dimension if it is to be successful. In fact, after making obligatory references to "dialogue and respect between cultures and religions" as "a necessary pre-condition for bringing the peoples closer," this chapter of the Barcelona Declaration goes on to identify the need for a strengthened program of exchanges of young people and students, teachers, clerics, journalists, scientists, trade unionists, businesspeople, as well as political leaders. It also spells out priority people-related areas, already referred to in the declaration's preamble, where strengthened cooperation can have an impact: migration, illegal immigration, terrorism, drug trafficking, organized crime, corruption, and the fight against racism and xenophobia.

While these are all noble aims, how do the signatories of the Barcelona Declaration intend effectively to reach them? The declaration is accompanied by a work program, which sets out in some detail proposals for implementing the priority actions agreed at the conference. Cooperation in the Mediterranean does not involve starting with a clean slate. Schemes such as the EU's MED programs already give financial support to creating decentralized networks for the exchange of know-how and experience in fields that include the media, urban management, higher education, investment, technology, and migration. The numerous agreements and conferences on sectoral policy areas that have already been entered into or held in recent years can be built on to achieve further progress. There are many of these: a Mediterranean Water Charter was adopted in Rome in 1992, the General Fisheries Council for the Mediterranean is concerned with management and conservation of fish stocks, a Mediterranean Tourism Charter was agreed in Casablanca in 1995, and a Mediterranean energy conference took place in Madrid in November of that year. These and other bodies, such as the Euro-Arab Business School in Granada, will play their part in the practical implementation of many of the proposals. Over and above this, the foreign affairs ministers of the signatory states are to meet periodically to review progress, with their meetings to be prepared by a Euro-Mediterranean Committee for the Barcelona Process at the level of senior officials; the European Commission will provide the input for this committee's work and will be responsible for appropriate follow-up. The Barcelona Declaration calls on parliamentarians, regional authorities, local authorities, and the social partners to arrange their own contacts. The European Parliament is invited to organize a "Euro-Mediterranean Parliamentary Dialogue."

The stage has thus been set for a period of intensive collaboration across and among the Mediterranean states, European and non-European. The success of the Barcelona process will depend in part on the ability of the Arab states involved to work together in promoting their own cooperative and integrative machinery; it is clear that a lack of cooperation among the southern and eastern Mediterranean countries will put the entire project in doubt. Recent history has shown that many of the divisions within the Arab camp have been the result of divergent approaches to the Middle East peace process: a period of further progress in resolving the many outstanding problems between Israel and its neighbors would thus certainly help the Barcelona process to bear fruit. Equally, however, the existence of the process should encourage the Arab-Israeli peace process by building confidence and helping to reduce some of the more glaring economic disparities that continue to exacerbate existing differences.

Israel, Palestine, and the Middle East Peace Process

In spite of the EC's careful and long-standing diplomatic and economic cultivation of the Arabs and its support for the Palestinians, Europe has also remained close to Israel. The Euro-Arab Dialogue, the Venice Declaration, and numerous EU expressions of support for a just and balanced peace notwithstanding, as the Middle East's only functioning democracy, Israel has always enjoyed the European Union's friendship and understanding, frayed though this may have become from time to time. Economic ties have always been strong. A 1975 trade agreement gave Israeli manufactured products free access to EC markets, and in 1989 complete free trade in the industrial sector was introduced. The Community has also provided a major market for Israeli agricultural produce. Financial protocols attached to the trade agreements have provided significant funding in the form of loans to the Israeli state. On a per capita basis, Israel bought more EU exports in 1995 than any other non-European country except Hong Kong. It is the European Union's largest trading partner overall in the Mediterranean after Turkey.

As this chapter has shown, the EU has tried to adopt an evenhanded approach in the Middle East peace process, arguing that both the Jewish state and the Palestinians have a right to secure existence in the region. Now that this principle has been accepted by all the parties, the European Union and its member states have become the major international contributor to the Palestinian Authority in the West Bank and Gaza, with grants from the EU's own budget helping to finance the administrative infrastructure and police and security apparatus needed to ensure that the fledgling Palestinian state can function. The European Commission operates offices in East Jerusalem and Gaza to channel its aid. A joint action under the Common Foreign and Security Policy provided EU finance and practical assistance to the Palestinians in organizing and observing the first elections to the Palestinian Council in January 1996. In 1994 the European Parliament set up an ad hoc delegation for relations with the PLO; this delegation has visited the territories, held discussions with Palestinian leaders, and taken part in the observation of the 1996 elections. The delegation became a standing body of the Parliament in January 1997 and is now called the Delegation for Relations with the Palestinian Legislative Council. In February 1997, the European Community signed an interim association agreement with the PLO; the first of its kind with an organization that does not represent a full-fledged state. Yasser Arafat and other senior PLO figures have been frequent visitors to the European Parliament in Brussels and Strasbourg for many years (even prior to the Israeli-Palestinian accords), often provoking Israeli government protests.

Turkey

Turkey was one of the very first countries to enter into a formal relationship with the European Community. Its association agreement was signed in Ankara in September 1963, just five years after the entry into force of the EEC Treaty, and came into force on 1 December 1964. The agreement contains a commitment to eventual full Turkish membership in the Community and is similar in content to that concluded with Greece in 1961 (and which led to Greece's accession in 1981). But the main aim of the association was economic, for it was always clear that actual membership would require Turkey to undergo a major economic and structural transformation. A gradual development of trade relations was foreseen, leading to free trade (and the freedom of movement of services and people) and an eventual customs union. A series of financial protocols provided ECU 695 million ($875 million) in loans to Turkey in the period 1964–1980.

If it seemed expedient to hold out the prospect of membership to Turkey in the early 1960s, not least because of Ankara's position as NATO's eastern bulwark during the Cold War, the attractions of accession were always more evident to the Turks than to the European Community. While membership was a long-term goal, it was always clear that integrating a country of around 60 million[22] people into the EC would be difficult, particularly because Turkey's per capita GNP, at $2,120,[23] is just over 10 percent of the EC average and its social and political development lags far behind that of the Community. Indeed, in the early years of its association, Turkey accepted that it could not expect immediate membership in the EC. But by 1987 it felt it was ready and in April formally applied to join the Community, though it must have realized that its application stood little chance.

Turkey's occupation of 39 percent of the island of Cyprus in 1974 and its refusal to bow to consistent international pressure to withdraw had already branded it as something of a maverick state. A return to military rule in 1980 and the freezing of the association agreement by the EC did not help its case either. Nor did the accession to the Community of its most bitter enemy, Greece, in 1981. Ankara's growing resort to force in dealing with its Kurdish separatist problem and its arrest of dissidents in the late 1980s and afterward—coupled with evidence of torture in its jails and other human rights abuses—further tarnished its reputation. The abrupt end of the Cold War in the late 1980s lessened its strategic importance to the West as a whole, and although it participated on the side of the allies in the 1991 Gulf War, its significance as a regional power began to wane.

Many of these factors undoubtedly weighed with the Commission, which in December 1989 delivered a negative opinion on the Turkish request for accession, but it was the economic implications of membership that the Commission stressed. While not formally ruling out the possibility of Turkey's joining the Community at some later stage and thus falling short of an actual rejection of the application, the Commission's opinion effectively consigned Turkey to the European anteroom: it would have to content itself with a separate if privileged status as a close associate of Community Europe. The Commission's opinion (a formal requirement that, under the EEC Treaty, must precede any political decision on a membership application) also served to let the Community's political leaders off the hook, since it was not they but the Commission that was opposing Turkish membership. Nonetheless, it cannot have been lost on the Turks that in 1975 the Council had overruled a similar negative Commission opinion on Greece's application.

The question of membership notwithstanding, the additional protocol to the Ankara agreement that came into force in January 1973 stipulated that a customs union was to be completed within a period of twenty-two years, that is, by the end of 1995 at the latest. A first attempt to achieve this goal was made in the form of a Commission proposal in 1991 designed to put into place a wide-ranging cooperation framework for relations with Turkey, including a customs union, financial cooperation, intensified political dialogue, and Turkish alignment with existing Community laws.[24] But on this occasion it was the Council that failed to achieve unanimity, rejecting the Commission's proposal. However, with the clock ticking toward the 1995 deadline, work continued, and in March 1995 the EU-Turkey Association Council adopted a decision implementing the customs union. In fact, the EU had already made virtually all the concessions on free trade that it had committed itself to under the original Ankara agreement, so the 1995 decision actually imposed more obligations on Turkey than on the European Union—in particular, requiring it to bring its laws and policies into line with those of the EU in fields such as competition, industrial policy, and intellectual property rights. The decision did not, to Turkey's dismay, tackle the question of free movement of persons, the achievement of which had also been foreseen under the 1973 additional protocol.

But before the new arrangements could enter into force, they needed to be ratified by the European Parliament. The EP had long been critical of Turkish human rights violations, including the arrest and imprisonment of members of the Turkish parliament. Indeed the EP's relations with the Turkish Grand National Assembly, with which it had had a formal link since the 1960s in the shape of a joint parliamentary committee under the terms of the Ankara agreement, had often been stormy—so much so in recent times that the usual twice-yearly meetings had been suspended altogether in 1994 and resumed only in June 1996. Parliament announced even before the signature of the March 1995 decision on a customs union that it would withhold its assent in the absence of clear commitments by the Turkish government on a number of questions.

Against considerable internal opposition, the government in Ankara did push through a raft of reforms during 1995, including a series of constitutional amendments strengthening the democratic rights of citizens, trade unions, and parliamentarians and a relaxation of the antiterrorism laws. As a result, two Kurdish members of parliament were released from jail and the promise given that four others could have their cases heard by the European Court of Human Rights. Seventy-nine other prisoners were set free by year's end as a result of the changes in the antiterrorism laws. The European Parliament was not overly impressed with these moves, believing they did not go far enough. Nevertheless, it acknowledged that the Turkish action represented progress and, under considerable political pressure from national EU capitals, ratified the customs union in December 1995, just days before the January 1996 deadline.

Events in 1996 rapidly soured the new relationship, however. In particular, Turkish actions in Cyprus in August and its continued harassment of its Kurdish population led the European Parliament to vote in September to freeze payments to Turkey under the financial protocol attached to the customs union and to call on the Commission not to finance projects in Turkey under the MED program.

In spite of the strains that persist, Turkey's economic relationship with the European Union is now closer than that of any other nonmember except Norway, Iceland, and Liechtenstein, whose membership in the European Economic Area gives them free trade (although not a customs union) and a range of related institutional and practical privileges (and obligations), including free movement of persons (see Chapter 3). While the customs union does not formally preclude eventual Turkish full membership in the EU, it seems highly unlikely that circumstances will change sufficiently to result in any further rapprochement between the two sides in the near future; certainly, the anticipated round of enlargement negotiations with the Central and Eastern European applicants and Cyprus will not include Turkey.

Cyprus and Malta

Of all the major islands in the Mediterranean—the Balearics, Corsica, Sardinia, Sicily, Crete, and Rhodes—only Malta and Cyprus are not part of the European Union. The EU has always adopted a certain parallelism in its relations with them, born of the recognition that they are both "European" states. Former British colonies, Cyprus gained its independence in 1959 and Malta five years later. Even before UK accession to the Community in 1973, both countries had concluded association agreements with the EC (Malta in 1970, Cyprus in 1972). Each of these agreements had as its ultimate aim the establishment of a customs union with the EU and in the meantime provided special terms for the two countries' exports of "Mediterranean" agricultural products (wine, early potatoes, and other fruit and vegetables) to the Community market as well as tariff-free entry for most of their manufactured goods. Both countries have benefited from a series of financial protocols aimed at strengthening their infrastructures.

This parallelism has led to a tendency to refer to the two independent island states of the Mediterranean in the same breath. This view that Cyprus and Malta are somehow linked to one another was reinforced when both tendered their applications to join the EU as full members within two weeks of one another, on 4 and 16 July 1990 (the European Council pledged to open negotiations with both states six months after the conclusion of the 1996 IGC, likely to be around the end of 1997 or beginning of 1998). Yet they have different histories, languages, cultures, and peoples and are as far apart from one another geographically as Ireland is from

Sweden. For the European Union, however, they present many of the same characteristics, particularly in terms of the implications of their membership applications. Although the Cypriot population of 726,000 people is just about double that of Malta (362,000), their per capita incomes are roughly similar (Cyprus is marginally the wealthier of the two) and both have highly educated and skilled workforces. Their agricultural output is Mediterranean in nature, and both rely heavily on tourism as a source of foreign exchange earnings. Neither would present major economic problems as members of the EU, although the institutional consequences of adding two ministates in the same league as Luxembourg should not be underestimated.

In the case of Malta, however, these considerations are currently somewhat academic. Until the late 1980s, Malta's ruling Labor Party was implacably opposed to EC membership. But in 1987 the pro-European Nationalist Party took power, and it was the government of Prime Minister Edward Fenech Adami that tabled the Maltese application for EU membership in 1990. Today, however, the application is on ice: in October 1996 a general election returned the Labor Party to power. With the party still opposed to membership, the country's new prime minister, Alfred Sant, has pledged to seek a special relationship with the European Union short of actual membership. It remains to be seen what form this will take and whether both major political parties on the island will one day unite on the issue of a renewed membership bid.

The situation in Cyprus is complex for other reasons. The island remains divided, with its northern, Turkish half still occupied by troops from mainland Turkey. United Nations forces patrol the border between the two sides, and the capital, Nicosia, is riven by a Berlin-style wall. Although northern Cyprus has declared itself to be an independent state (the Turkish Republic of Northern Cyprus), the European Union and every other country in the world, except Turkey, recognize only one Cyprus, whose legitimate government is now fully in the hands of the Greek Cypriots and whose territory extends to the entire island. Unlike Malta, all the major political forces in (Greek) Cyprus favor EU membership. But while it would be legally possible for the government of the Republic of Cyprus to negotiate entry terms on behalf of the entire island, in reality any attempt to accede to the European Union without having involved the Turkish Cypriot community would be politically untenable. The hope, of course, must be that a resolution to the "Cyprus problem" can be reached between the country's Turkish and Greek communities, making the application effectively a joint one. The carrot would be the huge economic advantages to the poorer, northern part of the island that membership would bring; the stick would be that failure to reach an internal settlement could result in the Greek Cypriot side's joining alone, condemning the north to permanent poverty as a separate state or as a province of Turkey.

What is clear at present is that the prospect of Cypriot accession negotiations is likely to concentrate the minds of both administrations on the island as never before. The hope for a settlement lies in the argument that a federal Cyprus of two largely autonomous states could function within the European Union (with its guarantees of free movement of goods, services, capital, and persons) in a way that would be difficult or impossible to achieve outside it. But it is also clear that any solution to the division of Cyprus, and the success of its EU application, will require the acquiescence of Turkey. The hope must be that the new relationship between Brussels and Ankara following the agreement on a customs union will be sufficient to persuade the Turkish government not to oppose Cypriot membership and to use its good offices to ensure that northern Cyprus agrees to a settlement deal with the south. The events of August 1996, when Turkish troops shot and killed a Greek Cypriot demonstrating on the demarcation line between the two sides, may or may not have helped to persuade the parties of the urgency of finding a solution sooner rather than later.

It is in the European Union's own interest that a way be found to admit Cyprus: the new Euro-Mediterranean partnership now being forged is aimed not least at bringing an end to conflict throughout the entire area, and a solution to the Cyprus problem would represent a significant step toward achieving what the Barcelona Declaration describes as the creation of an "area of peace and stability" in the Mediterranean. Brussels is likely to stick to its promise to begin negotiations six months after the end of the 1996–1997 intergovernmental conference. Whether they succeed or not will depend on progress in reconciling the island's two communities, and that, in turn, will be tied to the state of the EU's relations with Turkey.

Notes

1. *Bulletin,* 10–1972, p. 119.

2. Saleh A. Al-Mani', *The Euro-Arab Dialogue: A Study in Associative Diplomacy* (London: Pinter Publishers, 1983), p. 82.

3. European Parliament, *Fact Sheets on the European Parliament and the Activities of the European Union* (Luxembourg: European Parliament, 1993), p. 131.

4. Quoted in Bichara Khader, "Europe and the Arab-Israeli Conflict 1973–1983: An Arab Perspective," in D. Allen and A. Pijpers (eds.), *European Foreign Policy Making and the Arab-Israeli Conflict* (The Hague: Martinus Nijhoff, 1984), p. 166.

5. The dialogue's specialized working parties or committees covered seven areas: industrialization; infrastructure; agriculture; financial cooperation; trade; science and technology; and culture, labor, and social affairs.

6. See Tareq Y. Ismael, *International Relations of the Contemporary Middle East* (Syracuse, NY: Syracuse University Press, 1986), p. 106.

7. See Elfriede Regelsberger, "The Euro-Arab Dialogue: Procedurally Innovative, Substantially Weak," in Geoffrey Edwards and Elfriede Regelsberger (eds.), *Europe's Global Links: The European Community and Inter-regional Cooperation* (New York: St. Martin's Press, 1990), pp. 57–65.

8. *Bulletin,* 6–1980, pp. 10–11.

9. Ismael, *Contemporary Middle East,* p. 125.

10. I accompanied the five MEPs on their mission and remember calling on King Fahd at the palace in Riyadh at 2 A.M. The European parliamentarians were ushered in just as British foreign secretary Douglas Hurd and his staff were leaving.

11. See Eberhard Rhein, "Agreement with the Gulf Cooperation Council: A Promising If Difficult Beginning," in Edwards and Regelsberger, *Europe's Global Links,* p. 112.

12. Ibid., n. 7, p. 117.

13. Commission document SEC(90) 812, 1 June 1990, p. 2.

14. Commission document SEC(92) 401, 30 April 1992.

15. Commission document COM(93) 375, 8 September 1993, p. 4.

16. Commission document COM(93) 458, 29 September 1993.

17. Commission document COM(94) 427, 19 October 1994, p. 5.

18. The June 1992 Lisbon European Council meeting established three key criteria for urgent foreign policy cooperation: geographical proximity, overwhelming interest in the political and economic stability of a region or state, and existence of a potential threat to the Union's security interests.

19. COM(94) 427, p. 15.

20. *Bulletin,* 11–1995, pp. 137–145.

21. Ibid., p. 138.

22. The World Bank projects that Turkey's population will rise to 68 million in the year 2000 and 92 million by 2025.

23. Figures for 1993 from the *World Bank Atlas* (Washington, DC: World Bank, 1995). In fact, given the size of Turkey's "black" economy, the real figure is likely to be considerably higher. Even if it were double the official figure, however, Turkey would still have a per capita GDP about half that of Greece, the EU's current poorest member state.

24. Commission, *Dossier: Customs Union Turkey,* Brussels, 9 November 1995, p. 2.

5

The Transatlantic Relationship: The EU and North America

North America and Europe are, without any doubt, one another's most important partners. The reasons for this mutual dependency—some would say interdependency—are both obvious and complex. They range from the historic ties that have bound the two regions since long before the creation of the European Community to the simple fact that each is the other's largest overseas trading partner. But they also embrace the security dimension, as all but two of the European members of NATO (Turkey and Norway) are members of the EU, and certainly include the more difficult to quantify ideological affinity that spans the Atlantic. There is also the question of size: the EU and North America are the biggest and second biggest markets in the world and rank in the same order in terms of their international trade. Neither can afford to ignore the other.

This chapter is concerned with the transatlantic relationship in general terms, because that relationship is important not only to the partners involved but also to the rest of the world (witness the delays to the conclusion of the GATT Uruguay Round because of disagreements between the EU and the United States in its closing stages). But it also looks at a range of specific issues that have been the cause of friction over the years. Better than anything else, these disputes demonstrate the impact the EU and its doings have had on North America and illustrate why both sides take their relationship so seriously.

"North America," for the purposes of this chapter, consists of the United States and Canada (Mexico is dealt with in the chapter on Latin America). Each of these two countries maintains its own distinct relations with the EU. Each is represented in Brussels by its own ambassador to the Union, and the Union, for its part, has Commission delegations in both Washington, D.C., and Ottawa. Separate Transatlantic Declarations were concluded between the EU and Canada and the United States in November 1990. The EU has been linked to Canada since 1976 through a framework agreement covering trade relations as well as energy, monetary and economic

93

questions, cooperation on research and technology (Canada is the only non-European member of the European Space Agency), and nuclear cooperation. In December 1995 the EU-U.S. Transatlantic Declaration of 1990 was complemented by the New Transatlantic Agenda, a halfway house toward a genuine transatlantic treaty many have advocated for a number of years. A similar agenda was concluded between the EU and Canada exactly one year later.

Canada, as a midsize industrialized country, is important to the EU in the same way as are other midsize industrialized countries: as an economic and trading partner. But its geographical position, its membership in NATO and the G7 group of industrialized nations, its close ties to the United States, and its role as a member of NAFTA all combine to make Canada of particular interest to Europe. For its part, Canada is vastly more affected by the existence of the European Union and the effects of its policies than is the United States, and in some ways is a good example of how small or mid-size industrial economies must seek ways to accommodate their interests to those of economic giants like the United States, the EU, or Japan. In terms of sheer size, political importance, and economic clout, however, it is the United States that dominates the transatlantic relationship on the North American side. Their respective sizes have come to make the United States and the European Union in many ways equals, if not in the political then certainly in the economic sphere. Indeed, their relationship has increasingly come to be important not just for one another but for the whole world.

U.S. Role in the Integration of Europe

The United States, of course, was for many years the dominant partner in its relationship with Europe. Political scientists like Robert Keohane have described the United States' role as leader of the Western world as "hegemonic,"[1] a situation that persisted until relatively recently. Certainly, Europe was in no position in the immediate aftermath of World War II to go it alone without U.S. help. By the 1950s the United States and the new European Community (and indeed Western Europe as a whole) were very much in a patron-client relationship.[2] But at the same time, U.S. support and encouragement for European cooperation and unity became a major catalyst for integration. The United States was keen to see a high degree of economic cooperation among European nations so as to enable them to make the most effective use of Marshall Plan aid. A strong Europe was also a guarantee against Soviet expansionism. While different U.S. presidents and secretaries of state varied in the degree of enthusiasm they showed toward European integration efforts in the postwar period (Harry Truman and Dean Acheson were more skeptical, Dwight Eisenhower and

John Foster Dulles more positive), the general view from Washington was one of well-meaning benevolence.

The United States (along with Britain) was the first country to accredit a diplomatic representative to the European Coal and Steel Community and in 1956 established a separate mission to the ECSC headed by Ambassador Walton Butterworth.[3] Indeed some observers[4] believe that the high level of U.S. support for early efforts at European political integration may even have been counterproductive, contributing to the failure of the European Defence Community in 1954 to receive the endorsement of the French National Assembly: France, it is argued, had become suspicious that Washington's interest was in an Atlanticist Europe heavily dependent on the United States.

Despite the collapse of the EDC project, the successful negotiation and conclusion of the EEC Treaty rekindled U.S. interest. President Kennedy, speaking on 4 July 1962 at Independence Hall in Philadelphia, clearly articulated U.S. support for the moves toward European integration embodied by the Treaty of Rome. The United States, he said, regarded a strong and united Europe not as a rival but as a partner. Such a Europe, he went on, "will be capable of playing a greater role in the common defense, of responding more generously to the needs of poorer nations, of joining with the United States and others in lowering trade barriers, resolving problems of currency and commodities, and developing coordinated policies in all other economic, diplomatic and political areas." The United States, Kennedy said, saw Europe as "a partner with whom we could deal on a basis of full equality." It was up to the Europeans "to go forward in forming the more perfect union which will someday make this partnership possible."[5]

Kennedy's Euro-enthusiasm was motivated not least by his desire to have a solid, strong, and reliable partner to stand by the United States in the Cold War against the Soviet Union. To this end he encouraged British prime minister Harold Macmillan to apply for UK membership in the Community, which he saw as essential if the new Europe was to be Atlantic-oriented and a true ally of the United States. This was not to be, and President de Gaulle's veto of the British application in 1963 signaled the beginning of a decade in which EC-U.S. relations stagnated, indeed in which the European integration process itself seemed to mark time, largely in the face of Gaullist insistence on more intergovernmentalism and less supranationalism in Europe. U.S. involvement in Vietnam, President Richard Nixon's efforts to forge new relationships with the Soviet Union and China, and the internal polarization of U.S. society symbolized by the events of the Democratic National Convention in Chicago in 1968 and later the Watergate scandal, all conspired to shift the U.S. agenda away from Europe.

But the early 1970s saw a series of dramatic changes. The UK was finally admitted to the EC. The Vietnam War came to an end. The 1973

Arab-Israeli war and the resulting oil crisis presented Europe and the United States with a common problem. Changes in leadership on both sides of the Atlantic provided fresh views on questions of common concern: in the United States President Gerald Ford replaced Nixon, and in Europe Harold Wilson took over from Edward Heath, Valéry Giscard d'Estaing from Georges Pompidou, and Helmut Schmidt from Willy Brandt. And Japan emerged onto the world scene as a major economic player, presenting challenges to both the United States and the EC. But most significant, the resurgence of the European integration process after the stagnation of the 1960s, coupled with the greater economic power of the EC of nine, ten, and subsequently twelve states, made Europe for the first time a key player in the international arena. The United States began to find itself dealing with a partner that was starting to assume the characteristics of an integrated entity and not merely a collection of states cooperating with one another in the EC. Despite Henry Kissinger's gibe in the early 1970s that it was hard to do business with Europe because you never knew whom to phone, the EC's legal responsibilities for trade matters and its growing body of harmonized laws meant that the United States had no choice but to take it seriously—often as competitor as well as partner.

The Political Dimension of the U.S.-EU Relationship

Earlier chapters of this book have already made the point that the political and economic aspects of the EU's external relations can be hard to distinguish from one another. An exception deserves to be made in the case of Europe's relations with the United States, which can be relatively easily divided into the political on the one hand and the economic or commercial on the other. The EU collectively has always been sheltered under the U.S. security umbrella, independently of the fact that most of its members were also members of NATO and the United States has always implicitly expected broad support for its foreign policies from its allies. This has often been easy for the EU to do, because U.S. and European interests have tended to correspond. But there have been exceptions, and these have led on occasion to tensions between the two sides. It is not surprising that these have grown as the EU's own capacity for foreign policy articulation has evolved through the gradual development of European Political Cooperation.

Pre-1970 and the advent of EPC, there was simply no machinery to permit consultation or coordination of EC member states' positions in the foreign policy field. While the Community and the United States were able to wage their "chicken war" in the 1960s (see the section "Trade Disputes and Trade Agreements"), the EC was institutionally incapable of having a common view on, say, the Vietnam War, and of either supporting or opposing the U.S. position. After EPC, however, the EC became able to express collective opinions, and meetings between the two sides (at the level of the EPC presidency and the U.S. secretary of state) became regular events. Eventually, an institutional framework for consultation on all matters (including foreign policy) was established by the 1990 Transatlantic Declaration so that today clearly defined mechanisms exist to allow detailed consultation to take place and, where possible, positions to be coordinated.

> Both sides agree that a framework is required for regular and intensive consultation. They will make full use of and further strengthen existing procedures, including those established by the President of the European Council and the President of the United States on 27th February 1990, namely:
> - bi-annual consultations to be arranged in the United States and in Europe between, on the one side, the President of the Commission, and on the other side, the President of the United States;
> - consultations between the European Community Foreign Ministers, with the Commission, and the U.S. Secretary of State, alternately on either side of the Atlantic;
> - ad hoc consultations between the Presidency Foreign Minister or the Troika and the U.S. Secretary of State;
> - bi-annual consultations between the Commission and the U.S. Government at Cabinet level;
> - briefings, as currently exist, by the Presidency to U.S. Representatives on European Political Cooperation (EPC) meetings at the Ministerial level.
> Both sides are resolved to develop and deepen these procedures for consultation so as to reflect the evolution of the European Community and of its relationship with the United States.[6]

These mechanisms are mentioned in the EC-U.S. declaration but include as well the contacts pursued by the two sides' diplomatic representations in Washington, D.C., and Brussels. They also include regular biannual meetings (which began as long ago as 1972) between members of the European Parliament's standing delegation for relations with the United States and members of a corresponding delegation of the House of Representatives. The pace of all these meetings has accelerated over the years. Prior to the institutionalization of ties in 1990, most meetings (except those between Commission officials and their U.S. government counterparts, which tended to follow a six-month rhythm, and the twice-yearly EP–U.S. Congress encounters) were organized on an ad hoc basis. In the 1970s Commission president François-Xavier Ortoli visited Washington only once (in 1973) and Roy Jenkins twice (in 1977 and 1978). The return traffic was similarly irregular, with President Ford meeting President Ortoli once, on the occasion of a visit to NATO in Brussels in 1975, and President Jimmy Carter meeting President Jenkins at the Commission headquarters in 1976 and 1978. President Ronald Reagan, in office from 1980 to 1988, never went to the Commission's headquarters in Brussels, though the frequency of Commission presidential visits to Washington began to increase, with Jenkins going in 1980, Gaston Thorn in 1981 and 1983, and Delors paying annual visits from 1985 onward. Under the Reagan administration, even the biannual Commission-administration meetings were reduced to an annual schedule, resuming their old pattern only in 1990 along with the other changes instituted by the Transatlantic Declaration.

The longest-standing series of regular political contacts between the United States and the EU are those between the European Parliament and the U.S. Congress. Almost without interruption, these meetings have happened twice a year since 1972, making a total of well over forty by the mid-1990s. For the EP, its decision to constitute a permanent delegation to engage in systematic dialogue with the U.S. House of Representatives was the beginning of its own institutionalized system of interparliamentary relations that now extends to most countries in the world. But the U.S. link was the first (followed by a similar delegation set up a year later for relations with Canada). The two groups of parliamentarians (now around sixteen Europeans and up to fifteen from the United States) hold their meetings alternately in the EU and the United States. When the EP delegation travels to the United States, it usually precedes the interparliamentary meeting proper with a series of meetings in Washington with members of the U.S. administration and the Senate[7] and receives briefings from the Commission's delegation and the member states' ambassadors on current EU-U.S. differences. The actual meetings between the standing delegations from the two sides usually take place over a weekend away from Washington, in the home congressional district of one of the U.S. members. This allows the delegations to concentrate on their agenda without fear of distraction by House votes or other congressional business. When the U.S. delegation pays its return visit to Europe, usually in January, the meetings are sometimes held in the capital of the member state holding the presidency, thus allowing the U.S. members to meet some of the government ministers who will be conducting EU business over the subsequent six months. Alternatively, they take place in Brussels or Strasbourg, giving the U.S. delegation the chance to have discussions with members or senior officials of the Commission.

The agendas for the meetings generally cover a range of political and economic issues of interest to the two sides. Although the European Parliament had no real competencies in the field of external relations until the Single European Act came into force in 1987, this never stopped its delegations from discussing the most sensitive matters with their U.S. partners, from the details of individual trade disputes to the high politics of disarmament, burden sharing, or policy toward the Middle East, Cuba, or South Africa. It also never shied away from raising issues in bilateral relations it considered important, such as the fate of European individuals in jail in the United States or the long-standing irritant of U.S. visa requirements for European tourists visiting the United States (thanks in part to EP pressure on this issue and the good offices of members of the congressional delegation, the United States in the late 1980s introduced the visa waiver program, which now exempts most EU citizens from the requirement).

Foreign policy, long a difficult subject for discussion between the EC and the United States even after the advent of EPC, was always a central theme for frank debate between European and U.S. parliamentarians in the context of their meetings. Indeed since the late 1970s, during its visits to Washington the European Parliament delegation has always requested and invariably been granted briefings from the State Department, whose senior officials (often of the rank of deputy secretary of state) have provided details of U.S. policy. In November 1986 the president of the European Parliament, Pierre Pflimlin, visited President Reagan at the White House. The central theme of their discussion was U.S. policy following the agreement between Reagan and General-Secretary Gorbachev in Reykjavík on strategic arms reductions and the removal of cruise and Pershing missiles from European territory. Pflimlin wanted assurances, which Reagan gave, that this agreement would not prejudice the U.S. defense commitment to Europe.[8]

The overall number and intensity of political contacts between the United States and the EU have grown over the years and have never been as great as they are today. As U.S. hegemony has declined and European influence in the transatlantic relationship grown, the need to concert has become all the more important for both sides. Whether in reacting to the Tiananmen massacre or the Russian intervention in Chechnya or coordinating policy on the Middle East or Bosnia, neither the European Union nor the United States is today likely to undertake any action without first consulting the other (there are exceptions: the United States consulted neither the EU presidency nor individual Union member states when it launched cruise missile attacks against Iraq in September 1996, instead merely informing them). Although such consultation may not lead to a perfect harmony of approach, the results are likely to be no worse than the differences that need to be overcome among the member states of the Union itself. Totally divergent policy approaches like that on Cuba, for example, where the United States pursues a policy of total embargo and the EU believes in undermining the Castro regime through contacts and trade, are rare.

This was not always so. Until 1970 and the introduction of European Political Cooperation, there were no disputes between the United States and the EC per se; disagreements, by definition, were with individual member state governments, such as with Paris over French withdrawal from NATO's command structure or with various other European governments over their failure to support U.S. policy and actions in Vietnam. But once EPC came into being, disagreements became possible between the United States and the collective policy of the Community, where one had been reached. The first major differences of opinion occurred over the response to the 1973 Arab-Israeli war and the subsequent oil boycott. With its far greater dependence on Middle East oil, Europe felt obliged to take a more conciliatory approach toward Arab concerns. An EPC statement recognized that the Palestinians had "legitimate rights" in the region, and the Euro-Arab Dialogue was launched in an effort to develop better relations. Both these actions were taken against U.S. wishes. At the end of the 1970s, the United States expected stronger reactions from the Europeans in the wake of the Iranian hostage crisis and the Soviet invasion of Afghanistan. The European responses to these events were, of course, dictated by the need to find whatever level of agreement was possible among nine member states, all of which still had their own foreign policy interests and priorities. But for the United States, the early hopes that EPC would provide it with a real foreign policy partner were frustrated.

The situation was mixed throughout most of the 1980s. While the cooperation between the two sides over the invasion of the Falkland/Malvinas Islands helped to persuade the Argentineans that their case was hopeless on a diplomatic as well as a military level, Europe's growing interest in Latin America as a whole often brought it into conflict with U.S. policy in the area. Although Washington broadly supported the regime of Augusto Pinochet in Chile, convinced that it was the lesser of two evils, the EC was outspoken in its regular condemnations of human rights violations there. Similarly, in Central America the United States and the EC found themselves practically on opposing sides in the internal conflicts in El Salvador and Nicaragua.

Other events also saw the two sides of the Atlantic in frank disagreement. One example was the Soviet gas pipeline affair. Numerous European countries stood to benefit from an extension of the Siberian pipeline to Western Europe, and European companies were anxious to participate in building it. The United States opposed the plan and went so far as to extend its embargo on the USSR to European subsidiaries of U.S. firms and to other European companies that had licenses to use U.S. technology. This led to a concerted protest by the EC that eventually resulted in the ban's being lifted.[9] Another example was the failure of EPC in 1986 to adopt a strong policy in support of U.S. measures aimed at isolating Libya in retaliation for the latter's alleged involvement in a series of terrorist attacks (including one in Berlin on 5 April in which two people were killed and over 200 injured in the bombing of a discotheque). In the absence of what it regarded as a firm European response, Washington decided to bomb targets in Libya. However, both the French and Spanish governments denied the United States use of air bases on their territory (and even overflight privileges), and it had to launch its raid from Britain, whose government, under Margaret Thatcher, adopted a traditionally supportive approach.[10]

These examples provoke three observations. First, in relations between the United States and Europe, nontrade foreign policy issues have arisen and continue to arise in ways that are not usually the case in Europe's links with other regions or countries, namely, in sectors that have global political and/or security implications. Second, U.S. interests and policy can be prejudiced by strong European positions that do not accord with its own. Third, the *failure* of Europe to reach joint positions on critical issues can be just as injurious to U.S. foreign policy outcomes as a common policy that is not supportive of the U.S. line. The United States, in short, is best served by a united European position on foreign policy issues that accords with its own. While this may sound axiomatic, it is at the same time a measure of how important the EU has become as a foreign policy actor in its own right, even for the world's leading power. Probably the best single example of this was the Iraqi invasion of Kuwait. For the subsequent U.S.-led military operation, backing from the EC was an essential precondition, both within the United Nations and, for reasons of diplomacy, in the Arab world. Even though the lack of an effective security dimension to the EC's foreign policy meant that it was up to individual member states to contribute forces unilaterally, the Community was ultimately unequivocal in its political stance. The net result was a genuinely international operation rather than just a U.S. action, and the provision of the necessary legitimacy to the liberation of Kuwait and the later sanctions against the Iraqi dictatorship.

From the U.S. perspective, Europe's post-Maastricht Common Foreign and Security Policy offers the prospect of a full partnership and a more equitable sharing of the burdens, financial and political, of international power. Already the European Union has taken on a major share of the costs of supporting economic and political reform in the former Soviet Union, providing almost three-quarters of all international assistance to the CIS, through institutions such as the European Investment Bank and the European Bank for Reconstruction and Development and in the form of direct aid through humanitarian programs like the European Community Humanitarian Office (ECHO) and practical assistance schemes like TACIS. Similarly, the EU has financed over 60 percent of all aid to the countries of Central and Eastern Europe. But more important than financial help are the association and partnership agreements that the Union has concluded with almost all its eastern neighbors, offering them access not just to EU loans and aid but to its markets, its know-how, and its technology—and ultimately, in the case of the Central and Eastern European countries, to membership in the Union itself.

For the United States, EU action in this area makes a significant contribution to the stability of the region and thus serves U.S. interests and saves U.S. tax dollars. The same is increasingly applicable to the strategically vital Mediterranean, where Europe has committed itself (most recently at the November 1995 Barcelona conference) to help build and maintain economic and political stability. Chapters 3 and 4 have already dealt with these matters in depth. They deserve a mention here because they show how an increasingly assertive and coherent EU foreign policy benefits the United States by relieving it of burdens and responsibilities that it might otherwise have to bear. This is no less true as a general rule just because the European Union is not always successful in its efforts: U.S. involvement—in the former Yugoslavia, for instance, or in the potential conflict between Greece and Turkey over a disputed island[11]—may still be called for from time to time.

But such occasions are rarer now than they were, and the United States bears less of a burden. This same assertiveness has also come to mean that the United States can no longer assume the leadership role that it once enjoyed in many international fora. The United States and the EU now work closely together in organizations such as the UN General Assembly, the OSCE, the WTO, and numerous international conferences on issues ranging from the environment to the law of the sea. The EU is no longer merely a client of the United States and now often takes the lead on major issues in international gatherings. This can have advantages or disadvantages for U.S. policy, but whatever the outcome, it is a new fact of political life that Washington must now consider.

Much the same applies to EU responses to unilateral U.S. policies, where automatic acquiescence is no longer the rule. The European Union's countermeasures against U.S. action targeting EU companies with interests in Cuba (under the 1996 Helms-Burton legislation) are a case in point.[12] So is the EU's rejection of the terms of the 1996 Iran and Libya Sanctions Act (the D'Amato law), which would affect European firms doing business with those countries. Both these examples could result in rows on a scale not seen since the 1981–1982 gas pipeline affair, when U.S. extraterritorial legislation threatened European interests and the EC's reaction eventually forced Washington to back down. However, President Bill Clinton's decision in January 1997 to renew the suspension he granted in July 1996 under the provisions of Title III of Helms-Burton—under which foreign companies can be sued in U.S. courts—was a first sign of Washington's desire to avoid an escalation of the dispute. The presidential waiver followed a strongly worded declaration[13] in the form of a common position by the EU's Council in December 1996 calling for the respect of human rights and progress toward pluralist democracy in Cuba. Each side was thus attempting to minimize the risks of a protracted dispute by making conciliatory moves aimed at defusing the situation.

The Economic and Trade Relationship

The economic and trade aspects of the European Union's external activities have had an impact on the United States since the creation of the EC and played a part in the transatlantic relationship long before the EPC's first steps in building foreign policy. Indeed the economic relationship predates the European Community. The individual countries of Europe have been trading with the United States since colonial days. Many of the

United States' best-known companies were active as manufacturers and investors in Europe decades before the EC was created: Ford, General Motors, Coca-Cola, Woolworth, Kellogg, Hoover, Heinz, and many others were providing jobs and products to Europeans in Europe long before World War II.

Today's transatlantic trading relationship, and particularly the occasional disputes that sully it, must be seen against the background of the extraordinary degree of investment interdependence that exists between the United States and the European Union. Around 55 percent of all foreign direct investment in the United States is European (worth some $220 billion in 1993). A somewhat smaller but still significant percentage (over 40 percent) of total FDI in the EU stems from U.S. sources. This makes each the other's largest foreign investment partner. Since foreign investment plays such an important role in job creation in the target country or region, these figures enhance the part trade already plays in making the EU and the United States mutually dependent on one another for many millions of jobs on both sides of the Atlantic. According to the European Commission, in 1992 around 3 million people were employed in the United States by European-owned companies or their subsidiaries, compared with 2.3 million U.S. jobs that depended directly on U.S. exports to the EU.[14]

The bulk of EU investment in the United States is in the manufacturing, wholesale trade, and petroleum sectors; U.S. FDI in the European Union is concentrated in the manufacturing and financial/insurance sectors. In the late 1980s, many U.S. investors were tempted into the EU by the prospect of the internal market arrangements that came into force at the end of 1992: in some cases this may have been a hedge against the worry that the internal market might prove to be a barrier to continued free trade ("Fortress Europe"), in others the attraction of expanded business opportunities in the post-1992 Europe. Overall the climate for investment between the United States and the EU has been extremely benign. The U.S. anxiety about the level of Japanese investment and acquisitions in the United States, particularly during the 1980s, has not generally affected feelings toward European investors. However, the Exon-Florio amendment (Section 5021 of the 1988 trade act), giving the U.S. president new powers to block or delay foreign acquisitions or takeovers of U.S. firms in the interests of "national security," is a concern to the European Union.

The trading relationship, in contrast, has not been quite so free of friction. Trade is always political as well as economic, and some of the numerous disputes between Europe and the United States have served (if only temporarily) to sour relations between the two sides. The United States is the EU's largest trading partner, and if the EU barely takes second place to Canada as the United States' major partner, then it does so in quantitative but not qualitative terms (only some 45 percent of Canada's exports to the United States are manufactured products, the rest primary products; this compares to around 75 percent of EU exports to the United

States that fall into this category). Together, the EU and the United States account for around 40 percent of world trade. They have comparable GNPs: since its enlargement to fifteen members, the EU's total GNP amounts to some $7,300 billion, somewhat larger than that of the United States at around $6,400 billion. But the U.S. per capita GNP ($24,750) exceeds that of the European Union ($19,680).[15] Two-way trade currently runs at just over ECU 200 billion ($250 billion) annually, and since 1993 has been largely in balance (see Table 5.1).

None of this is surprising. On the contrary, it would be surprising if the two greatest industrial powers on earth were not closely linked economically. Europe was important for the United States long before the emergence of the EC.-U.S. involvement in two European wars did not happen out of altruism but out of a clear understanding that the United States' own economic and political stability was linked to that of Europe. What the arrival of the European Community changed was the institutional relationship. The United States had long been a close trading partner of individual European countries and before the existence of GATT had been free to fix its own trading terms with each of its partners. With the establishment of the EC, however, it faced for the first time a trading bloc, a customs union that imposed identical terms on all of its members. As we have seen, the United States was generally supportive of this development: if the EC led to a strengthening of the economic foundations of Western Europe, so Soviet influence would be more easily held in check. Moreover, a prosperous Europe could be expected to shoulder a greater share of the costs associated with the containment of the perceived Soviet threat, not least by being able to afford to make a substantive and worthwhile contribution to the NATO alliance.

The postwar period saw a proliferation of international organizations and agencies as part of the global effort to promote peace and economic development. Both the IMF and the International Bank for Reconstruction and Development (IBRD, better known as the World Bank) were established by the Bretton Woods agreement in 1944 in anticipation of the need for postwar reconstruction, and the United Nations Organization itself emerged immediately after hostilities ceased in 1945. It was followed by

Table 5.1   EU-15–U.S. Merchandise Trade, 1991–1995 (in ECU billions)

	1991	1992	1993	1994	1995
EU imports	97.0	92.8	90.7	100.0	103.6
EU exports	76.8	79.3	91.4	102.4	100.9
Total volume	173.8	172.1	182.1	202.4	204.5
EU balance	−20.2	−13.5	+0.7	+ 2.4	−2.7

Source: Eurostat

a host of other bodies (most of them limited to the Western world): the GATT, the Organization for European Economic Cooperation (OEEC, later OECD), NATO (and the Warsaw Pact), the Council of Europe, and numerous UN agencies such as the FAO, the World Health Organization (WHO), the International Atomic Energy Agency (IAEA), and more. Even before the first of the European Communities was set up in 1951, therefore, the United States and the future member states of the EC were working together, particularly in the economic field, as partners in a number of international fora. While the United States was by virtue of its size and strength the primus inter pares among the members of most of these organizations and set the agenda for much of the initial postwar period, it also developed the links, particularly with its Western European allies, that would come to serve it well after those allies had coalesced into a genuine European partnership. It is important to remember as well that although for at least the first twenty years after the war the United States remained the undisputed leader of the West and exercised the political and economic hegemony that came with that position, it shared with its European partners a belief in capitalism and free market economics and the political liberalism that accompanied them. Thus, in spite of an asymmetrical relationship between the United States and the EC in the early days of the Community's existence, the conditions obtained for a relatively harmonious development of their trading and economic relationship.

Trade Disputes and Trade Agreements

"Relatively harmonious" correctly describes the trade links that the United States and the EU have enjoyed with one another over the longer term. Although there have been numerous disputes, often involving a degree of genuine acrimony and resulting in mutual recrimination and sometimes retaliation, they have never upset the fundamental balance of the relationship and should not be considered all that significant when set against the total value and volume of trade between the two sides. Every major dispute has eventually been settled, if not to the satisfaction of both sides, then at least in a way that has allowed an eventual return to business as usual. Trade, after all, is not conducted between nations or governments but between businesspeople anxious to make money: governments may try to ensure the fairest possible conditions for the traders, but ultimately, in broadly capitalist economies, deals must be struck by the buyers and sellers even if conditions are not perfect. Since it is indisputable that trade flows and investment between the United States and the European Union have grown steadily in all key sectors over the years, it is clear that disputes and disagreements have failed to have any major effect on the qualitative and quantitative progress that has been achieved.

It does not lie within the scope of this chapter to enter into the details of all the numerous individual trade disputes that have occurred between the United States and the European Union.[16] Table 5.2 lists the main conflicts and their dates. Nevertheless, it may be interesting to look at a couple of examples of how specific disputes arose and were subsequently resolved. The first real trade feud to divide the United States and the EC was the so-called chicken war of 1963–1964. It is significant not just because it was the first, occurring only five years after the entry into force of the EEC Treaty, but because it was concerned with agriculture, an issue that was to lead to several further disagreements. The Community had decided to promote its domestic poultry industry by imposing levies on imported chicken. Under GATT rules, the EC became liable to compensate the United States for the loss of its traditionally high levels of poultry exports to the European market, but the two sides were unable to agree on an amount. The matter was referred to a GATT panel, but the United States was dissatisfied with the value of the compensation it proposed. Instead the United States took unilateral action, imposing retaliatory tariffs on a number of EC exports (including cognac and Volkswagen vans) in an amount that roughly equaled what the United States had lost in poultry sales. The "war" was thus honorably resolved, although the retaliation did not help U.S. chicken farmers, whose exports remained subject to the higher EC tariffs, and penalized cognac producers and a German auto manufacturer who were innocent bystanders. But a principle had been established: the European Community was willing to put its own interests before those of its patron, the United States, and to stand up for them.

Table 5.2   Chronology of Major EU-U.S. Trade Disputes

Years	Dispute
1962	Carpets and glass (U.S.)
1963–1964	Poultry (EC)
1969–1974	Steel trade (EC)
1981–1982	Soviet gas pipeline embargo (EC)
1981–1984	Wheat flour export subsidy (EC)
1981–1985	Canned fruit subsidies (EC)
1982–1986	Pasta subsidies (EC)
1982–1986	Mediterranean citrus imports (EC)
1982–1989	Steel exports to the United States (U.S.)
1985–1986	U.S. Wine Equity Act (U.S.)
1986–1992	Airbus (EC)
1986–1987	Compensation for Iberian enlargement (EC)
1987–	EC ban on hormones in meat (EC)
1988–1989	Canned fruit subsidies (EC)
1988–	Oilseeds subsidies (EC)
1991–	Audiovisual (EC)

Note: Parentheses indicate who caused each dispute.

A more recent dispute is interesting not just because of the issues and the two very different approaches to the fundamental principles involved, but also because it could have occurred only between two mature and equal partners sharing levels of technology and skills that placed them squarely in the same league. The dispute concerned European subsidies to Airbus, a genuinely pan-European project[17] that has enabled the European Union to compete in a field previously dominated by the United States, that of large passenger aircraft. The dispute originated in 1986 when the United States claimed that Airbus Industrie, the consortium that manufactures the aircraft, was receiving government start-up subsidies in contravention of the GATT civil aircraft code. The EC claimed that all loans to Airbus were repayable and that they were therefore not illegal. It countercharged the United States with indirectly subsidizing its own major aircraft manufacturers by providing them with massive defense contracts, research and development grants, and tax breaks. The United States responded by saying that its manufacturers had to shoulder the full cost of aircraft development and production (unlike the Europeans) and thus had fewer resources to invest in new technologies.

Negotiations dragged on for some six years. Initial U.S. complaints were followed by a fresh wave of EU government subsidies to help launch a new series of Airbus aircraft in 1988. These brought threats that Section 301 of the trade act would be invoked (which allows the United States to take unilateral action outside of the GATT procedures in response to allegedly unfair foreign trade practices) and that antidumping and countervailing duty cases would be brought before the GATT. A new element entered the dispute: exchange rate differentials. With the dollar falling against European currencies, particularly the German mark, Airbus production costs increased in dollar terms; since civil aircraft are priced in U.S. dollars, this had a negative effect on Airbus profitability. The United States objected to a German exchange rate guarantee scheme, which it saw as an additional indirect subsidy. The conflict was finally resolved in 1992: the two sides agreed that direct government support for civil aircraft development costs would be limited to 33 percent and to 3–4 percent of turnover in indirect support for manufacturers. The accord now forms the basis for a multilateral GATT agreement on civil aircraft.

Perhaps the longest-running dispute of all concerns the EU's ban on growth hormones used in beef rearing, adopted in 1985. The matter was immediately raised by the United States at the GATT, because it meant that U.S.-produced beef that had been subjected to the hormones could no longer be exported to the European Community. The ban had been agreed not least because of pressure from consumer groups and the European Parliament; in fact EC-commissioned reports in 1982 and 1987 and a WHO report in 1988 all showed no significant risk to human health from the use of hormones in beef. Neither a GATT standards code committee nor a technical experts group was able to resolve the issue; the EC postponed application of the ban until the beginning of 1989. Once it entered into force, however, the United States responded by invoking 100 percent tariffs on EC meat products worth $100 million.

After renewed discussions between the two sides, an interim agreement was reached in May 1989 to allow U.S. shipments of untreated beef to the EC. In the same year, European pork hams and tomato sauce were removed from the U.S. retaliation list, but in December of that year U.S. president George Bush signed the Harkin amendment calling for U.S. military bases in Europe to be supplied only with U.S. beef. Further consultations in December 1993 failed to bring progress. A scientific meeting convoked by the Commission in November 1995 concluded that five of the hormones banned by the European legislation were in fact safe for human consumption, but the European Parliament called on the EU to maintain its ban, despite threats by the United States to take the matter before the WTO. At the beginning of 1997, there was still no solution to a dispute that had lasted ten years.

As the list of disputes in Table 5.2 shows, the bulk of disagreements have been the result of actions taken by the EC, often under the Common Agricultural Policy. Such conflicts are likely to lessen thanks to the reform of the CAP in 1992 and the successful conclusion of the Uruguay Round. Another category of minor disputes, usually called trade irritants, exists at a more bilateral level (genuine disputes usually involve the intervention of GATT panels at some stage in their resolution). The European Commission publishes an annual booklet called *Report on United States Barriers to Trade and Investment* that highlights the myriad petty restrictions exporters and investors face when doing business across the Atlantic. These occur in areas that range from U.S. national security requirements and public procurement restrictions to technical barriers to trade and discriminatory taxation measures.

The New Transatlantic Agenda

It was the U.S. secretary of state James Baker who, in a speech in Berlin in December 1989, first mused out loud about the possibility that the EC and the United States might "work together to achieve, whether in treaty or some other form, a significantly strengthened set of institutional and consultative links."[18] But what would such a treaty contain? Nobody was quite sure. Instead, in November 1990, the Community and the United States signed the Transatlantic Declaration. It did not constitute a formal agreement, much less a treaty, and committed neither of its signatories to anything beyond more regular consultations. Although conceived as a compromise (similar declarations were signed between the EC and Canada and Japan, respectively), it quickly became clear that even on its own terms it did not go far enough. The idea of a genuine treaty did not go away. The possibility of a transatlantic free trade area was mooted. In studies, discussions, and speeches, the need for further developing the bilateral relationship between the European Union and the United States became a recurring theme. The adoption and entry into force of the Maastricht Treaty; the opening for business of the single market; the EU's role in reconstructing Central and Eastern Europe; the transatlantic standoff in the closing phases of the Uruguay Round negotiations; the accession of Austria, Finland, and Sweden to the EU—all these events served to heighten Washington's awareness of Europe's growing importance.

By the beginning of 1995, it was clear that a new step could not be further delayed. What finally emerged again fell short of a full treaty, but not by much. Called the New Transatlantic Agenda,[19] it was signed in Madrid in December 1995 by President Bill Clinton for the United States and jointly by Spanish prime minister Felipe Gonzalez (as president of the EU Council) and Commission president Jacques Santer on behalf of the European Union. Unlike the 1990 declaration, which was limited to rhetoric and a commitment to more regular consultations, the NTA singled out four areas for cooperation (see Appendix 4):

- "promoting peace and stability, democracy and development around the world";
- "responding to global challenges";
- "contributing to the expansion of world trade and closer economic relations"; and
- "building bridges across the Atlantic."

Attached to the NTA is a "Joint EU/U.S. Action Plan," in which the four areas for cooperation are translated from mere rhetorical goals into a series of detailed actions for implementation. It is worth highlighting here the principal actions proposed under each of these headings, since the success or failure of the European Union and the United States in putting them into effect between now and the turn of the century may well be taken as a test of their ability to work together. If the NTA and joint action plan fail to yield results, the largely declaratory nature of the EU-U.S. relationship may yet need to be reinforced through the conclusion of a more formal treaty. Given the relative specificity of some of the proposed actions, it will not be difficult to judge the performance of the partners in implementing them.

The first area for cooperation, "promoting peace and stability, democracy and development around the world," begins with a pledge to work together "boldly and rapidly" in promoting the peace and assisting in the reconstruction of the former Yugoslavia. This will be done through EU-U.S. cooperation to ensure respect for human rights and the rights of minorities, refugees, and displaced persons; respect for the work of the War Crimes Tribunal to ensure international criminal accountability; the establishment of a framework for free and fair elections in Bosnia-Herzegovina; and the implementation of the agreed process for arms control, disarmament, and confidence-building measures. The two parties also agree to continue to provide humanitarian assistance and help with reconstruction, and to support the Bosnian-Croat Federation.

Similar detail characterizes European and U.S. plans to act jointly in Central and Eastern Europe and in Russia, Ukraine, and the other new independent states, especially in promoting democracy, coordinating assistance, promoting environmental protection, and more. Other foreign policy joint actions include promoting the Middle East peace process; sharing responsibility in other regions of the world (such as various parts of Africa, Central America, the Caribbean, and the Far East); coordinating and working together in development cooperation and humanitarian assistance; supporting human rights and democracy; cooperating in international organizations; and working together in the fields of nuclear nonproliferation, international disarmament, and arms transfers.

The second goal, "responding to global challenges," commits the European Union and the United States to joining forces in meeting together "the challenges of international crime, terrorism and drug trafficking, mass migration, degradation of the environment, nuclear safety and disease." Again, the actions proposed are noteworthy for their detail. In the area of immigration and asylum, for example, the two sides intend to

- "develop a common stance on temporary protection in the United Nations High Commission for Refugees";
- "coordinate positions on the Conference on Refugees and Migrants in the Commonwealth of Independent States";
- "improve existing arrangements and exchanges of intelligence in areas of mutual concern, for example, forged identity documents and transport carriers' liability"; and
- "convene seminars in 1996 and compare the results of [their] respective studies on migration flows both into the U.S. and into the EU."

The most substantive of the action plan's sections concerns "contributing to the expansion of world trade and closer economic relations." Here, the partners agree to work toward strengthening the multilateral trading system by ensuring that the WTO functions properly (and completing work on the unfinished business of the GATT Uruguay Round, notably telecommunications and maritime services); promoting the liberalization of financial services; improving the level of protection for intellectual property rights worldwide; creating additional trading opportunities by improving access to their own and international markets; cooperating in harmonizing customs procedures; and combating bribery and corruption in international trade. But certainly the most ambitious part of this section concerns the creation of what is termed "the New Transatlantic Marketplace." Addressing squarely the numerous areas in EU-U.S. bilateral trade that regularly give rise to disagreements or friction, the parties preface their list of fourteen specific issues by agreeing to "carry out a joint study on ways of facilitating trade in goods and services and *further reducing or eliminating* tariff and nontariff barriers" (emphasis added). For the first time, in other words, the European Union and the United States intend to consider, in a *joint study*, the possibility of achieving a transatlantic free trade area. In the meantime, as part of a "confidence-building process," they will increase their efforts to resolve bilateral trade issues and disputes. The list of areas in which they will make these efforts covers nearly every contentious aspect of bilateral trade relations, from standards and certification to government procurement, from veterinary and plant health issues to telecommunications. The section concludes with an undertaking to create a joint working group on employment and labor-related issues intended to contribute toward the shared goal of encouraging job creation.

The final section, "building bridges across the Atlantic," sounds as if it may be a return to rhetoric, but in fact it sets out a series of practical proposals aimed at "deepening and broadening the commercial, social, cultural, scientific and educational ties" between the two sides. Chief among these is support for the Transatlantic Business Dialogue (TABD), the first meeting of which (involving CEOs and other leading European and American businesspeople) took place in Seville in November 1995; several of its ideas form part of the action plan. The second TABD was held in Chicago in November 1996, and annual meetings are planned for the future. Other proposals include broadening scientific and technological cooperation (not least through the negotiation, by 1997, of a comprehensive EU-U.S. science and technology agreement); strengthening "people-to-people links" by promoting educational exchanges, scholarships, internships, and so on; and supporting cultural cooperation (including transatlantic TV and movie coproductions, instituting an EU-U.S. literary prize, and using the Internet to make relevant material easily available to a wider public).

The New Transatlantic Agenda marks the first attempt by the European Union and the United States to identify and tackle an inventory of objectives perceived by both to be important not only in terms of their bilateral relationship but also of their roles as world leaders. If the two sides are successful in implementing all or even a significant part of the NTA, they will have gone a long way toward reducing the tendency they still have to become tied up in commercial and political disputes, with all the unnecessary acrimony—and often economic loss—that results. Moreover, they will be in a far stronger position to play a positive role in international affairs and to help resolve many of the major outstanding problems in the world than either would be acting alone. Long the most important of all international relationships, the EU-U.S. link could now be on the verge of entering a qualitatively new phase based on a genuine recognition of shared goals and a joint willingness to achieve them.

The European Union and Canada

The relationship between the European Union and the United States is one between two great powers, certainly in the economic sense and, since the demise of the Soviet Union, increasingly also in a political one. The EU's relationship with Canada is of a different order of magnitude. In many ways it is more typical of the great majority of the Union's links with the rest of the industrialized world. The United States is clearly exceptional in its status as the only country or entity that rivals and often surpasses the EU in economic and political importance. For the most part, Europe's size, strength, and economic muscle allow it to play a dominant role in its dealings with other countries. This is the case with Canada, as it is with Australia, Brazil, Argentina, and Korea, for example.

Nevertheless, Canada is unlike any other country with which the EU has to deal. With its population of some 29 million, it is equivalent in size and economic strength to a large state like California or New York; but unlike U.S. states, it must make its own way in the international arena. It has a relationship with the United States similar to that of Ireland to the United Kingdom or Luxembourg to Belgium: independence tempered by interdependence. However much Canada may rely on the United States economically—and it does so to the extent of around 70 percent of its trade—it attempts to play its own unique role as an international actor. Precisely in order to distinguish itself from its large neighbor, it seeks to demonstrate its sovereignty by giving its foreign relations a high profile.

Canada's history also places it in a special relationship with the European Union. As a former British dominion and still an active member of the Commonwealth, Canada has always had strong links to the United Kingdom. Until 1973, when it joined the EC, the UK was Canada's second biggest trading partner (after the United States); this role automatically fell to the Community once the common customs tariff became applicable to Britain. Canada moved swiftly to upgrade its links to the EC after the British accession had been agreed. In 1972 biannual high-level consultations between senior Canadian and EC officials covering bilateral and multilateral issues were inaugurated, and in 1973 Canada accredited a separate ambassador to the Community (until then the Canadian ambassador to Belgium had performed this function). The same year, the European Parliament and the Canadian House of Commons set up a formal institutionalized relationship involving annual meetings of parliamentarians, which has continued ever since.[20]

The EC-Canada framework agreement on trade and economic cooperation, concluded in 1976, was the only such agreement between the European Community and an industrialized country until the two framework agreements with Australia and New Zealand, on which negotiations were started in 1996 (see Chapter 7). Unlike the many other accords entered into by the Community until then, it did not offer concessions of any kind but rather established a *context* in which to situate an already mature relationship between two advanced industrialized societies. Its origin lay in the wish of the Canadian government to place its relationship with the enlarged EC on a formal footing. It established an institutionalized structure of regular contacts between the Canadian minister for international trade and the EC's external relations commissioner and set up a joint cooperation committee (JCC) of Canadian federal and provincial officials and their EC and member states' counterparts. Today several subcommittees and working groups concern themselves with specific areas of interest to the two sides, such as industrial policy, trade, and investment; other issues dealt with in this context include the environment and telecommunications and a range of sectoral matters such as metal and minerals, wood and paper products, and information technologies. The framework agreement does not attempt to establish any type of preferential trade regime between the two sides.

In 1990 the EC and Canada signed a Transatlantic Declaration. Similar to that concluded at the same time between the Community and the United States, the declaration sets out the principles on which the relationship is based and institutionalizes regular meetings between the Canadian prime minister on the one hand and the presidents of the EC Commission and Council on the other (though not at the twice-yearly rhythm Brussels and Washington agreed upon).

Trade (see Table 5.3), at around ECU 20 billion ($25 billion) annually, reflects Canada's position as a major producer of raw materials, with its exports to the EU dominated by wood and paper products and aluminum (it also supplies considerable quantities of aircraft and transport equipment); by contrast, its imports from Europe consist primarily of organic chemicals, aircraft, computers, cars, and alcoholic beverages. The EU is Canada's major source of non-U.S. foreign investment, accounting for

Table 5.3   EU-15–Canada Merchandise Trade, 1991–1995 (in ECU billions)

	1991	1992	1993	1994	1995
EU imports	10.4	9.5	8.4	9.9	11.7
EU exports	10.2	9.3	9.4	10.5	10.1
Total volume	20.6	18.8	17.8	20.4	21.8
EU balance	–0.2	–0.2	+ 1.0	+ 0.6	–1.6

Source: Eurostat

22.6 percent of total FDI; Canada in turn provides about 20 percent of FDI in the European Union.

None of this, however, can mask a long series of bilateral disputes that have involved everything from seal products to shoes to Canadian liquor board practices to old growth lumber to furs to fish. Many of the disputes have soured Europe's relations with Canada in ways that have had more of an emotional edge to them than Europe's numerous trade conflicts with the United States. Animal rights activists, environmental pressure groups, and human rights organizations all have identified issues in Canada (not always directly related to trade) that have resulted in EC action or the threat of it. The well-documented killing of baby seals in the early 1980s led to the imposition of an EC ban on seal products. The use of leg-hold traps for catching fur-bearing animals in Canada's far north resulted in similar EC action (though a postponement of an import ban until the end of 1996 may allow time for alternative trapping methods to be introduced). The European Parliament has been lobbied extensively by groups of Canadian native peoples concerned at the confiscation or alleged misuse of their lands by federal or provincial authorities. The extensive clear-cutting of old growth rain forest in British Columbia led to calls for a ban on lumber imports and provoked a fact-finding trip by MEPs.

But the most bitter dispute of all has concerned fishing in the rich waters of the Grand Bank off Newfoundland and in neighboring international waters, historically a destination for fishing crews not only from Canada but from many other countries as well, including EU member states. An agreement was reached in December 1992 regulating use of Canadian ports by Community vessels and covering stock conservation, enforcement, and management. Although endorsed by the EU, the agreement was never ratified by Canada. In September 1994 the Northwest Atlantic Fisheries Organization (NAFO) imposed a limit (total allowable catch, or TAC) on the quantities of Greenland halibut, or turbot, that could be caught. The EC was dissatisfied with the quota it was allocated: it had previously taken by far the largest share of the catch of turbot (which, unlike cod and other species, had not previously been regulated) and was now to be limited to just 12.59 percent of the 1995 TAC. In accordance with NAFO rules, it registered an official objection, not to the TAC itself (which it accepted on conservation grounds) but to its share of the overall allocation. Pending consideration of its objection, and again in accordance with NAFO rules, EU vessels continued to fish for Greenland halibut in international waters.

At the beginning of March 1995, armed Canadian "inspectors" boarded an EU trawler flying the Spanish flag, the *Estai*, arrested its captain, locked up its crew, and towed the vessel to port. The "turbot war," as it became known, had begun, bringing EU-Canada relations to an unprecedented low. Since the *Estai* had been fishing in international waters, the EU accused Canada of blatant disregard not only of NAFO rules but also of the

UN Convention on the Law of the Sea. The Canadians argued that the EU ship had been violating the TAC set by NAFO in 1994. Although the vessel was eventually released and a new agreement on fisheries enforcement and conservation was reached later in 1995, the political consequences lingered. In the words of Sir Leon Brittan, EC Commission vice president responsible for relations with Canada, "The recent dispute . . . will inevitably continue to have repercussions well outside the fisheries sector. Many in the EU were shocked by Canada's disregard for international law and by its apparent willingness to resort to gunboat diplomacy."[21]

In November 1990 the two Transatlantic Declarations between the European Community and the United States and Canada had been signed in Paris within hours of one another. No effort was made in December 1995 to maintain this parallelism when the EU and the United States signed the New Transatlantic Agenda, undoubtedly not least because of the prevailing coolness of relations between Brussels and Ottawa. However, the two sides began drafting a similar agenda in 1996. By midyear most of the work on the text had been completed, including a joint action plan similar to if not as extensive as that attached to the EU-U.S. NTA. But the agenda's conclusion was delayed because of the EU's insistence on including a fishing clause in the action plan's section on economic and trade relations. The two sides could not agree on mutually acceptable language for this provision, and the hope that the package could be signed at the Rome meeting of the European Council in June 1996 was thwarted.

Several more months went by before the two sides ironed out their differences. The Joint Political Declaration on Canada-EU Relations was finally signed on 17 December 1996 in Ottawa (the text appears in Appendix 5). In a dig at the United States over its Cuba policy, the declaration recalls the "common approach" of Canada and the European Union "in combating secondary embargoes," and commits the two sides to working together under the Action Plan "in order to avoid unilateralism and the extraterritorial application of laws." Canada was the first country to be directly affected by the Helms-Burton legislation (also called the Libertad Act) that targeted foreign companies with business interests in Cuba. By the time of the declaration's signature, several Canadian businesspeople had been banned under the new U.S. law from entering the United States because of their companies' involvement in Cuba.

The Joint Canada-EU Action Plan[22] attached to the declaration provides a detailed framework for cooperation. It is divided into four sections. The first of these—economic and trade relations—covers areas that include reinforcing the multilateral trade system, reinvigorating the bilateral economic relationship, and promoting employment and growth. The section on fisheries, the inclusion of which led to the delay in concluding the declaration, is anodyne in the extreme, with the two sides merely noting:

- The Agreed Minute of 20 April 1995 and the subsequent adoption of its different elements in the NAFO context;
- Canada's decision to reopen its ports to EU-registered fishing vessels effective 21 June 1996 and that Canadian and EU enterprises can enter into joint commercial ventures; They will follow up on the results of their bilateral fisheries negotiations of 1992 and 1995; They express their determination to adopt all the necessary measures with a view to the early ratification of the United Nations Agreement on Straddling Fish Stocks and Highly Migratory Fish Stocks.[23]

In the second section—foreign policy and security issues—Canada and the EU identify five areas for joint action: strengthening cooperation on Euro-Atlantic security issues; reinforcing cooperation on global issues (e.g., in the United Nations and in support of human rights and democracy); regional cooperation in areas such as the Balkans and the Middle East; development cooperation; and humanitarian assistance.

Transnational issues, the third area for joint action, include the environment, migration and asylum, fighting terrorism, combating drug trafficking and organized crime, and cooperating in legal matters and health. The fourth area, fostering links, concentrates on educational and cultural ties, cooperation in science and technology, encouraging business ties, and promoting people-to-people contacts.

Like the New Transatlantic Agenda and its joint action plan, the Canada-EU equivalent is a further element in the extensive series of informal but intense links that bind the European Union and its two North Atlantic partners. Relations between the EU and the United States and Canada may not be free of friction, but they are so close, and so interdependent, that cooperation is not an option but a requirement. Both joint action plans are designed not only to consolidate the interregional ties that already exist in almost every conceivable area of mutual interest, but also to give formal recognition to the idea that the European Union, the United States, and Canada together represent an extraordinarily powerful force around the world. By acting in concert, their combined influence and efforts can have a major impact in reducing, if not solving, many of the outstanding problems confronting the international community. For the European Union, a close and healthy relationship with its North American allies is a prerequisite if its broader ambitions on the global stage are to be realized.

Notes

1. See, for example, Robert O. Keohane, *After Hegemony: Cooperation and Discord in the World Political Economy* (Princeton: Princeton University Press, 1984).

2. Roy H. Ginsberg, *Foreign Policy Actions of the European Community: The Politics of Scale* (Boulder, CO: Lynne Rienner, 1989), p. 130.

3. In 1961 the responsibilities of the first mission were extended to all three European Communities (the EEC, ECSC, and Euratom), and the USEC (U.S. Mission to the EC) was born. Now renamed USEU, the mission numbers more diplomats and staff from other U.S. government departments than either of the other two U.S. diplomatic missions in Brussels, the embassy to Belgium, and the mission to NATO.

4. See, for example, Roger Morgan, *The United States and West Germany, 1945–1973: A Study in Alliance Politics* (London: Oxford University Press, 1974).

5. Quoted in Pascaline Winand, *Eisenhower, Kennedy and the United States of Europe* (New York: St. Martin's Press, 1993), p. 240.

6. "Institutional Framework for Consultation," *Declaration on EC-U.S. Relations*, 20 November 1990.

7. Although the Senate has always declined to set up its own delegation to talk to the EP or indeed to join the House delegation, individual senators meet the visiting MEPs when they come to Capitol Hill, and the majority leader gives a lunch in their honor. The Senate has also accorded the EP's delegation the rare (if symbolic) privilege of inviting it onto the floor of the Senate, a distinction granted only to the European Parliament and the parliaments of Canada and Mexico.

8. I attended the meeting in my capacity as adviser to President Pflimlin and was later called by President Reagan's chief of staff and told to regard Reagan's comments as completely off the record and in no way as constituting any formal assurance.

9. See Antony J. Blinken, *Ally Versus Ally: America, Europe and the Siberian Pipeline Crisis* (New York: Praeger, 1987).

10. A detailed account of the U.S. disagreement with the EC over Libya can be found in William C. Cromwell, *The United States and the European Pillar* (Basingstoke, England: Macmillan, 1992), pp. 122–130.

11. U.S. ambassador Richard Holbrooke's subsequent remark that the EU was "literally asleep" as Greece and Turkey came close to going to war in the Aegean in early 1996 was not appreciated in Brussels.

12. Under the countermeasures, judgments or administrative decisions based on foreign laws with extraterritorial application, such as Helms-Burton or d'Amato, are considered null and void within the European Union; any EU company or individual penalized under such laws may countersue U.S. companies or citizens who win cases against them in U.S. courts. The European Union also successfully requested the convening of a WTO arbitration panel to consider the conformity of U.S. extraterritorial measures with international trade rules.

13. *Agence Europe*, 2/3 December 1996, p. 3a.

14. Commission, *Partnership: The European Union and the United States in the 1990s* (Washington, DC: EC Delegation, 1994), p. 22.

15. These are 1993 figures taken from the *World Bank Atlas* (Washington, DC: World Bank, 1995).

16. An excellent analysis is given in chapter 4 of Kevin Featherstone and Roy H. Ginsberg, *The United States and the European Community in the 1990s: Partners in Transition* (New York: St. Martin's Press, 1993).

17. Airbus is manufactured by a consortium of companies from four EU countries: Aérospatiale of France, Deutsche Airbus of Germany, British Aerospace of the United Kingdom, and Construcciones Aeronauticas of Spain.

18. Quoted in Featherstone and Ginsberg, *The United States and the European Community*, p. 90.

19. Council of the European Communities, Press Release PRES/95/356, 3 December 1995.

20. The Canadian parliament canceled the scheduled meeting for 1996 over a row concerning the EP's contacts with the province of Québec.

21. Speaking in Ottawa on 2 May 1995. Quoted in *European Union News* NR (95) 21, Press Office of the EC Delegation, Ottawa, 2 May 1995.

22. Council of the European Communities, Directorate General E, Document 12909/1/96 Rev 1 (undated).

23. Ibid., I.2.j.

6

The EU and Latin America

Latin America,[1] like the United States and Canada, has a European heritage stretching back many hundreds of years. Its principal languages and religion reflect the continent's colonization in the sixteenth and seventeenth centuries by the Spanish and Portuguese. Later it experienced waves of European immigration, and not just from the two Iberian countries. These left an enduring legacy of European culture and ideology throughout the region that persisted long after the colonies became independent states. Although the nineteenth century saw the rise of U.S. political hegemony over Latin America, the region's economic, trade, and cultural relations remained strongly oriented toward Europe until well into the twentieth century. But the Monroe Doctrine, which in 1823 had espoused the concept of a Western Hemisphere free of European domination, eventually came to be accepted by the former colonial powers as a fact of political life. The European powers, particularly Britain and Germany, continued to play a major economic role in South America from 1918 to 1945 as traders and investors, but Germany's defeat and Britain's drastically reduced circumstances in 1945 left the United States the dominant economic and political influence in the region in the postwar period.

Beginning with the formation of the Organization of American States (OAS) in 1947, the U.S. role in Latin America became increasingly pervasive. Washington gave tacit support—as well as training and arms—to the military regimes that flourished in the region, not least because of their avowed anticommunism. U.S. FDI, trade, and ODA to the region also grew during the late 1940s and throughout the 1950s. The overthrow of the government of Fulgencio Batista in Cuba by Fidel Castro in 1959 only reinforced U.S. support for the authoritarian and anti-Communist regimes that replaced democracy in most Latin American states, including Brazil, Argentina, Uruguay, Peru, Bolivia, Chile, and most Central American states, in the 1960s and 1970s.

In the late 1950s, several European countries had started to revive their old contacts, and a trickle of investment began to flow toward the bigger Latin American economies—Argentina, Brazil, and Mexico in particular. But even after the creation of the European Economic Community in 1958, Europe made no coordinated efforts to address the growing needs of much of Latin America for development aid and cooperation. Although the EC responded to overtures from the Comisión Especial de Coordinación Latinoamericana (CECLA) by declaring 1971 Latin America Year and establishing a "mechanism for dialogue" involving annual discussions with the Latin American ambassadors in Brussels,[2] any genuine exchange was impossible. For one thing, the lack of effective regional integration mechanisms in Latin America left it fractured and disunited: the early attempts at intraregional cooperation—the Latin American Free Trade Association (1960), the Central American Common Market (1961), the Caribbean Free Trade Association (1965), and others—were at best forerunners of more serious efforts later on. In these circumstances who would be the EC's dialogue partner?

Furthermore, the EC itself had been in crisis for much of the 1960s, and the 1970s brought enlargement followed by the oil shock. When, in 1975, the Lomé convention was signed with the African, Caribbean, and Pacific countries, Latin America (like the developing countries of Asia) was relegated to "nonassociated" status. With U.S. influence still strong and most of the countries of South and Central America in the grip of unsympathetic and undemocratic authoritarian regimes, the EC paid little more than lip service to the region's needs for economic cooperation and ODA. The EC did conclude a nonpreferential trade agreement with Uruguay in 1974 and a first-generation trade and economic cooperation agreement with Mexico in 1975, and later in the decade it negotiated a similar agreement with Brazil (which came into force only in 1982). But compared to the development of the EC's relations with other parts of the developing world, such as the Mediterranean or ASEAN, this was a modest beginning.

Any further progress in developing relations was halted by the Argentinean invasion of the Falkland/Malvinas Islands in April 1982. With both the United States and the entire European Community backing Britain in the brief but bloody conflict, the war was quickly over. But in spite of the subsequent downfall of President Leopoldo Galtieri and the restoration of democratic government in Buenos Aires, other Latin American countries viewed the EC's support for Britain, acting to maintain its colonial possessions, as essentially an unfriendly act. In fact Spain (in 1982 not yet a member of the EC, although it had applied to join) threw its diplomatic weight behind Argentina during the conflict, and it was clear that a number of other Community governments would have preferred not to have had to choose between solidarity with a fellow member state and support for Argentina's desire to put an end to a colonial anachronism. But the Community's adoption of a policy perceived as inimical to Latin America's interests did nothing to bring the two sides closer.

It is no coincidence that the revival of European interest in Latin America occurred just as Spain and Portugal were on the point of joining the EC in the mid-1980s. The "solidarity which binds Europe and the overseas countries," as the EC Treaty's preamble puts it, had always tended to be selective: the countries that had benefited most from European Community "solidarity" had been the former colonial possessions of the member states. The Yaoundé convention of 1963 had been designed to provide for the needs of the territories with special links to the original Six, particularly France, and Lomé took this principle further by incorporating the former possessions of the UK following its accession in 1973. British membership also ensured a degree of special consideration for the countries of South Asia, as the next chapter shows. But Latin America had no privileged links to any of the Community's member states, and this (in addition to the considerations outlined above) was another central reason for Europe's neglect of its needs. U.S. hegemony was certainly a factor. So was the proliferation of authoritarian regimes and the lack of any effective integrationist trends in Latin America. But democracy and integration were hardly hallmarks of the ACP states either. What the latter did share— and what Latin America lacked—were their recent colonial ties to the European Community.

The EC's "return" to Latin America in the 1980s was therefore encouraged by Spanish and (to a lesser extent) Portuguese accession to the Community. Though these two countries joined only at the beginning of 1986, the membership negotiations had begun in 1979, and the Spaniards had always made clear their interest in Latin America. Once in, they succeeded in securing for themselves the succession to the post of commissioner responsible for Latin America and Asia, at the time held by former French foreign minister Claude Cheysson; in 1989 it passed to Abel Matutes, who had been a prominent figure in Spain's center-right Popular Alliance Party. The key job of director for Latin America and Asia in DG I at the Commission had already gone to a Spaniard shortly after accession (posts at this level in the European civil service are considered political and are often filled as a result of national or political party pressure).

However, if the considerable intensification of links between the EC and Latin America that has occurred since the mid-1980s is due in part to the Iberian accession, it is not exclusively so. As we shall see, the revolutionary conflicts in Central America had already inspired the European Community, along with the governments of the Central American states and the Contadora Group (comprising Colombia, Mexico, Panama, and Venezuela), to launch what was called the San José process with a ministerial meeting in the capital of Costa Rica in September 1984. Moreover, the adoption of the Single European Act in 1986 gave a new impetus to foreign policy making through the institutionalization of EPC; this was reinforced by the Maastricht Treaty and the creation of the CFSP in 1993. Growing integrationist tendencies in Latin America itself, including the establishment of Mercosur, the Rio Group, and the Central American Integration System (SICA), made the region at once more attractive to the Europeans, both economically and politically. Above all, the return to Latin America of democracy and a measure of political stability, along with the attractions of an emerging market, combined to make the consolidation of relations irresistible.

Today relations between the European Union and Latin America are pursued at a number of different levels. Political dialogue at the ministerial level exists with the Rio Group and in the context of the San José process (and is discussed in more detail later in this chapter). In Brussels, regular meetings take place between GRULA, the group of Latin American ambassadors accredited to the EU, and Coreper, the committee of EU member state permanent representatives to the Union. The European Parliament has played a long and distinguished role in promoting political dialogue, not least through its regular conferences with the Latin American Parliament, a consultative assembly with its seat in São Paulo that brings together parliamentarians from virtually every Latin America country. These conferences, which take place once every two years in venues alternating between Latin America and Europe, began in 1974. Their agendas have covered the whole range of issues affecting relations between the two regions, including trade, development, security, regional integration, human rights, the environment, the position of women, democracy, as well as the numerous conflicts that have occurred in Latin America over the past two decades. These European–Latin American parliamentary conferences have always been highly political in tenor and, until the debut of the San José process, constituted the only real political exchange between the two sides.

Indeed the very creation of the Latin American Parliament was probably inspired by the example of the European Parliament, which sent a delegation to visit a number of countries in the region in the 1960s.[3] For many years, the EP has maintained two specialist standing delegations, one for relations with the countries of Central America and Mexico, the other for South America. These have not only represented the EP at the regular conferences with the Latin American Parliament but have also paid frequent visits to the region. Particularly since Spanish accession to the EC in 1986, the role of these delegations has grown substantially as they have come to act as a kind of parliamentary lobby group, developing close relations with the Commission as well as with the GRULA. In the late 1980s and early 1990s, EP delegation members served as observers at the numerous elections that marked the return to democracy of many countries in the region, including Nicaragua, El Salvador, Panama, and Chile. The participation of MEPs as observers, always at the invitation of the countries concerned, was a recognition of the close involvement of the European Parliament's delegations in the search for solutions to the region's internal conflicts.

The all-party pressure exerted by the delegations' members has ensured the adoption of frequent resolutions on Latin American issues and helped to assure parliamentary support for European Union budgetary measures in favor of Latin America. Among these measures was the creation of the Institute for European–Latin American Relations (IRELA), a Madrid-based think tank that provides research and other practical and documentary backing for EP members as well as the Council and Commission. In recent years, the European Parliament has become an almost compulsory stop for visiting Latin American heads of state, who use the institution as a platform for appealing for European Union support.

Trade—the linchpin of the EU–Latin America relationship, as it is with so many other parts of the world—is subject to a variety of bilateral and multilateral agreements. Development aid is also an important aspect of the relationship, with the EU and its member states accounting for the lion's share of all ODA flowing into the region (some 60 percent in 1993). Both trade and development are discussed below in the sections dealing with Central and South America. Unlike its dealings with regions closer to home, such as Central and Eastern Europe or the Mediterranean, the EU's approach to Latin America has been less global and more localized and problem-specific in nature. For one thing, Latin America does not present the same security considerations for the European Union as the latter's immediate neighbors do and is therefore of less strategic concern. For another, the differentiation in Latin America's integration efforts (see Table 6.1) has required an approach focused more on specific regions than on the countries as a group. But this is likely to change as the current trend toward "open regionalism"—in which numerous Latin American countries are simultaneously members of more than one regional trade grouping—develops into the panregional cooperation now being actively espoused (for example, by merging all existing subregional trade agreements into a Latin American free trade area by the end of the century[4]).

Central America and the San José Process

It was the numerous conflicts in the Central American isthmus that in the 1980s first drew the European Community back to Latin America as a matter of policy. The conflict in Nicaragua between Sandinistas and Contras following the revolution in 1979 and the worsening civil war in El Salvador between leftist groups and the country's successive military-backed

Table 6.1   Regional Groupings in Latin America

Designation	Member Countries	Role/Characteristics
Rio Group	Argentina, Bolivia, Brazil, Chile, Colombia, Costa Rica, Ecuador, Mexico, Paraguay, Peru, Uruguay, Venezuela	Major Latin American group for political coordination. Holds political dialogue with European Union. Grew out of merging of Contadora and Lima Groups.
Latin American Integration Association (LAIA)	Same as Rio Group (minus Costa Rica)	Loose association aimed at fostering regional integration.
Andean Pact	Bolivia, Colombia, Ecuador, Peru, Venezuela	Free trade area with variable common external tariff.
Central American Integration System (SICA)	Costa Rica, El Salvador, Guatemala, Honduras, Nicaragua, Panama	Planned common external tariff and free movement of people (Costa Rica and Panama not fully integrated). Central American Parliament.
Group of Three (G-3)	Colombia, Mexico, Venezuela	Free trade area (1995). Latin America's main oil-producing states.
Southern Cone Common Market (Mercosur)	Argentina, Brazil, Paraguay, Uruguay	Free trade area/customs union. Common external tariff. Negotiating free trade agreement with EU. Chile and Bolivia are associate members.
North American Free Trade Agreement (NAFTA)	Canada, Mexico, United States	Free trade area. Not strictly a Latin American grouping, this free trade area includes one major Latin American country, Mexico. Chile is considering association or membership.

regimes were the prime focus of EC attention; the situation in other countries in the region, notably Guatemala and Honduras, also rated concern. The Europeans saw the growing instability of the area as inimical to their broader interests: there was a fear that because the United States supported the repressive Salvadoran governments and the Nicaraguan Contras, the Soviet Union might be tempted to intervene. If that were to happen (say, through the direct supply of arms or materiel) there was a real risk that the United States would feel impelled to act militarily, sending troops or resorting to bombing (indeed, the United States carried out army exercises in Honduras near the Nicaraguan border in 1983 and 1984 and mined

Nicaraguan ports in 1984). Not only would this heighten superpower tensions, but it would also reduce the likelihood of progress in nuclear disarmament talks between the United States and the USSR, an issue close to the hearts of several EC governments facing domestic protests against the installation of U.S. cruise and Pershing missiles on their territories. Moreover, there was also genuine abhorrence in Europe, given particular expression in numerous resolutions in the European Parliament, at the slaughter of civilians caught up in the conflict and at the human rights violations being perpetrated by all sides.

While the European Parliament had expressed its concern at the worsening situation in a number of resolutions and parliamentary questions in 1981 and 1982,[5] and the Commission had stepped up financial, technical, and food aid to Central America (Nicaragua alone was the fourth largest recipient of EC food aid to Asia and Latin America during 1976–1988, with only India, Bangladesh, and Sri Lanka receiving more[6]), it was the European Council, meeting in Stuttgart in June 1983, that effectively committed the EC to becoming a participant in the search for peace. In declaring their support for a political resolution to the conflicts in the region based on the principles of noninterference, respect for human rights, and democracy, the heads of government threw their weight behind a peace initiative launched earlier that year by the Contadora Group. They followed up on this declaration of support in a number of ways, the EC's troika meeting with the foreign ministers of the Contadora Group countries at the United Nations in New York in September 1983 and an EP delegation (accompanied by the Parliament's president, Piet Dankert) visiting Costa Rica and Nicaragua in January 1984. A later attempt by the center-right Christian Democrats in the EP to shift parliamentary support more toward U.S. policy in the region failed.[7]

The European Community became actively involved in September 1984, when the ten European foreign ministers (plus those of the two applicant countries, Spain and Portugal) traveled to San José, Costa Rica, to attend a meeting of the Contadora Group and the Central American states to discuss peace initiatives. This meeting, which became known as San José I, was the first in an annual series that continues to the present day and gave its name to the San José process. While the September 1984 meeting was devoted largely to discussion of restoring peace and democracy to Central America and the institutionalization of an interregional dialogue to help achieve that end, it was an early experience of a "new approach that would subsequently lead to a widening and deepening of EU relations with the whole of Latin America, and thus help to increase the scope for political, economic and trade cooperation between the two regions."[8] It was also remarkable for the absence of the United States. Here was a high-level gathering of foreign ministers of twelve European countries and their counterparts from the Contadora Group and Central America, meeting in a region Washington considered its own backyard, but with no U.S. government representation (a letter to participants at San José I from U.S. secretary of state George Shultz, warning them not to agree to measures that might help the Sandinistas, was ignored[9]). The San José process remains one of the earliest and most successful instances of European Political Cooperation and is all the more noteworthy for having preceded by almost two years the subsequent institutionalization of EPC in 1986 under Title III of the Single European Act.

San José I was followed just over a year later by a second conference, held in Luxembourg in November 1985. This was the start proper of the "process," the participants agreeing to turn the ministerial meetings into annual events. It also added practical results to the previous year's commitments: a trade and cooperation agreement was signed with all the countries of the isthmus (the five members of the Central American Common Market, plus Panama). The accord, which came into force in March 1987, institutionalized the dialogue between the European Community and the Central American countries and pledged EC support for integration efforts in the region. Its goals were to encourage investment and private-sector cooperation; to provide help in developing the region's energy resources and infrastructure; to support export promotion, marketing, and quality control with a view to improving the region's trading potential; and to prioritize development aid by emphasizing integrated rural programs, food supply security, education, and public health. To ensure effective implementation of the projects and programs established under the agreement's terms, it set up an EC–Central America Joint Committee to meet in the intervals between the annual ministerial gatherings.

For the European Community, the San José process thus initially combined an economic element, epitomized by the cooperation agreement and aimed specifically at the countries of Central America themselves, and a political element, involving both the Central American states and the Contadora Group, focused on achieving an end to the civil wars in the region. The overall strategy was simple: by encouraging economic growth through the provision of aid and the facilitation of trade, the social and political situation could be ameliorated. Moreover, supporting regional dialogue and integration efforts would help to consolidate economic gains and provide expanded opportunities both for the Central American states and for the larger Latin American community. The resulting climate of increased economic stability and mutual regional support would foster a return to peace, democracy, and social justice. Once achieved, that would lead to a scaling down of superpower tensions in the area, benefiting not only the Central Americans themselves but also the wider world, including the European Community.

Peace finally came to Nicaragua following the February 1990 elections and the defeat of the Sandinista government. Twelve years of civil war in El Salvador came to a close with the Chapultepec peace treaty of January 1992. In September 1996 the guerrilla insurgency in Guatemala ended following thirty years of conflict, with a final peace agreement signed in December 1996. It would be facile to suggest that the EC's involvement through the San José process was the key to ending the years of bloodshed and human rights abuses in Central America. Indeed the governments of the region were not all that impressed by the Community's willingness to match its rhetoric with action, and particularly by what they perceived as often less than generous financial help and trade concessions. The terms of the 1985 cooperation agreement and the levels of ODA flows were both considered wanting by the beneficiary states.[10] It was only in 1988 that the Community's aid to Central America exceeded ECU 100 million ($125 million) for the first time, itself a modest enough sum. Nonetheless, the diplomatic support and encouragement of the EC, which acted with an extraordinary degree of unity throughout the San José process, provided essential moral and political backing to the efforts of the Central Americans and the Contadora Group. An example of this was the creation of the Central American Parliament, or Parlacen. A regional consultative institution concerned with issues related to security, peace, democracy, human rights, the narcotics problem, and integration, it was conceived at the first of the summits of the Central American presidents (known as the Esquipulas conferences) in 1986. The Parlacen project quickly won the enthusiastic backing of the European Parliament, which provided much of the practical help and administrative know-how as well as financial support to get the project off the ground in October 1991.

The San José IX conference in February 1993 saw the conclusion of the successor agreement to the 1987 trade and cooperation accord. A third-generation agreement, it incorporates a conditionality clause, a feature of most new institutionalized arrangements between the European Union and third countries, making benefits subject to respect for democracy and human rights. It also contains an evolutionary clause, allowing the agreement to be extended or added to by mutual accord without the need for total renegotiation. In addition to extending the terms of the 1987 agreement, the new deal includes aid for refugees and programs in support of democracy and human rights.

EU cooperation in the economic sphere now includes areas such as energy, investment, transport, and science and technology, including data processing. Development cooperation is aimed especially at farming, fisheries, the environment, sanitation, and the fight against drugs. Central America has become the largest recipient of EU aid per capita in the world. (Overall, however, the United States remains the largest aid donor to the area, one of the few regions or countries where this is the case; for Latin America as a whole the EU is by far the biggest supplier of ODA, accounting for around 60 percent of the total, compared to 15 percent for the United States.[11]) The agreement confirms trade preferences already granted at the beginning of 1992, under which nearly all of the region's farming and fisheries products, including coffee, enter the EU duty free. Only bananas, Central America's biggest single export, are partially excluded.

While coffee and bananas still comprise around 60 percent of total Central American exports to Europe, nontraditional products have recently come to assume a greater proportion of the total, up from 23 percent in 1988 to 39 percent in 1992. This diversification to products including pineapples and melons as well as shellfish and textiles is important, not least because of the susceptibility of bananas and coffee to fluctuating world market prices. The renewal of the Lomé convention in 1989, however, which extended the special treatment of banana imports from the ACP countries, led to the effective imposition of a quota on imports from Central America. Following a successful complaint by a number of Latin American countries (including Costa Rica, Guatemala, and Nicaragua) against the GATT, a partial solution was reached in 1994. Nevertheless, the banana issue remains an irritant to current EU–Central American relations.

The twelfth San José conference took place in Florence in March 1996 and set a new focus for the EU's activities in the isthmus. Practical and financial help will be concentrated on three priority areas. Funds will be used to support the reinforcement and modernization of the rule of law (notably in human rights and in strengthening democracy and the institutions of state); to support social policies (particularly in relation to the economic and social rights of citizens); and to boost Central America's capacity for integrating into the international economy (by supporting regional integration, the diversification of exports, and the role of the private sector). The frequency of the San José conferences is to be reduced to once every two years, with a greater role devolving to the EU–Central America Joint Committee set up under the 1993 accord. As it approaches the millennium, the San José relationship is entering a new phase, no longer driven by the need to find solutions to the bloody conflicts of the 1980s but instead by a desire to consolidate and build on what has been achieved.

The position of Cuba in Latin America remains complex. Long the only Communist country in the hemisphere, it is today the only nondemocratic state in the region and represents a problem for all of Latin America, in whose councils it still does not play a full part. It is a member of the Association of Caribbean States but spurned a 1996 offer by the Rio Group to become an observer country. While the European Union has provided humanitarian aid and numerous EU companies have invested in the country (inter alia, in the tourism, sugar, and oil-refining sectors), talks the EU began with Cuba in 1995 to negotiate a cooperation agreement broke down in May 1996. The major sticking point appears to have been Havana's unwillingness to accept the now mandatory EU human rights clause, and in particular the European insistence on a reform of the country's penal code barring the political opposition.[12] The Cuban regime also reacted coolly to EU offers to provide material and technical assistance in reforming the country's political and economic systems.

The European approach contrasts strongly with that of the United States, which continues to levy an economic embargo of the country. Indeed, the passage into law in 1996 of the Libertad Act not only strengthened the embargo but led to a major row between Washington and Brussels. The law penalizes foreign companies that conduct business in Cuba involving property or land allegedly confiscated from U.S. citizens by the Castro regime. The EU, along with numerous other countries, considers the extraterritorial reach of Helms-Burton illegal under international law and in breach of WTO rules, as well as politically unsuited to bring about change in Cuba. The European Union's policy of cooperation and contact with Cuba is designed to encourage and persuade the Castro regime to undertake reform. Certainly thirty-five years of U.S. economic embargo have proved singularly unsuccessful in achieving this aim.

The Rio Group and South America

The Rio Group was formed in 1986 and rapidly became the major Latin American forum for political coordination[13]. The group's genesis lies in the merging of the two groups concerned with finding solutions to the conflicts in Central America. As we have seen, the first of these, the Contadora Group, came into being in 1983 and comprised Colombia, Mexico, Panama, and Venezuela. In 1985 four South American countries, Argentina, Brazil, Peru, and Uruguay, set up the Lima Group to provide support for the Contadora process. The two groups together became known as the Group of Eight and renamed themselves the Rio Group in 1986. They held their first summit meeting in Acapulco, Mexico, in November 1987 and declared their aims to be regional political cooperation, closer regional integration, support for democracy, and a greater international role. Later Bolivia, Chile, Ecuador, Paraguay, and Costa Rica joined the Rio Group (with Jamaica as an observer), making it the most comprehensive if informal grouping in Latin America, accounting for 90 percent of the region's population and a similar proportion of its GDP.

The European Community had begun an informal dialogue with the original Group of Eight even before the Acapulco summit, with a meeting of the foreign ministers of the EC and Rio Group taking place on the margins of the UN General Assembly in New York in September 1987. Informal encounters between the two groups continued in various venues (often on the margins of the San José meetings) until December 1990, when the Declaration of Rome institutionalized the dialogue in the form of an annual meeting of foreign ministers with the task of dealing with all issues of mutual relevance. The major issues dominating the agendas have been the debt problem, Latin American integration efforts, drug trafficking, and general trade questions. The Rio Group includes members of all the principal integration organizations in Latin America (the Andean Pact, Mercosur, the Group of Three oil-producing states—Colombia, Mexico, and Venezuela—and SICA) plus Chile and has thus come to constitute an overarching dialogue partner for the EU and a key forum for its own members.

As other chapters of this book have made clear, the end of the 1980s and start of the 1990s was a period of unparalleled change in the post–World War II era. In Europe the Single European Act had not only set the EC on course for a single market, but it had also provided a quasi-institutional umbrella for joint foreign policy making, in the guise of EPC. The Maastricht negotiations had been launched and would lead to a timetable for implementing the Economic and Monetary Union and to still greater cooperation in foreign policy. Negotiations had started with the EFTA countries with a view to creating a European Economic Area—in essence, an extension of the planned single market to include the seven Western European countries that did not belong to the European Community. Of these seven, four would enter into accession negotiations with the EC, and three would become members in 1995.

As the very design of the European Community was being redrawn, so was that of Europe in a larger sense. The collapse of the Soviet Union and its allies presented the EC with opportunities but, more immediately, challenges, not least of a financial nature. Germany became reunited, and the Community gained 18 million new citizens overnight. The Gulf War reminded Europe of the importance of its neighbors to the south and of the need to reinvigorate the Middle East peace process. The outbreak of civil war in the former Yugoslavia confronted the incipient Common Foreign and Security Policy with its first practical test.

While all this was going on, there was a natural concern in other parts of the world, notably Asia and Latin America, that the European Community was becoming increasingly Eurocentric. But in Latin America change was also rampant. To some degree, the end of the Cold War affected the conflicts in Central America; the end of the civil wars in Nicaragua and El Salvador was certainly influenced by the demise of the Soviet Union and its surrogate, Cuba, as actors in the region. Countries in Latin America increasingly were casting away their military or authoritarian governments in favor of democracy. Regional integration efforts began to take on new life. The U.S.-sponsored Summit of the Americas, which brought together the heads of state of the member nations of the Organization of American States in Miami in December 1994, agreed to the aim of creating a free trade area to cover the entire Western Hemisphere by 2005. The current complex network of partly overlapping free trade areas and customs unions seems likely to merge eventually into a single whole.

Although the European Community did indeed seem caught up in domestic and local preoccupations for a few years, it never allowed Latin America to disappear from its sight. Economic as well as political developments in the region assured Europe's continuing interest in encouraging integration and providing aid and cooperation. The EC's exports to Latin America grew by two-thirds from 1990 to 1994, against only 16 percent to the world as a whole. Similarly, annual investment flows from Europe to Latin America were 30 percent higher during the first three years of the 1990s than they had been during the 1980s.[14] In other words, Latin America's potential as a market was becoming evident. During the same three-year period, the EC and its member states provided over $8 billion in aid and cooperation to the region, more than the total for the whole of the 1980s and representing well over half of all aid to Latin America.[15] It is thus clear that the EC was not neglecting the region.

The growth in the EC's economic and trading ties to Latin America must be seen in perspective, however. Other trading powers, especially the United States and Japan, have capitalized even more on the opportunities that the region presents. Although European trade with Latin America has increased substantially in absolute terms (see Table 6.2), it declined as a percentage of total world trade with the region over the period 1990 to 1994; by contrast, the share of U.S. trade increased by some 15 percent, while that of Japan remained steady. The same applies to foreign direct investment. While European investment flows to Latin America increased on an annualized basis during the early 1990s compared to the previous decade, they fell markedly as a proportion of overall FDI to the region[16] and represented less than one-third of overall U.S. investment in Latin America (in the 1980s the EC's member states had been the biggest single source of foreign investment).

The EU does continue to command a clear lead in the field of cooperation: financial and technical assistance, humanitarian aid, the environment, and economic cooperation. The Union's ODA is divided between that supplied by its member states bilaterally and the part administered by the Commission. At the bilateral level, each EU member state has its own priorities, often based on historical considerations. Italy, for example, has been the major single donor to Argentina, reflecting the significant Italian emigration to that country; Spain provides Cuba with almost half of its total ODA receipts; and France has been the biggest bilateral donor to Mexico. Among EU countries, Germany is the leading individual donor to the majority of Latin America states. The Commission attempts to take member states' bilateral assistance into account in determining recipient countries and the types of aid it provides. Its ODA is based on 1991 guidelines covering aid

Table 6.2   Latin American Trade with the EU-15, United States, and Japan,
              1990–1995 (in U.S.$ millions)

	1990	1991	1992	1993	1994	1995
EU-15						
Imports	34,506	34,201	33,858	27,415	34,527	37,963
Exports	21,712	24,085	28,294	29,790	36,526	40,277
Balance	−12,794	−10,116	−5,564	2,375	1,999	2,314
United States						
Imports	64,209	62,566	68,368	74,468	88,211	—
Exports	49,423	58,913	71,312	73,589	87,850	—
Balance	−14,786	−3,653	2,944	−879	−361	—
Japan						
Imports	8,796	9,072	7,976	7,773	8,904	—
Exports	9,257	11,211	13,974	14,984	16,667	—
Balance	461	2,139	5,998	7,211	7,763	—

Sources: IRELA; Eurostat

to Latin America and Asia as well as new guidelines for the period 1996–2000 aimed specifically at Latin America.[17] As a result of the Maastricht Treaty's amendments, the EC Treaty (Article 130x) now formally requires the member states and the European Union to coordinate their development policies. That the EC's member states have succeeded in cooperating so closely with one another in the San José process and in their dialogue with the Rio Group bodes well for similar cooperation in the field of ODA in Latin America as a whole.

In the mid-1990s, the Commission was responsible for channeling aid worth around ECU 0.5 billion ($630 million) annually to Latin America, nearly half of it through nongovernmental organizations (NGOs). Financial and technical assistance was being concentrated on the rural sectors of the poorest countries, but money was also going to numerous other areas, such as antinarcotics programs, democratization, and the promotion of public administration, as well as projects involving women, children, and minority groups and human rights in general. Humanitarian aid was being diversified away from an emphasis on food aid and more toward emergency aid to respond to natural disasters or the results of conflict situations. In 1992 the EC set up the European Community Humanitarian Office, which currently administers such aid on a global basis; Cuba has been the single major beneficiary in Latin America. Further aid is being directed toward environmental projects, including alleviating urban blight and protecting tropical rain forests.

But the most interesting developments have been taking place in the field of economic cooperation, assistance designed to promote economic growth and activities through the encouragement of joint ventures, scientific and technological collaboration, investment promotion, and business co-operation. The EU has set up a number of agencies and programs to facilitate this type of cooperation. In Latin America these include AL-INVEST (to encourage business cooperation and promote investment between the EU and Latin America), ALFA (Latin America Academic Training, aimed at financing academic exchanges and scholarships to allow students to pursue research in Europe), and training programs for businesspeople and public administrators. The European Community Investment Partners (ECIP) program, which is active elsewhere in the world, too, supports joint venture projects through financing via a network of financial institutions and banks.

Recent efforts at coordinating the ODA objectives of the EU's individual member state donors, both with one another and the Union as a whole, should lead to a more rational and cost-effective use of aid flows to Latin America. Moreover, the growing movement toward integration within Latin America itself is likely to foster the creation of regional plans and mechanisms for making better use of ODA receipts through greater coordination and the creation of joint projects and cross-border cooperation. At the same time, there is little chance of further growth in total European aid flows toward Latin America. The current climate in most EU member state capitals is not conducive to any increase in the overall size of ODA allocations, and Latin America will have to fight to maintain its share of existing funds.

Within the Rio Group, the European Union has concluded a variety of agreements over the years, most recently a series of third-generation accords with its principal partners in the region, Mercosur, the Andean Pact, and Mexico. In looking at the EU's links with these areas as they exist at present, it is important to remember that they are dynamic. Not only has there been a series of new agreements concluded since the end of the 1980s, but substantial new links have recently been concluded or are now in the process of negotiation. And even these are likely to require constant adaptation over the coming years as the integration process within Latin America continues to progress.

Mercosur

The Southern Cone Common Market (Mercado Común del Sur) includes two of Latin America's three biggest economies, Argentina and Brazil, as well as Paraguay and Uruguay. Chile became an associate member in 1996[18] (and also signed a framework cooperation agreement with the EU, similar in scope to that concluded with Mercosur in December 1995 and described at the end of this section). Bolivia joined Chile as an associate at the end of 1996. The European Union is Mercosur's biggest trading partner and its major source of investment. The group has achieved a high degree of economic integration, with a customs union and a common external tariff. It is the largest economic grouping in the world outside the "big three," with a total GDP of some $650 billion in 1993. While this may represent only 10 percent of the GDP of the EU or NAFTA, it is greater than that of China, Russia, ASEAN, or South Asia (represented by the South Asian Association for Regional Cooperation, or SAARC). With a total population of 200 million (not counting Chile and Bolivia, as associate members, and Venezuela, which has expressed interest in joining) and economic growth rates similar to those in the booming Asian economies, Mercosur has enormous potential. It already represents by far the fastest-growing export market for the EU. In 1994 Brazil and Argentina jointly took around 27.5 percent of their imports from and sent 26.4 percent of their exports to the European Union (although this represented only 2.4 percent of the EU's total trade).[19]

All of Mercosur's constituent states have third-generation trade and cooperation agreements with the European Union, and all benefit from the numerous programs put in place and financed by the EU to promote scientific and technical cooperation, business, joint ventures and investment, academic and cultural cooperation, and so on. A political dialogue is maintained within the framework of the Rio Group as a whole.

But with Mercosur's transition from a largely cooperative grouping to a full-fledged customs union, the European Commission drafted a proposal in 1994 for upgrading the bilateral relationship, arguing that "Mercosur seems to be a new growth centre of worldwide importance and one of strategic importance to Europe."[20] Its conclusion: in the longer term, an interregional association between the EU and Mercosur should be established, to be preceded by an interregional framework agreement on trade and economic cooperation. Armed with a negotiating mandate from the Council, the Commission opened talks with Mercosur in 1995, and an agreement was signed in Madrid in December of that year. The first accord ever between two customs unions, it is designed to pave the way for an eventual total liberalization of trade between the two sides (probably some time after the year 2000) and also institutionalizes a regular political dialogue at the ministerial and presidential levels separate from that with the Rio Group. It can be seen as a first step toward the possible establishment of a European Union–Latin America free trade zone, which might eventually encompass NAFTA as well.

The Andean Pact

The five Andean states—Bolivia, Colombia, Ecuador, Peru, and Venezuela— formed their regional association in 1969. After a relatively auspicious beginning, the group stagnated throughout much of the 1980s, becoming at best a loose forum for cooperation and dialogue. But in the 1990s it took out a new lease on life, transforming itself into a free trade area, beginning with Colombia and Venezuela in 1992 and adding the remaining members in 1995. A variable common customs tariff was also introduced. In spite of their free trade agreement, the five countries still display major asymmetries, and the long-term viability of the group may be in doubt.[21] Peru and Ecuador have still not solved their border dispute (which flared up into fighting in 1995), and Venezuelan and Colombian troops clash frequently on their common frontier. Moreover, individual Andean states have other ambitions: Venezuela and Colombia are also members of the Group of Three, along with Mexico, and hope to join an expanded NAFTA (though Colombia's hopes in this respect received a setback in 1996, when the country was denied certification by the United States for its failure in combating narcotics trafficking). Bolivia has now concluded an association with Mercosur, and Venezuela has been seeking a similar agreement to join Mercosur. In spite of these difficulties, however, the five countries concluded the Act of Trujillo in March 1996 setting up an Andean Community; intended to emulate the EU's integration model, it will have a secretariat based in Lima, and an elected Andean Parliament and a full-fledged customs union are to be in place within five years.[22]

The European Community concluded a third-generation agreement with the pact states in 1993 (the first EC accord with any of Latin America's subregions was concluded with the Andean group in 1983). Under the latest agreement, the subregion's states profit in particular from EU funds designed to protect the environment and to help in the fight against drugs. Indeed four of the five Andean countries have benefited from duty-free access to EU markets since 1991 as part of an incentive scheme to discourage the growing of coca in favor of product diversification (only Venezuela is excluded from this concession). European countries have become the main source of FDI in the Andean region, and the EU and its member states have devoted a higher proportion of their ODA flows to the area than to any other subregion of Latin America, accounting for about 37 percent of the total over 1980–1992.[23]

Mexico

Mexico is the EU's second largest single trading partner in Latin America (after Brazil), even though almost 80 percent of the country's total trade is with the United States and it accounts for a mere 0.7 percent share of total EU trade (1995). However, EU imports from Mexico have remained stagnant for many years, while its exports have grown steadily, giving it a massive trade surplus with an export-to-import ratio that reached 2.5:1 in 1994 (although a drop in EU exports in 1995 reduced Mexico's deficit somewhat). From 1991 to 1995, Mexico took more EU exports than any other Latin American country except Brazil. Always heavily dependent on the United States economically, Mexico's part in the North American Free Trade Agreement has tied it still more closely to the hemisphere's dominant economy. But Mexico remains a key Latin American power. Its dependence on the United States is tempered by its 1991 free trade agreement with Chile and its participation, with Colombia and Venezuela, in the Group of Three oil-producing states, which became a free trade area in 1995. It has similar trade arrangements with Costa Rica and Bolivia. It also played a central role in the creation of the Association of Caribbean States, an organization set up in 1994 that brings together the thirteen members of the Caribbean Common Market (Caricom), the Group of Three, and the Central American Integration System, plus Cuba. Within Latin America, therefore, Mexico is well placed to take advantage of future moves toward closer regional integration. The ten-year transitional periods for the implementation of the free trade accords with its various neighbors fit with the planned 2005 deadline for a hemisphere-wide free trade zone.

In the wider context, Mexico is also a member of APEC, the Asia-Pacific Economic Cooperation forum. It is a contracting party to the WTO and was admitted to the OECD in 1994. In short, Mexico has become a modest international actor in its own right. If its current economic reform program is successful, it stands to increase its weight in the regional fora to which it belongs and make a greater international impact.

It is against this background that the Commission began negotiating a far-reaching cooperation agreement with Mexico in October 1996 involving an intensified bilateral political dialogue (including meetings at presidential, ministerial, and parliamentary levels), moves toward reciprocal trade liberalization (to be negotiated in detail after the agreement is signed) and stepped-up economic cooperation, and cooperation in a wide range of other fields. Bearing many of the hallmarks of the EU's agreement with Mercosur, the agreement will be unique in the sense that it promises to be the most detailed accord to be worked out with an individual Latin American country. The European Community signed its first agreement with Mexico as long ago as 1975 and concluded a third-generation framework cooperation agreement in 1991 (the first to contain the conditionality clause making its continuance subject to respect for human rights). Through liberalizing trade and creating a new framework for political dialogue and economic cooperation, the new accord is expected to promote confidence among European investors and businesses that wish to establish production facilities in Mexico. It is also likely to encourage Mexican exporters to view the European market as a realistic alternative to NAFTA and its Latin American neighbors and thus to begin reducing the significant trade imbalance with the EU that currently exists.

The Future of EU–Latin American Relations

Latin America is at a turning point in its history. Generations of external dominance and internal authoritarian rule are being replaced by integrationist trends and democratic government. But both are fragile because of their interdependence. Democracy can flourish only in a climate of economic stability and growing prosperity. Economic and political integration, in turn, are unlikely to make genuine progress in the absence of open and democratic societies in the region. There is no guarantee that new economic and social crises, resulting from the impact of rapid structural adjustment and economic liberalization, may not lead to a return to authoritarian government in one or more Latin American countries, destroying at least part of what has been achieved during the 1980s and 1990s.

Stability in Latin America is obviously in the European Union's interest. A stable, prosperous, and integrated region will offer enormous opportunities by providing export markets, a base for investment, and a strong partner in the wider international arena. The attention that the EU has paid to the region over the past decade reflects those interests and may go some way toward helping to consolidate the progress that has already been made. Perhaps the most extraordinary aspect of Europe's recent involvement is the speed with which it has happened. After having virtually no formal or institutionalized links in the mid-1980s, the EU ten years later found itself with a network of ties and agreements spanning every aspect of political and economic cooperation with Latin America. It also finds itself a welcome and sought-after partner. This chapter has shown how this transformation has come about. What happens next, however, will depend more on the Latin Americans themselves than on what Europe can do to help them.

Notes

1. "Latin America" refers, of course, to the Hispanic countries of the Americas. While Cuba is generally considered to be part of Latin America, the English-, French-, and Dutch-speaking Caribbean island states are not; nor are Belize, Guyana, and Suriname (all linked to the EU through the Lomé convention). French Guiana is an overseas department of France and thus technically part of the European Union.

2. Riordan Roett, "Latin America, Europe, and the United States," in Susan K. Purcell and Françoise Simon (eds.), *Europe and Latin America in the World Economy* (Boulder, CO: Lynne Rienner, 1995), p. 178.

3. See Karlheinz Neunreither, "The European Parliament: An Emerging Political Role?" in Geoffrey Edwards and Elfriede Regelsberger (eds.), *Europe's Global Links: The European Community and Inter-regional Cooperation* (New York: St. Martin's Press, 1990), p. 176.

4. As proposed by nineteen Latin American presidents meeting in 1994. See Susan K. Purcell and Françoise Simon, "The Impact of Regional Integration on European–Latin American Relations," in Purcell and Simon, *Europe and Latin America*, p. 58.

5. See, for example, the European Parliament's "Resolution on the Political Situation in Nicaragua," *Official Journal* C 117, 12 May 1980, p. 45; "Written Question on Relations with the Central American Countries," *Official Journal* C 267, 19 October 1981, p. 3; "Resolution on the Situation in Nicaragua," *Official Journal* C 182, 19 July 1982, p. 59.

6. Hazel Smith, *European Union Foreign Policy and Central America* (London: Macmillan, 1995), p. 100.

7. Ibid., pp. 83–84.

8. Institute for European–Latin American Relations (IRELA), *Ten Years of the San José Process* (Madrid: IRELA, 1994), p. 22.

9. See Veerle Coignez, "A Test-Case of Consistency: The San José Dialogue," in Reinhardt Rummel (ed.), *Toward Political Union: Planning a Common Foreign and Security Policy* (Boulder, CO: Westview, 1992), p. 109.

10. Ibid., p. 110.

11. See statistical tables in IRELA Dossier no. 51, *European Cooperation with Latin America in the 1990s: A Relationship in Transition* (Madrid: IRELA, 1994), pp. 56–58.

12. Pascal Fletcher, "EU Halts Talks on Cuban Economic Cooperation," *Financial Times* (U.S. edition), 8 May 1996.

13. IRELA base document, *The European Union and the Rio Group: The Biregional Agenda,* BD-EU/RIO 3/95 (Madrid: IRELA, 1995) p. 6.

14. Ibid., pp. 7–8.

15. IRELA, *European Cooperation with Latin America*, p. 6.

16. IRELA, *The EU and the Rio Group*, p. 70.

17. Commission, "Guidelines for Financial and Technical Cooperation with the Developing Countries in Latin America and Asia During the Period 1991–95," in *Official Journal* C 037, 13 February 1991, p. 3. Commission, *The European Union and Latin America: The Present Situation and Prospects for Closer Partnership, 1996–2000,* COM(95) 495 final, 23 October 1995.

18. Chile has concluded a free trade agreement with the other Mercosur states, under which all tariffs will be removed by 2004, but it is not part of the customs union.

19. Eurostat, *External Trade* (monthly statistics), April 1996.

20. Commission, *The European Community and Mercosur: An Enhanced Policy*, COM(94) 428 final, 19 October 1994, p. 12.

21. Purcell and Simon, "The Impact of Regional Integration," p. 56.

22. Sally Bowen, "New 'Andean Community' to Be Modelled on EU," *Financial Times* (U.S. edition), 12 March 1996.

23. IRELA, *European Cooperation with Latin America,* table 12.

7

The EU and Asia

Asia, of course, is a big place. Traditional definitions have it starting at the Urals and stretching east to the Kamchatka peninsula and Japan, and southeast from Asia Minor all the way to the Indonesian archipelago and beyond to the Philippines. In view of its size, political geographers divide it into East Asia (including China, Mongolia, Japan, and Korea), Southeast Asia (including the ASEAN countries[1] and Indochina), South Asia (including all of the Indian subcontinent), and Central Asia (Kazakhstan and the neighboring republics of the former Soviet Union). This excludes vast tracts of Asian Russia, as well as the Middle East and Turkey (Asia Minor, or Southwest Asia) and Australia and New Zealand, sometimes referred to as Australasia. Southwest Asia (Turkey, the Middle East, and the Gulf states) has already been discussed in Chapter 4 and the Central Asian republics in Chapter 3. This chapter examines the EU's links with its principal partners in the region: China, Japan, Korea, ASEAN, and the Indian subcontinent. It also touches briefly on Indochina and the two antipodean countries, whose uninterrupted status as Western democracies in the Asia Pacific region has tended to set them apart from their neighbors until relatively recently.

The continent of Asia shows all the variety that its size suggests (it is home to half the world's population) and has none of the ethnic homogeneity that at least partly defines most other continents. The differences in the economic and political development of its constituent nations—from the richest to the poorest on earth, from authoritarian to democratic—call for an extremely differentiated approach on the part of the European Union. The result has been a series of largely bilateral relationships, with the partial exception of that with ASEAN, and a less integrated overall strategy toward Asia than the EU has adopted elsewhere.

Europe has been present in Asia for centuries, and this fact alone is key to understanding the close relationship that continues to exist between today's European Union and much of the region. All of today's South Asia once made up the British Raj; Britain was also the colonial power in Burma (now Myanmar), the Malaysian peninsula, and part of the Indonesian archipelago, and through Hong Kong it came to play a dominant role in controlling the trade routes to the Orient. France was present in Indochina (today's Vietnam, Cambodia, and Laos), the Netherlands in Indonesia, Portugal in Macau and Timor, and Spain in the Philippines. Britain, France, and Germany all were active in China in the nineteenth century, and the Dutch and Portuguese played their parts in introducing Japan to European influence long before the Meiji restoration.

One of the lasting consequences of this colonial legacy has been the widespread familiarity of Asians with European culture and language. The almost universal ability today of South and Southeast Asian elites to use English as a working language is in part the result of two centuries of contacts with Britain, not just of the more recent emergence of English as the international language of commerce. Until recently, a high proportion of those elites received their tertiary education at European universities. Asian governmental systems and civil service structures usually emulated European examples, even in those countries that were never colonized. Japan based its bureaucracy on the German *Beamtentum* of the nineteenth century and its current parliamentary system on the European rather than the U.S. model. Even China, that least Western of Asian nations, owes its present system of government to Karl Marx, a German.

Asia and Europe are geographically contiguous. The overland trade routes pioneered in the era of Marco Polo brought exotic products from South Asia and the Far East to Europe many hundreds of years ago. Asian art and culture followed other exports westward. All of this made—and makes—Europe's relationship with Asia and its peoples unique. Today individual European states maintain their own bilateral links throughout the region. But as has been the case elsewhere, European integration has increasingly meant that those bilateral ties have come to take second place to a more comprehensive relationship in which the EU has become a principal partner for most Asian countries. Trade, of course, is the foundation for this relationship. But especially in the developing countries of South and East Asia, the EU is present as a major aid donor and provider of technical and other assistance. A political dimension exists, too: the European Union has developed political ties (usually in the form of meetings at the foreign ministerial level) with most of its major partners, including Japan and, more recently, China. The Euro-Asian summit, held in Bangkok in March 1996 between the leaders of the EU countries and those of the principal nations of East and Southeast Asia, was the first of a series designed expressly to provide a regular institutionalized framework for political dialogue between the two regions.

The overall importance of Asia as a trading partner for the EU is clear from Table 7.1. Statistics have to be treated with caution, and nowhere

Table 7.1   EU-15 Trade with Principal Asian Partners, 1995 (in ECU billions)

	EU-15 Exports	EU-15 Imports	Total Trade	Balance
Japan	32.9	54.3	87.2	–21.4
ASEAN	36.7	34.5	71.2	2.2
China	14.6	26.3	40.9	–11.7
Hong Kong	15.8	7.1	23.0	8.6
Taiwan	10.1	11.8	21.9	–1.7
South Korea	12.3	10.9	23.2	1.4
India	9.4	7.8	17.3	1.5
Pakistan	2.1	2.0	4.1	0.1
Total	133.2	153.5	288.6	–20.3

Source: Eurostat; EC Commission

more so than when dealing with a heterogeneous region such as Asia. Globally, EU trade with all of Asia (excluding Australia and New Zealand, Central Asia, and Southwest Asia) amounted to around ECU 296 billion ($370 billion) in 1995, making the continent as a whole by far Europe's most important trading partner (see Figure 7.1). Of course, Asia is not a single partner but a variety of countries and regional groupings. Nevertheless, the statistics do reveal a number of interesting and valuable facts. After the United States and Switzerland, Japan is the EU's third most important bilateral partner (ECU 87 billion in two-way trade in 1995). Collectively, however, the countries of East Asia (China, Hong Kong, South Korea, and Taiwan, with a total trade volume with the EU of some ECU 109 billion) push Japan into fourth place. ASEAN, the most developed of Asia's regional organizations and one with which the EU has had a cooperation agreement since 1980, did a total of ECU 70 billion worth of business with the Union in 1995, putting it well ahead of China and making it, after the United States and Japan, the EU's third biggest non-European trade partner. But even ASEAN cannot truly be regarded as a single partner: it has no common customs tariff, no common trade policy, and is not even a customs union or a free trade area (though it plans to be one by 2008 and to have lowered average tariffs among its members to 5 percent by 2003).

Single partner or not, the figures make clear that the countries and regions that comprise Asia are vital to the EU's economy. They also show something else: the EU runs a significant trade deficit with Asia overall and with most of its constituent regions, making the European market an essential element in the expansion of many of Asia's individual economies (though the EU does have healthy surpluses with individual countries, notably Hong Kong, South Korea, and Singapore). Over the period 1984–1994, trade increased threefold with the Far East and doubled with Japan. This growth mirrors the expansion in the economies of these countries. And that is a key reason Asia has become so important to the European

Figure 7.1   Global EU-15–Asia Trade: Comparison with Principal EU Partners, 1995 (in ECU billions)

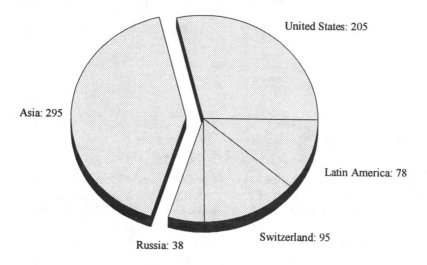

United States: 205

Asia: 295

Latin America: 78

Russia: 38

Switzerland: 95

Source: Eurostat

Union: it is a region with huge economic potential that offers European exporters and investors boundless opportunities. The reverse is equally true: the opportunities offered to Asia's exporters through access to the EU's internal market (particularly in the manufacturing sector, which is now contributing most of the region's new prosperity) are providing the basis for a fundamental shift away from traditional Third World production patterns toward more diversified economies. And while trade is central to the Euro-Asian relationship, the EU has also contributed to the development of the poorer and less-industrialized Asian countries through a range of development programs that have made available over $35 billion in aid since 1976.[2]

The Framework of EU Relations with Asia

As it did with most other regions of the world, the EC began institutionalizing its links to Asia many years ago. Details of the agreements and what they have meant for the countries concerned are discussed below, in the sections devoted to the different regions of Asia. It is clear that in the absence of more cohesive regional structures in Asia, the EU will have no alternative but to pursue its relationships with most parts of the continent on a bilateral basis. Nevertheless, in 1994 the Commission took an important step toward adopting a more global approach with the publication of a strategy paper.[3] For the first time, it formally recognized that the EU needed to pay more attention to its relations with Asia. According to the strategy paper, the Union needed to strengthen its economic presence throughout the continent if it wanted to maintain its leading role in the world economy. Political dialogue had to be stepped up commensurate with Asia's growing economic importance, not least with a view to ensuring that the region would not threaten stability in the post–Cold War world. The promotion of democracy and human rights should be an EU goal in the area, and the Union should seek to contribute toward regional conflict resolution and arms control and nonproliferation. A further goal should be the encouragement of a sound business and investment climate in Asia, and the Union should participate in the economic reforms taking place in countries like China and Vietnam, which were in the process of moving from centrally planned to market-based economies. Finally, the Union and its member states would have to continue to contribute through development cooperation and ODA programs toward helping raise the economic level of Asia's poorest areas. And in all its activities, the Union needed to raise its own profile in the region through a coordinated program of public relations.

The Commission's strategy has been endorsed by both the European Council (at its Essen meeting in December 1994) and the European Parliament. There was a growing awareness in the Commission during the early 1990s—reinforced by Asian diplomats in Brussels and by Asia specialists within the EU's institutions themselves—that the EU was becoming rather too involved with events in its own immediate neighborhood and tending to neglect the wider world. Indeed, the events in Central and Eastern Europe took the EC by surprise in the late 1980s and, understandably, absorbed much of its intellectual and financial energy throughout the early 1990s, as Chapter 3 of this book has shown. While this was never intended to result in any deliberate neglect of other parts of the world, virtually no new agreements, either global or sectoral, were concluded between the EC and any Asian country between 1988 and 1993.[4] The concentration on Europe during this period (more than twenty first- and second-generation agreements were negotiated and signed with the various states of Central and Eastern Europe and the CIS from 1988 to 1994, not counting four treaties of accession) took all the Commission's human resources in DG I and DG IA as well as the political energy of the Council and the European Parliament, which was required to ratify the new agreements. At the same time, of course, the Community was deeply involved in its most radical internal reorganization since its inception, in the form of the negotiations on Economic and Monetary Union and political union, which were to lead to the Maastricht Treaty.

The Commission's new strategy is based on a number of considerations that take into account Asia's size and the diverse nature of its component parts. At its root lies the recognition that Asia is home to half the world's population and that according to World Bank estimates 50 percent of the growth in the global economy in the year 2000 will come from East and Southeast Asia alone. Around 400 million Asians (roughly equivalent to the EU's total population) will by that date enjoy disposable incomes as high or higher than the average European. This will present both opportunities and challenges in the economic sphere. In the words of the strategy paper, "The Union needs to select priority sectors for economic cooperation which reflect its own comparative advantage, e.g. banking, energy, environmental technologies, transport equipment, telecommunications, etc."[5] At the same time, it must recognize that the economically tripolar world—the EU, the United States, and Japan—will soon be replaced by a truly global economy in which many more actors, many of them Asian, will be participating as equals; in this context the role of the WTO as guarantor of an open and rule-based international trading system will be vital. Europe therefore has every interest in encouraging a "dialogue of equals"[6] with its Asian partners, both bilaterally and with multilateral organizations like ASEAN, APEC, and SAARC. This dialogue will extend beyond the economic to the political: security in the Asia Pacific region, conflict resolution (e.g., in Cambodia or over the Spratly Islands), human rights issues—all areas in which Europe has both the experience and the resources to make itself a useful partner. Indeed, these and related issues were central to the agenda of the first Euro-Asian summit held in Bangkok in March 1996. The summit—due to be repeated in London in 1998 and in Seoul in 2000 and thus likely to become a regular institution—may come to be seen as the apex of the dialogue being proposed by the Commission, dealing as it does with economic and political issues alike.

But while the medium-term prospects for much of Asia are bright, a large part of the continent remains severely underdeveloped and poverty and malnutrition are rife. From 1976 to 1991, the EC and its member states were the second biggest providers of ODA to Asia, making available just under $30 billion in aid compared to Japan's $35.2 billion (the United States contributed just $10.6 billion over the same period). While Japan concentrated its assistance on its immediate neighbors in East and Southeast Asia, the EC was by far the biggest aid donor to the countries of South Asia ($18 billion), making almost double Japan's contribution ($9.7 billion) and three times that of the United States ($6.7 billion). This fits well with the EU's traditional role as the world's largest collective ODA provider, but Asia (with the exception of Papua New Guinea and some of the Pacific island states) is not included in the ACP framework for development cooperation and does not benefit proportionately from EU help. The Commission has proposed that the EU's focus should be on the poorest countries and that the Union and its member states pool their experience to target the most needy populations in "poverty alleviation strategies." It singles out China, Mongolia, Cambodia, Laos, Vietnam, India, Bangladesh, Bhutan, and Nepal as falling into this category. The political situation in Myanmar and Afghanistan currently rules them out as beneficiaries, but both will eventually qualify and may indeed become recipients of special EU assistance programs once they achieve stability.

The future of the EU's relationship with Asia will depend largely on developments throughout the continent and indeed in the wider Pacific area, to the extent that APEC makes progress as a functioning forum for trans-Pacific economic cooperation. Such developments in turn stand to be influenced by what the Union does and the efforts it is prepared to make both in helping individual Asian countries help themselves and in being an active economic and political partner in those countries' own efforts to forge closer ties among themselves and avoid damaging conflicts. To some extent, the European Union's success in deepening and solidifying its own integration will play a part in aiding Asian growth. For one thing, Asia's current export-led boom can be sustained only as long as there are open and prosperous markets in the wider world to which it can sell—and in the medium term that means Europe and the United States. For another, the EU remains the world's best model of regional integration, and one that already serves as an example to ASEAN and, to a lesser extent, SAARC. If the EU continues to prosper, its markets will provide one essential outlet for Asian exports; if it continues to integrate, it will give courage to those in Asia who believe that regional cooperation will help to reduce the likelihood of conflict and increase the region's prosperity.

Association of Southeast Asian Nations

ASEAN came into being in 1967, bringing together five Southeast Asian nations (Indonesia, Malaysia, the Philippines, Singapore, and Thailand) in a loose pact designed to promote economic and social cooperation, safeguard stability, and resolve regional differences. It was reinforced in 1976 by the Treaty of Amity and Cooperation in Southeast Asia and again in 1992, when the fourth ASEAN summit agreed to launch a free trade area, with complete trade liberalization to be phased in over a fifteen-year period. Brunei joined the group in 1984; Vietnam in 1995; and Myanmar was due to accede in July 1997. ASEAN has a population (400 million) slightly larger than that of the European Union, but its total GNP of just under $400 billion (in 1992) is dwarfed by the EU's GNP of over $7,000 billion. ASEAN as a regional organization is characterized by a high degree of asymmetry: its second smallest member, Singapore, accounts for about 0.75 percent of the group's total population but over 9 percent of its GNP, with per capita GNP at $15,750 (close to the EU average). At the other end of the scale, Indonesia has almost 47 percent of the population but contributes just 30 percent of total GNP; its per capita GNP of $670 places it among the world's poorer countries. ASEAN's two more recent members, Brunei and Vietnam, add to the extraordinary range of economic and political disparities among the members. Brunei, with a population smaller than that of Luxembourg (around 300,000), is one of the world's richest nations and second in Asia only to Japan; the 68 million people of Vietnam, by contrast, are among the poorest in Asia, with a per capita GNP of just $220 (one-third that of Indonesia).

Because of these asymmetries, ASEAN does not pretend to the same degree of integration as the EU. Within their own region, the ASEAN states cooperate largely on a voluntary basis, not in pursuit of legal obligations arising from treaty commitments. Economic cooperation is central to their efforts, but programs exist for cooperation on social issues, preserving and promoting their cultural heritage, and eliminating the production and distribution of narcotics. A 1994 action plan for science and technology aims at expanding cooperation in food science, microelectronics, biotechnology, and alternative energy research. On the institutional level, ASEAN has no executive comparable to the European Commission, no parliament, no court of justice. It does not legislate centrally and has no true common policies and no internal market. Even external trade is not subject to common rules, so the EU has to negotiate sectoral trade agreements separately with each of the group's member states. An annual meeting of foreign ministers, the ASEAN Ministerial Meeting, decides on policy and oversees its implementation. Between meetings, business is entrusted to the ASEAN Standing Committee, chaired on a rotating basis by one of its foreign ministers. Specific issues are dealt with by committees of officials or experts. Each member government maintains a national secretariat to deal with ASEAN matters, and a permanent ASEAN secretariat, based in Jakarta, acts as a clearinghouse and coordination office for the various governments and ASEAN bodies. The ASEAN Interparliamentary Organization holds an annual general assembly attended by parliamentarians from the member countries (Brunei, which does not have a parliament, sends observers). From time to time, the heads of state or government gather for summit meetings.

Although they are not comparable organizations, the European Union has had close ties with ASEAN since 1978. In that year it organized the first EC-ASEAN ministerial conference in Brussels, paving the way for the 1980 EC-ASEAN cooperation agreement. In October 1979, just after the first European elections, the European Parliament received a delegation of AIPO members during its plenary session in Strasbourg; the meeting turned out to be the first of an annual series of encounters between the two parliamentary bodies.[7]

The cooperation agreement concluded between the European Community and the five countries concerned as member countries of ASEAN contains three main headings: commercial cooperation, economic cooperation, and development cooperation. Commercial cooperation commits the parties to cooperate in solving mutual problems relating to trade, including in commodities; improve access to one another's markets for manufactured and primary products; encourage joint ventures and, through trade promotion measures, the expansion of two-way trade; and consult in cases where new measures that may harm the other party's trade interests are being considered. Economic cooperation aims at encouraging investment, scientific and technological progress, opening new markets and supply sources, and creating employment opportunities. At the heart of this cooperation is the encouragement of businesses in the relevant sectors to work together; investors are to be assured equitable treatment on the basis of nondiscrimination. Development cooperation recognizes that ASEAN is a developing region and therefore pledges the Community and its member states to expand their aid; specifically, it proposes concentrating on projects concerned with food production and supplies, development of the rural sector, education and training facilities, and the promotion of ASEAN regional economic development and cooperation.

A joint cooperation committee is set up to oversee and ensure the implementation of the agreement's aims. On the EU side, the JCC is represented by the Commission and assisted by officials from the member states; it meets usually every eighteen months, with intermediate contacts taking place between the ASEAN ambassadors in Brussels and the Commission. In 1994 the JCC set up five subcommittees, on trade, science and technology, economic and industrial cooperation, narcotics, and forestry. But contacts between the two sides are not limited to the JCC. Since the first meeting of foreign ministers from the two sides in 1978, ten further such encounters have taken place. Recently, the full ministerial meetings have been supplemented by EU-ASEAN senior officials meetings, at which the EU governments are represented by their political directors. In addition to these strictly bilateral gatherings, the EU[8] is one of seven dialogue partners invited to attend the ASEAN post-ministerial conference held each year after the annual meeting of the association's foreign ministers. They also attend the ASEAN Regional Forum, which was set up in 1994 to discuss regional security issues (although new membership criteria established in August 1996 may in future exclude the EU, which is not judged to play a security role in the region; instead, the UK and France would attend on an individual basis).

This close relationship between ASEAN and the European Union has developed during a period of extraordinary political and economic change in Southeast Asia and around the world. When it began, all five ASEAN partners were still very much developing countries; the Vietnam War was just over; Laos and Cambodia were in political disarray if not outright civil war; the region was awash with political and economic refugees;

insurgency was a major problem in several ASEAN countries; human rights violations were frequent. All these issues have been at the heart of discussions during the political dialogue at the foreign ministerial level, and many of the problems that once beset the region have now eased or disappeared. The European Union has played its part in these changes, both diplomatically and economically.

Recently, two issues have been a source of some disagreement between the two sides. The question of East Timor, a former Portuguese colony annexed by Indonesia in 1975 just as Portugal was preparing to grant it independence, has vexed relations for a number of years, particularly since the Dili massacre of 1991, in which Indonesian troops opened fire and killed 100 people. Condemned by Amnesty International and other human rights organizations, Indonesia has also been called upon repeatedly by the European Parliament to end its oppression, which has so far cost the lives of an estimated 100,000 Timorese (according to local Catholic bishops, violence and famine together may have accounted for double that number of deaths, or one-third of the entire East Timorese population[9]). The lack of any progress on this dossier, coupled with a noninterference approach adopted by Indonesia's ASEAN partners, has been the main reason that the 1980 cooperation agreement has not been upgraded since. However, because the issue of East Timor concerns only one of the ASEAN members directly, the EU and member states have pressured Indonesia on a bilateral basis, and it has overshadowed EU-ASEAN relations as a whole only to a limited extent. More generally, the question of human rights has surfaced frequently, with the Europeans insisting on the principle of individual and political rights and the ASEAN side (like most other Asian countries) on the primacy of economic and collective rights, which they believe must have precedence so long as the problems of poverty and development have not been resolved. While neither side is prepared fully to accept the other's arguments, they agree to differ.

The other issue on which the two sides disagree is policy toward Myanmar. The EU's approach has been to isolate the military regime in Yangon, which has controlled the country since it seized power following free elections in 1988; ASEAN, by contrast, has adopted a policy of "constructive engagement" toward the military regime. At their 1994 meeting in Karlsruhe, Germany, the foreign ministers of both EU and ASEAN agreed for the first time that this combination of approaches may have helped generate some improvement in the situation in Myanmar. However, a new wave of repression swept through the country in the spring of 1996 with the arrest and imprisonment of numerous members and supporters of Aung San Suu Kyi's opposition party and winner of the 1988 elections, the National League for Democracy. These events, together with the death in police custody of the Danish honorary consul in Yangon, have hardened the EU's stance toward Myanmar and provoked some tension with ASEAN.

This is likely to be exacerbated if, as planned, Myanmar becomes a full member of ASEAN in 1997.

But while the political dialogue has been important—particularly because, despite its shortcomings, it has been one of the few examples of this type of cooperation between regional groupings—trade remains the central plank in the EU-ASEAN relationship. The EU is ASEAN's third most important trading partner overall and its second source of imports. ASEAN's growth as an economic power is seen in the changing composition of its exports: in 1980 two-thirds of what it sold abroad was in the form of raw materials such as rubber, manioc, and timber. Today more than three-quarters of its exports are manufactured goods. Most of Asia started to benefit from the generalized system of preferences as long ago as 1971, when the EC became the first entity to introduce such a scheme. By 1992 70 percent of GSP imports into the EC were coming from Asian countries, a quarter of them from ASEAN. This preferential access to the EC's markets (GSP affords tariff-free or reduced tariff entry; see Chapter 8) undoubtedly encouraged ASEAN's exporters; although the scheme will be less advantageous in future as tariffs in general are reduced in the wake of the Uruguay Round, the climate that it fostered—and that was so successfully exploited by ASEAN (and other Asian) countries—will only encourage further export-led economic growth in the region.

Trade may be the main facet of EU-ASEAN economic ties, but the Union has been active in other fields, too, notably in encouraging investment and supporting business. The European Community Investment Partners scheme aims at providing start-up aid to small and medium-sized enterprises that wish to establish joint ventures or other types of cooperation. European Business Information Centres, located in the ASEAN capitals, provide information to local and EU companies on the legal, financial, and technical aspects of doing business in the two regions. The European Investment Bank has, since the entry into force of the Maastricht Treaty, been authorized to operate in the ASEAN region and by 1995 had already made loans of ECU 58 million ($73 million) and ECU 54 million ($68 million) respectively for natural gas projects in Thailand and Indonesia and ECU 48 million ($60 million) to finance modernization of Davao airport in the Philippines.[10] The EU has also helped finance a number of regional technology centers to enhance ASEAN's scientific and technological base through the transfer of know-how and the promotion of research. Centers already running cover timber technology, energy management, and environmental technology, and others are planned.

Japan

Japan has long taken the European Union seriously as an economic partner—not surprisingly so, since Europe has been one of its most lucrative markets. But it is the United States that has been Japan's closest Western partner since World War II. By providing security guarantees, the United States has always been able to exert a degree of pressure in other areas of its relationship with Japan, including the economic. There have been times when this has not always been apparent: the United States and Japan have had their share of trade conflicts, and the size of the Japanese surplus vis-à-vis the United States has often led to serious arguments between Washington and Tokyo. Indeed the U.S. approach toward perceived Japanese unfairness—the absence of the level playing field in everything from market access to employment practices—has led to an often extraordinarily aggressive approach by U.S. policymakers toward Japanese trade practices. However, Tokyo has succeeded in walking a fine line between its obligations toward the United States in the political and security fields and its determination to maximize its profits from the U.S. market. The Japanese are aware that the U.S. military umbrella has spared it the need to devote more than a fraction of its budget (technically limited to 1 percent under Japan's "peace constitution") to defense; at the same time, it knows that the U.S. security commitment is not entirely altruistic, and that while it benefits enormously it does not have to reciprocate to the extent that its dependent security relationship might suggest. Nonetheless, there can be no doubt that the United States remains Japan's most important political and economic partner and that this is due to the peculiar postwar relationship between the two countries.[11]

No such client-patron relationship exists between Japan and the European Union. As is the case with most of its other industrialized partners, the EU has no institutionalized association with Japan beyond a joint declaration signed in July 1991. Trade forms the centerpiece of the relationship. But while Japan is the Union's second biggest supplier of goods, it constitutes only the latter's third biggest market (Switzerland, with its population of 6.8 million, buys more from the EU than does Japan, with its population of 125 million). Indeed, this disparity between imports and exports, resulting in a chronic deficit of major proportions for the EU in its trade with Japan, has overshadowed links between the two sides since the 1970s. Europe is of course not alone: Japan's trade surplus with the United States has been consistently higher still. But the trade imbalance has tended to dominate the EU's ties with Japan, simply because there has not been any other dimension on which to build; in the case of the United States, by contrast, trade problems constitute part of a more complex relationship.

For many years, Japan's own position as a weak foreign policy actor meant that the European Community, with a similarly underdeveloped role in this field, did little to pursue a political dialogue with Tokyo. Nor did other issues of political significance affect the relationship: Japan was a democracy, did not violate human rights, was not involved militarily outside its own borders, paid its dues to the United Nations, put in place a generous ODA program, and was generally a model world citizen. Its only international dispute, for which it sought U.S. and European diplomatic support, involved the (still unresolved) question of ownership of the four southern Kuril islands, occupied since the end of World War II by Russia but claimed by Japan. The dialogue that began to take shape in the early 1970s, therefore, concerned economics. In 1974 the Commission set up a delegation in Tokyo. The Japanese, however, initially refused to accord the delegation head equivalent diplomatic rank to that enjoyed by the ambassadors of the EC's member states; not until 1990 was delegation head Jean-Pierre Leng accredited to the emperor instead of the foreign minister. Also in the early 1970s, a series of biannual ministerial-level meetings was instituted between Tokyo and the Commission.

If the first few years of EC-Japan relations were fairly calm, the second half of the 1970s ushered in a prolonged period of crisis. The Japanese viewed the European market (along with the United States) as a prime destination for its industrial and technological exports. It needed to establish surpluses in these markets to pay for its imports of raw materials, including oil, on which it was heavily dependent, and to cover its deficits in services, especially shipping and tourism, technology imports, ODA expenditure, and capital exports. The success of Japan's export offensive, encouraged by an undervalued yen and the presence of a panoply of domestic measures that ensured that its own market remained difficult or impossible for foreign exporters to penetrate, rapidly led to the accumulation of huge surpluses in Japan's trade with the European Community. The specific disputes, which covered trade in products ranging from automobiles, steel, and bearings to TVs, videorecorders, and alcoholic beverages, became increasingly politicized, and from 1976 to the end of the 1980s they were the subject of constant, often acrimonious negotiation. Both the EC Commission and member state governments used every opportunity to impress on their Japanese counterparts (ministers and officials from the Ministry of International Trade and Industry, visiting trade delegations, the Keidanren [employers' federation], diplomatic representations, etc.) their concern at what they considered to be an unacceptable situation.

In spite of the vigorous criticism of Japan's tactics, its competitors always recognized that its success as producer and exporter was worthy not only of condemnation but also of emulation. As early as 1979, there were reportedly 10,000 Japanese businesspeople living in Europe compared to only 1,500 European businesspeople in Japan.[12] Japanese technology and design was ahead of that in Europe, and European firms began to scrutinize Japanese management methods. A European parliamentary delegation that visited Tokyo in 1978 concluded that the EC should examine the reasons for Japanese success so that it could learn to improve its own performance.[13] Despite undiplomatic comments by senior Europeans (like that of Sir Roy Denman, the EC's ambassador in Tokyo, who claimed in 1979 that

Japan was "a country of workaholics who live in . . . rabbit hutches,"[14] or French prime minister Edith Cresson, who in 1991 described Japan as "an adversary . . . whose overwhelming desire is to conquer the world"[15]), Europe's experience with Japan since the mid-1970s did engender a good deal of constructive introspection. Klaus Grewlich maintains that "there cannot be the slightest doubt that Europe owes its revitalization to a large extent to Japan," arguing that the Japanese economic challenge was instrumental in the reevaluation of European economic structures that led, inter alia, to the decision to establish the single market.[16]

Both sides were undoubtedly aware that a lack of mutual understanding was part of the problem. Europeans failed to understand Japanese cultural and business processes, and the Japanese were unable to comprehend why the Europeans did not do more to help themselves, for example, through greater product innovation or more effort to design their goods to appeal to Japanese consumers. A number of schemes were set up to ameliorate this perceived communication gap. In 1979 the Japanese foreign ministry started an annual essay competition to identify and bring to Japan fifty young Europeans to take part in a two-week educational program covering Japanese economics, politics, culture, and society. The European Community Visitors Programme (ECVP) was extended to include Japanese invitees (it had previously been confined to those from the United States): "multipliers" from the worlds of politics, industry, journalism, and academia were given two-week individual trips to Brussels and Strasbourg and two national capitals to learn about aspects of the EC.[17] The Commission launched a scheme (the Executive Training Programme, or ETP) to enable young European businesspeople to spend eighteen months in Japan learning the language and gaining hands-on experience working for Japanese firms. The Commission also finances an annual trip to Brussels for leading Japanese journalists, who are exposed to an intensive agenda of meetings and seminars designed to help them understand the EU. More generally, there is now a range of cooperative ventures and projects involving Japan and the European Union that cover activities including research and development, export promotion, information and communications, the environment, and more.

The European Parliament's delegation visit to Tokyo in 1978 (mentioned above) turned out to be the forerunner of an institutionalized parliamentary relationship that continues to this day and that has provided an interesting political complement to the primarily trade-centred relationship between the EU and Japan. In 1979, following its election by direct universal suffrage, the EP set up a standing delegation for relations with Japan; in turn, the Japanese Diet created the Japan-EC Parliamentary League of Friendship. The EP's delegation (initially chaired by Sir Fred Warner, a former British ambassador to Tokyo) quickly became one of the most important of the Parliament's numerous interparliamentary delegations, attracting to its ranks senior MEPs who had a particular interest in Japan. What was more surprising, however, was the strong attraction the Diet's friendship association held for senior members of both the House of Representatives and the House of Councillors. Chaired for many years by the late Tadashi Kuranari, a luminary of the Liberal Democratic Party (LDP) and foreign minister in 1986–1987, it included over the years a host of senior Japanese politicians, many of whom had been or subsequently became government ministers. Among them was the present chairman, Tsutomo Hata, who was prime minister in 1994; Taro Nakayama, foreign minister from 1989 to 1991; Koji Kakizawa, foreign minister in 1995; Yoshiro Hayashi, minister of finance in 1994–1995; and Kosuke Hori, minister of education in 1990.

Meetings, known as parliamentary conferences, have been held on an annual basis almost without interruption since 1979, alternating between venues in Tokyo and the EP's working places in Brussels, Luxembourg, and Strasbourg. While the trade dispute of the moment has always figured centrally on every agenda of the two-day meetings, these conferences have been particularly noteworthy for the more political themes they have dealt with. Issues discussed have included Afghanistan and Indochina, nuclear disarmament, Asian Pacific security, development aid, the breakup of the Soviet Union and its likely repercussions, Japan's possible membership in the UN Security Council, and much more besides.[18]

Because of the presence on the Japanese side of numerous senior political figures close to the government and main opposition parties, the conferences have come to represent probably the single most important regular channel of political contact between the European Union and Japan, at least until recently. This has been especially true of the conferences held in Tokyo, which inevitably have a much larger Japanese attendance than those that take place in Europe. To the extent that members of the European Parliament can be said to offer a reasonably representative cross-section of prevailing political views in the EU, the Japanese Diet members have thus been exposed to them.

That said, these meetings are in no sense negotiating sessions. Nonetheless, the Japanese political establishment takes them seriously. Moreover, the framework in which the annual conferences are held allows each side to profit from its partner's ability to facilitate other contacts. EP members use their visits to Tokyo to meet senior Japanese government ministers and are invariably guests at a reception given by the prime minister; Diet members visiting the EU usually hold meetings with the president and other members of the Commission and have on occasion had the opportunity to meet ministers representing the Council presidency. In July 1996 a Japanese Diet delegation visiting the European Parliament in Strasbourg held detailed exchanges with Commission president Jacques Santer and vice president Sir Leon Brittan as well as with their parliamentary counterparts; they invited the EP's president, Klaus Hänsch, to pay an official visit to Tokyo in November 1996 and arranged for the agenda to include an official call on the emperor.

None of this is to say that no political relationship existed at other levels between the European Community and Japan; but the examples of cooperation are relatively few, and the priority accorded to ministerial-level meetings, let alone bilateral summits, has been traditionally low compared to those with, say, the United States. Until 1991, indeed, there was a stronger institutionalized political relationship between the EC and ASEAN than existed with Japan. The EC-Japan Declaration,[19] signed in July 1991 in The Hague, went some way toward recognizing this lacuna. In addition to setting out the guiding principles for the relationship (including "equitable access" to one another's markets and a statement on basic values shared by the two sides), it establishes an institutionalized framework for consultation, including an annual summit meeting between the Japanese prime minister and the presidents of the Commission and Council and regular ministerial meetings to cover specific domains. In spite of the 1991 declaration, however, the political relationship remains weak. The annual summits have not taken place regularly, ostensibly because of problems over timing and venues. According to the Commission's 1995 communication on the future of the EU-Japan relationship, *Europe and Japan: The Next Steps,* the regular ministerial meetings that have taken place have not led to much qualitative improvement. On substance, the communication says, the dialogue "has hardly proceeded beyond the level of exchanges of views and information and there have been few examples of concrete cooperation."[20]

The European Union's relationship with Japan is clearly of the utmost economic importance to both sides. For Japanese exporters and investors, the EU and its internal market have long been central to their strategies and immensely profitable into the bargain. For European business, Japan remains a potential prize of enormous value, but one that has yet to be won. "Fortress Europe" was an illusion that never materialized; the walls of "Fortress Japan," while cracking, have still to be fully breached. The Commission's *Next Steps* sees the EU's future strategy toward Japan primarily in terms of a reinforcement of the political dialogue, which it believes will not only have value in its own right but will contribute to improving the bilateral economic relationship. Now is the time to adopt such an approach, the Commission believes, because Japan has started to emerge on the world scene as an active player, not least through participating in numerous UN-sponsored actions (e.g., in Cambodia, Mozambique, and Rwanda) and in contributing through the G-24 to the reconstruction of Central and Eastern Europe. To parallel its upgrading of the political relationship, the EU will have to strengthen economic collaboration, especially in the domains of deregulation, competition, and industrial cooperation, and pursue ways of supporting EU investment in Japan (in

1993 just 7.6 percent of corresponding Japanese investment in the EU[21]) and reduce the "knowledge imbalance," which, the Commission believes, remains a disadvantage for Europeans attempting to do business in Japan.

China

China never had the reservations about the European Community shown by the other great Communist power, the Soviet Union. While the USSR and most of its satellites refused even to recognize the EC, let alone enter into agreements with it, the end of China's Cultural Revolution and its subsequent open-door policy toward the rest of the world quickly led to the development of close ties with the Community. China's leaders, indeed, lent their specific support to European integration efforts, viewing the EC variously as a useful economic partner, a factor for stability, and an irritant for the Kremlin, with whom their relations were extremely cool in the 1970s. China and the EC established diplomatic relations in 1975 and rapidly negotiated a trade and economic cooperation agreement, which was signed in 1978. In 1980 China gained access to the EC's generalized system of preferences and by the 1990s had become by far the leading beneficiary of the scheme (which applies to over 130 countries). In 1985 a new agreement provided an expanded framework for trade and economic cooperation. China is now the EU's third most important non-European trading partner. Providing some 15 percent of China's imports, the EU is a bigger supplier than the United States, making it China's second most important source of overseas imports after Japan (Hong Kong and Taiwan excluded).

The mutual economic and trade relationship is obviously crucial. For China, European technology, manufactured goods, know-how, and investment constitute a vital part of its plans for economic growth and modernization, and Europe's markets offer a key outlet for its products. For Europe, China offers a vast and expanding market with almost unlimited potential. According to the European Commission, EU-China trade has increased by a factor of fourteen since the beginning of the Chinese reform process. There is every prospect that China will overtake Japan as the biggest Asian economy within a few years (the IMF and the World Bank consider that on the basis of purchasing-power parities, China's economy is already equal to that of Japan). Within a generation, China is likely to become the world's biggest economy, if present trends continue. The European Union is already running a significant trade deficit with China (ECU 11.7 billion, or $14.6 billion, in 1995), a deficit that has grown every year since 1988, echoing the pattern set by Japan in the 1970s.

But unlike Japan, China is a nuclear power and will play an increasingly important part in Asian and global security considerations. For this reason, the EU, like the United States and other countries, has a keen interest in developing a positive political relationship with Beijing. This has for some time been hampered by concern about China's human rights record. A prolonged period of gradual relaxation in China came to an end in June 1989 with the violent intervention of Chinese troops against students and others encamped in Beijing's Tiananmen Square in a massive demonstration calling for greater freedom and democratic reforms. The EU's outrage at these events led to a virtual freeze of relations for a year or more and slowed a number of initiatives under way, including progress toward reintegrating China into GATT (a move supported in principle by the EU). Although relations have gradually returned to normal since the Tiananmen incident, the European Union has remained wary of China's continued disregard for human rights, including the treatment of the jailed leaders of the 1989 movement. As mentioned in previous chapters, since that time, the Union has made it a policy to include human rights clauses in all new agreements signed with third countries and has made a point of raising the human rights question, both generally and in relation to specific cases, in the various fora in which Chinese and EU or member state politicians or officials take part.

Beijing has responded uncertainly to attacks on its human rights record, making concessions here while continuing to act tough there. In the wake of the Tiananmen killings, the Chinese authorities seemed anxious to rebuild their shattered international image. The European Parliament's delegation for relations with China—which had held meetings with its counterpart delegation from the National People's Congress (NPC) on an annual basis since 1980—was due to pay a visit to China in the autumn of 1989. The visit was canceled by the European Parliament, as were nearly all other planned high-level contacts between the EC's institutions (and those of the Community's member states) and the Chinese. But Chinese diplomats in Brussels quickly began a campaign to persuade the members of the EP's delegation to reconsider. Over a period of several months during the winter and spring of 1990–1991, a number of contacts took place between the delegation chairman and his staff and the Chinese ambassador and other diplomats.

Eventually a deal was struck: the delegation would travel to China in September 1991, thus helping to restore the shattered relationship. But the delegation agreed to the visit only after its own conditions had been met. These included a firm insistence on being allowed to raise the question of human rights and the fate of the imprisoned Tiananmen dissidents with the Chinese leadership in Beijing and to be able to travel to Tibet to hold discussions with religious and other Tibetan officials. China honored the delegation's wishes. In Beijing the delegation met Prime Minister Li Peng and handed over a list of names of prisoners with a request for information as to their health and whereabouts, it met the minister of justice and discussed the question of prison conditions and the inadequacies of the Chinese legal system, and it brought up the matter of human rights in general during its meetings with members of the NPC. Subsequently, the EP members became the first foreign parliamentary delegation ever to visit Tibet, where (although closely chaperoned) they heard firsthand native Tibetans' grievances against their Han Chinese rulers.

Human rights are central to the EU's relations with China, now and in the future. In a 1995 communication on China, the European Commission proposed a three-pronged approach to the issue. The European Union should support efforts to open up and liberalize all aspects of Chinese life; by doing so, it will encourage the development of a civil society based on the rule of law. It should continue to raise human rights issues in bilateral dialogue with China. Finally, it should involve the international community in the dialogue in multilateral fora like the United Nations.[22] Related to this question is the position of Hong Kong and Macau, whose people—ruled for many generations by Britain and Portugal, respectively—will in future be dependent on Beijing. Both of the former colonial powers have sought guarantees from China that the freedoms and human and civic rights enjoyed by the populations of the two territories will remain unaffected by the handovers (in 1997 and 1999, respectively). While assurances have been given, the EU will be observing the situation extremely closely. Any substantial moves by Beijing to renege on the terms of the joint declarations (which essentially guarantee both territories special status for a fifty-year period, during which they will continue to be responsible for their internal affairs and remain entitled to act as separate economic entities internationally) would have dire consequences for the European Union's relations with China. Tensions are already mounting over Beijing's avowed intention to reverse the recent democratic reforms in Hong Kong that led to the direct elections of a proportion of the colony's legislative council (Legco) for the first time. Beijing argues that these elections took place after the joint declaration was signed and are therefore an attempt by Britain to alter the status quo ante.

Hong Kong is currently among the top ten trading partners of the Fifteen, and is home to substantial European investment. China has agreed that the territory should maintain its own economic and trade policy after it reverts to Chinese sovereignty and keep its membership in the WTO. The European Commission's Hong Kong office will be allowed to continue to operate. Macau's 490,000 people have been granted Portuguese (and therefore EU) citizenship by Portugal and would thus have the right to take up permanent residence in Europe should the situation in the territory deteriorate. Hong Kong's 5.5 million residents have not been given UK passports but will retain their right to visit the UK without visas. Beijing's actions in the two territories will do much to determine the nature of China's future political and economic relationship with the EU. Both sides appear to recognize that the transfer of sovereignty in Hong Kong will be seen as a litmus test of Chinese credibility in the wider international context.

The EU will watch China's actions particularly closely in Taiwan, the other major territory that China wishes to reclaim. Taiwan ranks fifth among the EU's trading partners in Asia. Nevertheless, the European Union has never recognized the Taipei regime and maintains no Commission office there. Ostensibly, the EU supports Beijing's "one China" policy, while seeking to maintain cordial, if informal, relations with the island. But that could change if it becomes apparent that China is failing to honor its pledges toward Hong Kong and Macau. The European Parliament, many of whose members have been intensively lobbied by the Taipei government, has already called for Taiwan to be admitted to various UN agencies (though not yet to the organization itself). So far, the EU and its member states have resisted such calls.

Also at stake for China is its application to join the World Trade Organization. The EU is in principle supportive of the application (pending since 1986) and has taken a leading role in the negotiations. At the EU's suggestion, some of China's commitments under an eventual agreement could come into effect over a specified period of time after entry into the organization, reflecting that the country is still in transition toward becoming a developed market economy. But as of early 1997 final agreement had yet to be reached. The Commission is also anxious to ensure that the bilateral EU-China dialogue on trade should be continued and intensified, with more frequent meetings of the existing Trade and Economic Working Group (set up in 1993) covering an expanded range of sectors. There is every reason for the European Union to take steps to avoid facing the same type of trade conflicts that it confronted twenty years ago with Japan. Dealing now with issues like technical barriers to trade, competition, non-discrimination, and financial services may help to avoid problems later. At the same time, the Commission is keen to see the EU develop its cooperation with China, particularly in areas linked to reform of all areas of Chinese society; these include economic and social reform, cooperation among private-sector actors (i.e., businesses), and so-called human resource development, which includes education and training (the Commission has already set up a China-Europe International Business School in Shanghai to help train business leaders). Other areas for cooperation are the environment and science and technology.

These and other initiatives are now European Union policy. Their success will become apparent in the medium term as the EU's relationship with what will soon be Asia's leading economy develops. Although issues such as human rights will remain problematic, China's own undoubted interest in becoming an accepted member of the international community may encourage it to conduct itself carefully. The more deeply involved the

EU becomes through a combination of cooperation and support for Chinese development, the steadier and less accident-prone the relationship will be.

Korea and Indochina

As with the other newly industrialized countries of Asia, Europe's involvement with the Republic of Korea has grown substantially over the past decade. Korea occupies fourth place, just behind Hong Kong, among the EU's Asian trading partners. This relationship is also a great deal more balanced than those with Japan, China, and Taiwan, with each of whom the Fifteen run substantial trade deficits. Nevertheless, while EU-Korea trade is currently in broad equilibrium, there has been no lack of conflicts in the relationship. Since the early 1980s, the EU and its member states have deployed the whole arsenal of trade weapons against the Republic of Korea, including antidumping litigation, minimum price regulations, imposition of quotas, voluntary export restraints and countervailing duties.[23] The EU has in particular targeted Korean exports of textiles, clothing, steel, electronics, and footwear, and it has also been concerned at the growth of subsidized shipbuilding in Korea.

More recently, however, the climate has improved, and in 1995 the Commission negotiated a far-reaching cooperation agreement with Seoul. Initialed in Bangkok on the margins of the March 1996 Euro-Asian summit and signed in Brussels in October 1996, the agreement steps up political as well as economic cooperation and commits Korea to opening up its financial services market. The agreement involves a number of concessions by the Seoul government, which had been anxious to secure EU backing for its application to join the OECD (it received the support and was admitted to the organization in October 1996). Among these was a Korean commitment to end discrimination against access to its domestic markets, which in the past had led to the exclusion of European companies from numerous potentially lucrative contracts. As with other agreements of this type, political contacts are institutionalized, with regular high-level ministerial meetings envisaged. The Republic of Korea remains wary of North Korea, despite a recent relaxation in tensions, and values the political support of the EU. Neither the Union itself nor any of its member states maintains diplomatic relations with North Korea.

No relations exist either between the EU and Myanmar (though individual member states maintain diplomatic ties). Ever since the military suspended the constitution in September 1988 and the popular leader of the opposition, Aung San Suu Kyi, was arrested, the EU has adopted an isolationist policy toward the Yangon government (as discussed earlier in the chapter). When constitutional rule is eventually restored, the EU can be expected to play a major role in providing development assistance and economic cooperation to this desperately poor country. Cambodia and Laos have both received considerable aid from Brussels in the past few years, and the Commission has now concluded cooperation agreements with both countries. A wide-ranging economic cooperation agreement was signed with Vietnam in 1995, making it the only ASEAN member state with which the EU has a separate bilateral agreement (see the section on ASEAN above). Vietnam, like Cambodia and Laos, has received growing amounts of humanitarian and development aid over the past few years. The Commission has now proposed that the best experience of the Union and its member states be pooled in "poverty alleviation strategies" aimed at the Indochinese countries and the poorest of the other Asian states.[24]

South Asia and SAARC

When, after the 1973 enlargement of the EC, the scope of the Yaoundé convention was extended from the former French and Belgian possessions to include those of Britain, India and its southern Asian neighbors were left out. The EC-ACP link remained limited to African, Caribbean, and Pacific states. The sheer size of the South Asia region (and India in particular) would have created significant disturbances in the EC-ACP relationship had the region joined. Instead, the Commonwealth countries of South Asia (as well as Malaysia and Singapore) were covered by a joint declaration of intent[25] signed at the time of British accession to the EC. This ensured that the enlarged Community would make appropriate provision in its development planning for the region, even if not in the same institutionalized form as for the ACP. These countries, like others elsewhere in Asia and those in Latin America, are known as the "nonassociated developing countries."

Despite the existence of the South Asian Association for Regional Cooperation, established in 1985 by the Dacca Charter, the EU's relations with the countries of the region have remained bilateral in nature. SAARC members—Bangladesh, Bhutan, India, the Maldives, Nepal, Pakistan, and Sri Lanka—have not been able to cooperate among themselves to the same degree as do the ASEAN states. A proposal contained in a 1988 European Parliament resolution[26] that SAARC should take the initiative in proposing the conclusion of a multilateral cooperation agreement with the EC, akin to that with ASEAN, fell on deaf ears, apparently not least because the organization's members believed that more intraregional cooperation would have to come first.[27]

The range of links at the bilateral level is, however, extensive. While cooperation initially focused on food and development aid, since the 1970s it has expanded into a wide variety of other fields. Nevertheless, with an average per capita GNP of just over $300 (compared with a figure of some

$28,000 for Japan, say), the countries of South Asia rank among the world's poorest, and the EU has accordingly treated them and continues to treat them as developing countries. Indeed the first major EC programs aimed at the region concentrated specifically on urgently needed food aid through the so-called Operation Flood scheme (supplying primarily skimmed milk powder to India) and other country-specific measures involving dairy products, vegetable oils, and cereals.

But along with the emergency alleviation of hunger, the EU attended to project aid for the neediest areas. The idea was to help people help themselves by providing resources and training in areas such as soil and water conservation, fertilization techniques, animal husbandry, sustainable forestry, and dairy production methods. As a result, EC-supported dairy development projects in India during the 1980s, designed to reduce dependence on skimmed milk powder and butter oil donations, were replaced in the 1990s by help in financing milk collection networks for the now functioning dairies. Dependence on outside help was being successfully replaced by an increasing degree of self-sufficiency.

Europe has been by far the largest aid donor to the subcontinent. By 1995 around ECU 1.8 billion ($2.25 billion) had been made available by Brussels for development assistance (including humanitarian aid) and economic cooperation to India alone, a sum that did not include bilateral aid from individual EU member states. The impact of this aid was greater than its value, since wherever possible grants were made on the basis of matching funds from the countries concerned or NGOs, often realizing projects that would not otherwise have been fundable. In South Asia India was the biggest beneficiary by a considerable margin, followed by Bangladesh, Pakistan, and Sri Lanka.

But trade has also played a central role in the relationship between Europe and the region. All the countries of South Asia have benefited from GSP privileges since 1971, and all have concluded trade and cooperation agreements with the EU, in addition to sectoral accords covering items such as textiles, clothing, and sugar. India indeed now has a third-generation partnership and cooperation agreement that came into force in 1994, succeeding two earlier agreements from 1973 and 1982. A commercial cooperation agreement was concluded with Pakistan in 1976, followed by an updated agreement covering economic and development cooperation as well as trade in 1986. A third-generation accord is due to enter into force in 1997. The EU's agreements with Sri Lanka date from 1975 and 1994, that with Bangladesh from 1976 and with Nepal from 1995. In 1987 the Stabex scheme (stabilization of export earnings; see Chapter 8) was extended to Bangladesh and Nepal, making them the first countries outside the ACP to benefit from the scheme.

The SAARC countries constitute practically the only Asian region with which the EU's trade (running at around ECU 24.5 billion, or $30.5

billion, in 1995) is in balance. Nevertheless, the total represented less than 9 percent of EU trade with Asia overall. Though small, the volume of trade has been rising at a rapid pace in recent years: EU exports to and imports from India, for example, increased by some 20 percent from 1994 to 1995. There is room for considerable further growth, too: while the EU is India's biggest market, its exports (principally textiles and clothing) accounted for less than 0.8 percent of that market in 1995. How quickly such growth can come remains unclear. India (as a highly competitive developing country in the textiles and clothing sector) is about to lose some of its GSP concessions and moreover faces stiffer competition in these products from Turkey, which in 1996 entered into a customs union with the EU.[28]

In 1992 the Council adopted a new, more comprehensive approach to Europe's relations with the nonassociated developing countries.[29] Development aid is in future to be concentrated on the poorest countries, and within them on the poorest sectors of the population. Economic cooperation will be aimed at those countries with the potential for high growth. The intention is to improve the business and regulatory environments of the partner countries with a view to encouraging trade and investment. Moreover, the EU will support the protection of human rights, democratization, administrative and judicial improvements, environmental protection, trade liberalization, and the promotion of regional cooperation. The southern Asian countries are among the main targets of this approach today.

Political dialogue with the SAARC countries has been relatively limited, although regular meetings at the foreign ministerial level have taken place, particularly with India and, to a lesser extent, Pakistan, for many years. However, apart from a joint statement on political dialogue agreed between the EU and India in 1994, there is no institutionalized dialogue like that between the EU and ASEAN. The lack of political cohesion among the SAARC members themselves, characterized not least by the uneasy relationship between India and Pakistan and their dispute over Kashmir, makes the organization unsuitable as a political dialogue partner. It also helps to explain why the SAARC states were not invited to participate at the 1996 Euro-Asian summit in Bangkok. The Asian side included the ASEAN group, at whose initiative the meeting was called, as well as Japan, China, and South Korea. The EU has proposed extending the next summit, due to be held in London in 1998, to the South Asian countries.

In the meantime the Union has already begun to take a series of initiatives designed to bolster its relations with the area, and India in particular. In the immediate aftermath of the Bangkok summit in March 1996, the EU's troika of foreign ministers visited Delhi, where they assured the Indian government that the "comprehensive Asia-Europe partnership"[30] that had been forged in Bangkok meant what it said (in fact, the summit's final statement referred throughout to "Asia" and "Europe" without defining either of the two regions more precisely). But more important, the

Commission has now drawn up a new strategy paper on revitalizing relations with India and has started negotiations with Pakistan and Bangladesh on revamped and more comprehensive accords to replace the now aging trade and cooperation agreements. If Asia as a whole has only recently moved to the forefront of the European Union's concerns following several years of Eurocentrism, then South Asia has been the last part of the continent to do so. But that period now seems to be past, and the last few years of the twentieth century are likely to see EU–South Asia relations enjoy something of a renaissance.

Australia and New Zealand

Not properly part of Asia geographically yet moving increasingly toward their Asian neighbors in an economic and even political sense, Australia and New Zealand are among the few countries in the world for which the European Union has become less rather than more important since the 1980s. Both countries remain largely European in terms of their populations and culture. New Zealand's European population is still predominately of British origin, as is Australia's, though the latter is now leavened by significant numbers of other European nationalities, especially Italians and Greeks. Both countries have begun to see increasing immigration from Asia in recent years, and both have important indigenous minorities as well. Until 1973, when the United Kingdom joined the European Community, Australia and New Zealand were both heavily dependent on Britain and other EC countries for their trade. This dependency was particularly dramatic in the case of New Zealand, 33 percent of whose trade in 1970 was with Britain alone. By 1988 this figure was down to 8 percent, and trade with the whole of the EC amounted to only 19.5 percent of New Zealand's imports and exports. In the case of Australia, the figures show 16 percent of its trade was with the UK in 1970, compared to 5.5 percent in 1988. The country's trade with the EC as a whole decreased by half over this period.[31]

Japan is now the major trading partner of the two countries. However, both the European Union and the United States (in second and third places) remain important partners, as do each of the two neighbors for one another (they have a customs union). The result of almost a quarter century of separation from Britain is thus a more balanced trading relationship with the world as a whole. Europe has come to assume merely an important rather than a dominant role in the economic lives of Australia and New Zealand. By contrast, the two antipodean nations have relatively little weight as trading partners for the EU. Australia ranked twenty-first in order of importance in 1995, accounting for just 1.4 percent of the European Union's total trade, and New Zealand came in forty-ninth, with just

0.3 percent. Although the EU's trade with New Zealand is relatively balanced, it enjoys a significant trade surplus with Australia, selling twice as much as it buys. No longer the primary trading partner of either Australia or New Zealand, the EU remains by a considerable margin the biggest single source of foreign investment for both countries.

For both Australia and New Zealand, the European Union's Common Agricultural Policy has been the dominant factor in the change in their relationships with Britain and the rest of the EU. On joining the EC in 1973, the UK accepted the principle of Community preference in the agricultural field, and although it negotiated lengthy transition periods for Australian and New Zealand farm products, import quotas were gradually reduced. New Zealand was particularly hard hit, since Britain had represented the single biggest market for its key exports of butter, cheese, and sheepmeat. Moreover, farm products (including wool and sheepskins) accounted for and indeed still account for the bulk of New Zealand exports, while Australia has been more successful in diversifying its export palette. The latter is now the world's biggest exporter of coal, and its mineral wealth and growing manufacturing sector have helped it offset a proportion of its lost agricultural exports to Europe. Both countries have been vociferous opponents of the CAP, however, not only because of the impact it has had on their European export markets but also because of the effects the policy has had in the wider world. EC subsidies have enabled European farm exports to compete directly with antipodean products on world markets, adding insult to the injury already caused by the quotas and import levies that decimated Australian and New Zealand sales to the United Kingdom and the Community. Both countries were active in the Cairns Group of agricultural exporting countries in pressuring the EC to reform its farm policy, pressure that probably contributed to the CAP changes that finally enabled the GATT Uruguay Round to come to a successful conclusion (see Chapter 1).

While Australia and New Zealand certainly believed they had a legitimate grievance with respect to the CAP and the effects it had on their respective export markets, the European Community could point to the inordinately high level of tariff protection applied by both countries to their imports of industrial goods. Although these have come down over recent years and are to be further reduced by the end of the century, they are still substantially above equivalent EU levels. In theory, low EU tariffs on manufactured goods offer both Australia and New Zealand the opportunity to break into Europe's lucrative internal market; but in spite of diversification, neither country has so far developed a significant industrial goods sector to take advantage of this opportunity. New Zealand is still dependent to the tune of around 70 percent of its exports on farm-related products, and even in Australia the figure remains high, at around 50 percent. It is perhaps somewhat bizarre that as late as 1995, Australia's single biggest export to the European Union should be wool (accounting for about 17 percent of total Australian sales to the EU).

In the absence of any global agreements between the EU and Australia and New Zealand, a variety of contacts were developed over the years, including regular ministerial meetings and an interparliamentary link between the European Parliament and the parliaments of the two countries. A Commission delegation, responsible for relations with both Australia and New Zealand, was set up in Canberra in 1981. But in 1996 the Commission proposed that framework agreements for trade and cooperation be concluded with both countries, and the Council issued negotiating directives. The accord with Australia would cover cooperation in economic, industrial, scientific, and "other fields of common interest."[32] The agreement's proposed subsections were to cover trade cooperation, cooperation in capital movements, economic and industrial cooperation, science and technology, information and communications, education and training, the environment, development cooperation, precursor chemicals and money laundering, and statistical cooperation. The framework agreement with New Zealand would follow the same pattern. Both accords would be managed by joint committees, and would be evolutive in nature, that is, they could be expanded and prolonged by mutual agreement and would thus not require formal renewal.

At the beginning of 1997, negotiations were stalled over the EU's insistence that the agreements, like all others concluded with third countries, should include a routine human rights clause. Both the Australians and New Zealanders considered this to be a slight on their reputations (or believed that their treatment of their respective minority populations was being challenged). The Commission argued that the EU was not questioning its partners' records but merely being consistent: if an exception were made for Australia and New Zealand, everyone would want an exception. But once these differences have been resolved and the accords signed, the EU's relationships with Australia and New Zealand will be on a formal footing for the first time.

Notes

1. Brunei Darussalem, Indonesia, Malaysia, Philippines, Singapore, Thailand, and Vietnam.

2. These figures include aid provided by the member states of the EU plus that donated directly from the EC budget and administered by the Commission.

3. Commission, *Towards a New Asia Strategy,* COM(94) 314 final, 13 July 1994.

4. Among the only exceptions were two sectoral agreements (one on nuclear fusion, the other on the environment) with Japan, concluded in 1989, and the EC-Japan Declaration of 1991.

5. Commission, *Strategy*, p. 24.

6. Ibid., p. 18.

7. Today's European Parliament maintains a standing delegation for relations with the member states of ASEAN, the Republic of Korea, and the countries of Southeast Asia.

8. The EU is represented at these meetings by the troika and a member of the Commission.

9. See the *Economist,* 2 February 1996, p. 18.

10. Commission, *The European Union and Asia*, "Europe on the Move" series (Brussels: European Commission, 1995), p. 7.

11. For a discussion of the U.S.-Japan relationship, see Mike Mochizuki et al., *Japan and the United States: Troubled Partners in a Changing World* (Washington, DC: Brassey's, 1991); and Francis Fukuyama, *The US-Japan Security Relationship After the Cold War* (Santa Monica, CA: Rand, 1993).

12. Albrecht Rothacher, *Economic Diplomacy Between the European Community and Japan 1959–1981* (London: Gower, 1983), p. 325.

13. European Parliament, *Report on the Results of the Visit by the European Parliament Delegation*, Document 666/77, 1978.

14. Reported in the *Economist*, 9 April 1979.

15. Reported in ibid., 18 May 1991.

16. Klaus Grewlich, "The Impact of 'Europe 1992' on Japan's Relations with Europe," in T. David Mason and Abdul M. Turay (eds.), *Japan, NAFTA, and Europe: Trilateral Cooperation or Confrontation?* (New York: St. Martin's Press, 1994), p. 93.

17. The European Community Visitors Programme has since been extended to cover participants from all over the world; over 100 invitees now visit the EU annually under the program, which is jointly administered by the Commission and the European Parliament.

18. Summary reports of the annual parliamentary conferences are prepared by the Secretariat of the European Parliament but are not published in the *Official Journal;* however, they are not confidential and can usually be obtained on request from the Secretariat in Brussels.

19. *Bulletin,* 7/8–1991, p. 109.

20. Commission, *Europe and Japan: The Next Steps,* COM(95) 73 final, 8 March 1995, p. 7.

21. Ibid., p. 22.

22. Commission, *A Long Term Policy for China-Europe Relations*, COM(95) 279 final, 5 July 1995, p. 5.

23. See Ji-hong Kim, "The Structure of Korea's Trade with the EC Countries," in Soogil Young and Moonsoo Kang (eds.), *The Single European Market and Its Implications for Korea as an NIE* (Seoul: Korea Development Institute/Friedrich Ebert Stiftung, 1991), p. 201ff.

24. Commission, *Strategy*, p. 24.

25. Attached to the final act of the act of accession.

26. European Parliament, *Resolution on Economic and Trade Relations Between the EC and SAARC*, Session document A2–212/88.

27. K. K. Bhargava and Ross Masood Husain, *SAARC and European Union: Learning and Cooperation* (New Delhi: Har-Anand Publications, 1994), p. 52.

28. See Shada Islam, "EU Moves to Calm South Asian Anger," *European Voice* 2, no. 9, 29 February 1996.

29. Council framework regulation no. 443/92, 25 February 1992, *Official Journal* L 52, 27 February 1992, p. 1.

30. "Statement by the Chairman of the Asia-Europe Meeting, Bangkok, 2 March 1996," *Bulletin,* 3–1996, pp. 129–132, para. 3.

31. Figures from David G. Mayes, "The Implications of Closer European Integration for Australia and New Zealand," in David G. Mayes (ed.), *The External Implications of European Integration* (Hemel Hempstead: Harvester Wheatsheaf, 1993).

32. *Negotiating Directives for a Framework Agreement for Trade and Cooperation Between the European Community and Australia*, in European Parliament Notice to Members no. 8/96, 20 June 1996 (PE 217.868), p. 2.

8

The EU, Lomé, and the Developing World

Lomé, capital of Togo, has given its name to a series of agreements, the Lomé conventions, that have come to constitute one of the European Union's most significant and enduring external activities. A coordinated and institutionalized system of trade and aid measures aimed at improving the economic and social conditions of a sizable group of developing countries, Lomé is the centerpiece of the EU's efforts to provide help to the Third World. But although it covers seventy African, Caribbean, and Pacific states, Lomé is not the only framework for EU help to the developing world. Earlier chapters of this book have already touched on aspects of the EU's development policies toward other parts of the world. Indeed, a significant part of Europe's relationship with Latin America and Asia has been concerned with providing help in the form of trade concessions and various types of development cooperation to the LDCs (less-developed countries) and LLDCs (least-developed countries) in both regions. Much of the EU's relationship with the Mediterranean has centered on that region's need for support in achieving its development goals. A string of trade and cooperation agreements, stretching back in some cases to the 1970s, has provided an institutionalized framework for many of these relationships. In the case of the southern and eastern Mediterranean countries, which still qualify as LDCs, the European Community concluded the first preferential trade agreements as long ago as the 1960s and by the early 1970s had converted these into cooperation agreements, replete with financial protocols providing economic assistance.

But today's Lomé convention is the direct descendant of the oldest of all the Community's efforts in the field of development policy. The 1957 Treaty of Rome stated in its preamble the original EEC's intention "to confirm the solidarity which binds Europe and the overseas countries and . . . to ensure the development of their prosperity, in accordance with the principles of the Charter of the United Nations." This pledge was given practical effect in Part Four of the Treaty itself ("Association of the Overseas

Countries and Territories"), which provided the legal basis for an association between the Community and the overseas colonies and territories of its member states. In Article 131 the member states

> agree to associate with the Community the non-European countries and territories which have special relations with Belgium, France, Italy and the Netherlands.[1] . . .
>
> The purpose of association shall be to promote the economic and social development of the countries and territories and to establish close economic relations between them and the Community as a whole.
>
> In accordance with the principles set out in the Preamble to this Treaty, association shall serve primarily to further the interests and prosperity of the inhabitants of these countries and territories in order to lead them to the economic, social and cultural development to which they aspire.

Subsequent articles in Part Four of the Treaty spell out the special treatment that the Community will give to the associated countries. First, member states are to trade with the associated countries on the same basis as they trade with one another (Article 132.1). This is nonreciprocal, to the extent that the associated countries need only apply to their trade with the EC as a whole the same conditions that they apply to the specific Community country with which they have a special relationship (i.e., the colonial power). However, the associates must also apply these conditions to their trade with *each other*. Second, the EC pledges to abolish all customs duties on imports from the associated countries (Article 133.1). Again, this is nonreciprocal: the partner countries must merely ensure that their duties on imports from any EC member state (or other associated state)—which they may impose "to meet the needs of their development and industrialisation or produce revenue for their budgets" (Article 133.3)—are no greater than those levied on goods from the colonial power (the most-favored-nation principle). Third, the Community pledges to "contribute to the investments required for the progressive development of these countries and territories" (Article 132.3). An "Implementing Convention" annexed to the Treaty spelled out the Community's responsibilities for contributing to the social and economic development of the associated countries. It established the European Development Fund (EDF), the mechanism (administered by the Commission, though not part of the EC's budget) through which the member states would channel aid to the recipient countries.

In a legal sense, the provisions of Part Four of the Rome Treaty are curious. That they were included in an internationally binding treaty meant that the Community had *committed* itself to helping the beneficiary countries over the longer term: there could be no reneging on these commitments, nor could they be unilaterally amended. This guarantee remained a characteristic of the subsequent Yaoundé and Lomé conventions and served to make them unusually reliable development instruments. At the same time, however, the original Part Four provisions were included in the EEC Treaty without any consultation of the putative beneficiaries, who simply found themselves, for better or worse, associated to the Six rather than just to their colonial masters. This was largely the result of French pressure during negotiations to set up the EEC, since it was to France that the bulk of the associated countries owed allegiance (and France that stood to gain economically and politically through ensuring that its colonies and territories would benefit from its own membership in the Community). While not all of the other original member states (particularly those without colonies of their own) were necessarily enthusiastic about contributing to the support of French colonies, they accepted it rather like they accepted the Common Agricultural Policy, also of benefit largely to France: it was part of the price exacted by Paris for agreeing to join a Community likely to be dominated economically by Germany.[2] Like the Treaty of Rome itself, the association provisions of Part Four were of unlimited duration, although the provisions of the implementing convention (and with it, the EDF) had a validity of only five years. Part Four also made no mention of what would happen to associated countries once they achieved independence; however, the Commission considered that they would retain their status unless they specifically renounced it.[3]

In the event, eighteen of the original associates, all of them African states, did become independent between 1958, when the EEC Treaty entered into force, and 1963, when the first tranche of EDF funding expired. All of them were keen to continue their association with the Community. What had started as a French-inspired plan to offer support to the colonial possessions of the EEC's member states (principally France itself) now required the Six to consider their response to eighteen *independent* ex-colonies. In short, the Community needed to define an approach to the developing world. The result of their deliberations, the Yaoundé convention of 1963, was in a very real sense also the starting point for the European Community's subsequent global role in the field of development cooperation. This chapter is devoted mainly to an examination of the EU's relationship with the ACP countries under the Lomé conventions, the successor agreements to Yaoundé. But it also shows how parts—if not all—of the EU-ACP relationship have come to be paradigmatic for most of the Union's other efforts in the field of development cooperation elsewhere in the world.

Origins of a Development Policy

The Yaoundé convention of 1963 was concluded with eighteen African countries (including Madagascar) that had recently won their independence from France and Belgium.[4] Known as the Association of African and Malagasy States (AAMS), they did not include all the territories associated with the EC under Part Four of the Treaty, some of which remained dependent and continued to be covered by the Rome Treaty's implementing convention. (One former colony, Guinea, had broken off its relations with France in 1958 and refused association both under Part Four and Yaoundé; however, it did join the Lomé convention in 1975.) The 1963 agreement, named after the capital of Cameroon, where it was signed, was thus nominally between equal, sovereign states: the EC, acting as an entity, on the one hand and the members of the AAMS on the other. The AAMS had set up a coordination council at the ministerial level, a coordination committee at the ambassadorial level, and a secretariat, and it attempted to negotiate the terms of their association jointly. However, they had little negotiating experience or bargaining power,[5] and the text of the final Yaoundé convention (negotiated on the EC side by the Commission) was very much a reflection of what the Six wanted (and were prepared to give).

While Yaoundé was not merely a continuation of Part Four association, it did take over the latter's main features: nonreciprocal trade arrangements designed to benefit the AAMS in their relationships with the Community (though not necessarily with each other), and continued help in the form of development assistance, worth ECU 730 million ($912 million) in the five years from 1963 to 1968, and a further ECU 905 million ($1,130 million) from 1968 to 1973, plus loans from the European Investment Bank. Where it differed was in its professed aims, the nature of its trade regime, and the institutional arrangements to oversee its operation.

Yaoundé at least in theory set up a more equitable relationship between the African signatories and the EC. The convention was aimed at "promoting the economic, social and cultural progress of their countries,"[6] implying that it was designed for the mutual benefit of the parties (i.e., both ACP and EC states) and was not just a matter of the rich helping the poor. The reference to "cultural progress" implied a dimension to the relationship that went beyond the merely economic. In fact, of course, the economic dimension remained key. Here, in a departure from the Part Four association, the convention was less equitable. It guaranteed each AAMS country free access to the markets of the Six but no longer insisted that the same preferential terms should exist among the associates themselves. Free trade was guaranteed from South to North but not from South to South (although since there was not much trade among the African countries anyway, this had no immediate effect beyond giving the lie to the idea that all the Yaoundé signatories, European and African, were equal).

Again true to the idea that the convention was an agreement between sovereign states, a series of joint institutions was established. An association council, comprising the EC's Council and Commission and one member of the government of each AAMS state, was the main decisionmaking body; an association committee, consisting of one representative of each of the Six and the AAMS, plus the Commission, oversaw the operational aspects of the agreement. Both council and committee were supported by a secretariat. A parliamentary conference, made up of an equal number of parliamentarians from the European Parliament and the AAMS parliaments, reviewed an annual report from the council, though it had no formal powers. Disputes were dealt with by a court of arbitration.

In fact, the Yaoundé institutions were almost certainly too sophisticated for the job they had to do. Most of the rules governing the relationship between Europe and the AAMS were fixed in the text of the convention, and decisions on implementation of the financial assistance under the European Development Fund were ultimately taken by the Commission and the EDF committee of national officials. There was thus little of practical value for the institutions to do during the lifetime of the two Yaoundé conventions (the second, an extension of the first, ran from 1969 to 1974). Nevertheless, the creation of formal bodies of this kind became a hallmark of the European Community's contractual links with countries and regional groupings and served to underline its integrationist approach to international relations generally.[7]

Yaoundé I and II covered, coincidentally, the ten-year period leading up to British accession to the EC in 1973. It had become clear as early as 1969, when President Pompidou gave London the green light for a renewed bid to join the Community, that eventual UK membership would have to entail a substantial upgrading of the existing Yaoundé arrangements. Not only would several British dependencies qualify for Part Four association under the Rome Treaty, but an even larger number of its former colonies, now independent members of the Commonwealth, would seek the same treatment from the enlarged EC that the AAMS enjoyed.

But other factors also contributed to the conviction that a revamped Yaoundé convention would need to go beyond just the "trade and aid" formula of the past. For one thing, a commodity price boom in the early 1970s made the EC more conscious of the need to maintain harmonious relations with the Third World countries that were its principal suppliers; for their part, the LDCs concerned were becoming more aware that they now had greater bargaining power than hitherto. Another element was the growing conviction that the "North-South dialogue" and the calls for a "new international economic order (NIEO)"[8] were more than mere rhetoric and needed to be translated into action as a response to the genuine needs of the developing world. A third factor—and one that was itself a reaction to calls for an NIEO—was the system devised by the UN Conference on Trade and Development in 1970 to offer tariff preferences to developing countries as encouragement to their fledgling industries to export to the industrialized world. In 1971 the European Community became the first to apply this system, known as the generalized system of preferences, to the

G-77 group of developing countries. By doing so, it effectively extended
to a far wider range of countries the concessions it had previously granted
only to its AAMS partners, thus eroding at least in part the benefits of the
Yaoundé association.

It was clear, therefore, that the Yaoundé convention would need to be
followed by something more imaginative if it was to satisfy the rising expectations of a growing group of developing countries. The successor
agreement to Yaoundé, the first of the Lomé conventions concluded in
1975 with forty-six African, Caribbean, and Pacific states, thus contained
a number of innovations. Before going on to consider in depth the Lomé
arrangements and their implications, however, it is worth looking in
greater detail at the nature and field of application of the GSP, a yardstick
against which all trade-related aspects of development policy must be
measured and a system that has had a profound influence on EU development policy more generally.

The Generalized System of Preferences

The European Community's introduction in 1971 of a system of generalized preferences for trade with the developing countries was part of a new
awareness in Europe and the rest of the industrialized world that the problems of development were universal and required a global approach. The
GSP was designed to promote the industrialization and economic development of LDCs and LLDCs by according them special customs treatment
(tariff and duty reductions or exemptions, though sometimes accompanied
by quantitative restrictions) for their exports of finished or semifinished
industrial products and processed agricultural goods. The GSP did not
cover primary products or commodities. The first scheme, which lasted
from 1971 to 1980, was somewhat restrictive in scope, though the EC
granted progressively more liberal GSP access as time went on. Tariff reductions were initially accorded on a fairly extensive range of specified
processed foods (covering some 350 tariff headings), and complete tariff
exoneration was applied to industrial products (subject to annual country-
by-country ceilings).

When the scheme was renewed in 1980 for a further ten-year period,
the LLDCs received an improved deal for their agricultural products
(bringing them all roughly into line with the terms the ACP countries enjoyed). But the GSP still did not apply to products covered by the Community's Common Agricultural Policy, and the concessions granted under
the EC's preferential accords with the ACP and Mediterranean countries
meant that GSP access for some products from other countries remained
limited. By contrast, quotas on manufactured items from the thirty-six least-
developed countries were lifted completely. In the case of more sensitive

industrial products, a flexible system was introduced for other LDCs, making tariff quotas dependent on each individual country's level of competitiveness. Textiles benefited from the GSP to the extent that the exporting country had concluded a voluntary restraint agreement with the Community. By 1983 65 percent of the exports to the EC under the GSP came from just ten countries (Brazil, Romania, Kuwait, India, Hong Kong, South Korea, China, Malaysia, Venezuela, and Thailand), many of which were by then firmly in the category of newly industrialized economies (NIEs).

Partly to make the scheme more helpful to the poorer developing countries, the emphasis during the latter half of the 1980s was on achieving greater differentiation in the application of the system. Based on objective economic and other criteria, countries could be excluded from GSP benefits in respect of products in which they showed themselves to be particularly competitive. Poorer countries could expect to pick up extra quotas for given products as relatively richer LDCs became subject to lower ceilings. As a result of this shift of emphasis, some major LDCs, such as India and China, have started to lose some of their GSP privileges as their economies have grown and become more competitive.

The 1980 scheme continued past its normal revision date of 1990, and the EU's new GSP entered into force only in 1995. It consolidates the GSP's role as a development instrument by simplifying its administrative procedures, improving the distribution of its benefits, and assigning it new goals in the social and environmental fields. Under the new scheme, products are no longer automatically entitled to zero tariffs but are "modulated" according to the "sensitivity" of the individual item. In effect, the more sophisticated the product (probably reflecting the sophistication of the economy producing it), the higher the tariff: for example, electronics or cars from eligible countries will receive only a 30 percent reduction on the normal tariff for such products. Only the most basic manufactured items will still be admitted duty free. Moreover, a new "graduation" mechanism allows GSP benefits to be withdrawn from countries that have developed a recognized degree of competitiveness in respect of a given production sector. Hong Kong, South Korea, Singapore, and some oil-producing countries will be the first to be affected by phased GSP withdrawals, and they and other more advanced countries are likely to lose all GSP benefits by 1998. Countries will also be liable to GSP exclusion if they are shown to be involved in practices such as forced labor or the export of prison-manufactured products or if they fail to enforce controls on narcotics trafficking or money laundering. By contrast, additional preferential benefits will be available to poorer countries that comply with ILO conventions in the social field and with international conventions on tropical timber.

The new GSP arrangements highlight the EU's policy of concentrating on the poorest countries by offering complete exemption from duty for

their industrial products as well as admission of a wide range of their agricultural products duty free. The arrangements will not benefit the ACP
countries, of course, even though they are all nominally eligible for GSP:
without exception, the Lomé convention provides the ACP better terms
than the best on offer under GSP. Moreover, as the EU has progressively
extended the number and scope of its bilateral and multilateral trade and
cooperation agreements, a great many other developing countries outside
the Lomé framework now enjoy tailor-made preferential trade arrangements, which give them equivalent or better access to European markets
than that afforded under the GSP. Together with the successful conclusion
of the Uruguay Round of GATT negotiations and the resulting global lowering of tariffs, these considerations mean that the overall value of the system has continued to become more marginal to all but the poorest developing countries.

Launching the Lomé System

Lomé has come to be equated with EU development policy as such not
least because of its scope. The African, Caribbean, and Pacific countries
that are today associated with the European Union under the convention
number no fewer than seventy, close to 40 percent of the entire membership of the United Nations. They include all of sub-Saharan Africa (except
for South Africa), most of the independent Caribbean states, and eight Pacific island nations (see Table 8.1). The modest beginnings under Part Four
of the EEC Treaty and the two Yaoundé conventions have thus grown to
represent the world's biggest institutionalized link between the developed
and developing worlds, worth ECU 46.5 billion ($58 billion) in EDF aid
(including EIB loans) from 1958 to 1999. As a *package* of trade, aid, and
related measures, the Yaoundé-Lomé arrangements "have been glorified by
some as important markers on the road to a new international economic
order, and described by others as tools of Western imperialism and neo-
colonialism;"[9] more often, though, they are regarded as a generally positive if increasingly flawed model for North-South relations.

The transmutation of the Yaoundé association into the broader and
more complex Lomé relationship (described at the beginning of this chapter) was the result of lengthy negotiations. These took place in two phases.
The first of these involved the EC's own member states (and in particular
the original Six and Britain during the latter's accession negotiations); the
second occurred after UK accession, when the enlarged Community as a
whole negotiated with the existing mostly francophone AAMS states on the
one hand and the prospective new Commonwealth members on the other.

It had always been clear that not all the Commonwealth LDCs would
be considered for membership of an expanded association: the Yaoundé

Table 8.1   Lomé Convention: African, Caribbean, and Pacific States

Southern Africa
  Angola, Botswana, Lesotho, Malawi, Mozambique, Namibia, Swaziland, Zimbabwe

Central Africa
  Cameroon, Central African Republic, Congo, Gabon, Equatorial Guinea, Sao Tome and Principe, Zaire

Eastern Africa and Horn of Africa
  Burundi, Djibouti, Eritrea, Ethiopia, Kenya, Rwanda, Somalia, Sudan, Tanzania, Uganda, Zambia

Sahelian and Coastal Western Africa
  Benin, Burkina Faso, Cape Verde, Chad, Côte d'Ivoire, The Gambia, Ghana, Guinea Bissau, Guinea, Liberia, Mali, Mauritania, Niger, Nigeria, Senegal, Sierra Leone, Togo

Indian Ocean
  Comoro Islands, Madagascar, Mauritius, Seychelles

Caribbean
  Antigua and Barbuda, Bahamas, Barbados, Belize, Dominica, Dominican Republic, Grenada, Guyana, Haiti, Jamaica, St. Kitts and Nevis, St. Lucia, St. Vincent and the Grenadines, Suriname, Trinidad and Tobago

Pacific
  Fiji, Kiribati, Papua New Guinea, Solomon Islands, Tonga, Tuvalu, Vanuatu, Western Samoa

convention had already specifically limited new applications to countries "whose economic structure and production" were comparable to those of the existing members; moreover, new applications were subject to approval by the existing membership. While the new circumstances that prevailed in the early 1970s meant that the Yaoundé formula needed substantial revision in a number of areas, none of the existing signatories were keen to see the basic membership profile of the AAMS altered as part of a new agreement, and the British did not insist. As a result, Commonwealth states such as India and Pakistan (countries certainly not comparable to existing Yaoundé members) were excluded a priori, in spite of their very real development needs. Indeed, as regards the admission of new members, the wording of the new Lomé convention, once it emerged, was identical to that of the original Yaoundé agreement.

The treaty of accession between the UK, Denmark, Ireland, and Norway and the Six, signed in 1971, listed the twenty Commonwealth countries in Africa, the Indian Ocean, the Caribbean, and the Pacific that would be eligible for association on the same basis as the AAMS; it also referred (in its Protocol 23) to the Community's willingness "to extend and strengthen the trade relations with the developing independent Commonwealth countries in Asia." These Asian countries (and, later, the countries of Latin America) eventually became known as the nonassociated developing countries (see Chapters 6 and 7). But British accession to the EC in 1973 was not automatically accompanied by an immediate successor agreement to Yaoundé. With the principle of who could join established in the accession treaty, the actual negotiations for a new and enlarged association could merely begin.

It took eighteen months to hammer out the first Lomé convention. Before the negotiations even got under way, a period of discussion had taken place among the AAMS and the newly associable Commonwealth states. The outcome was a new, wider grouping calling itself the ACP, or African, Caribbean, and Pacific states; the word "association," with its overtones of continued dependency on the former colonial powers in the EC, was dropped. Although there was initially some friction between the francophone and anglophone members and between the African and Caribbean states, which had somewhat different development agendas, the ACP established a joint secretariat in 1974. In spite of its size (the ACP initially comprised forty-six states), the necessity of presenting a common front in negotiations with the European Community did much to encourage solidarity among its members. Nevertheless, the ACP held 453 coordinating meetings among themselves and 183 joint negotiating sessions with the EC during the course of the talks.[10]

The resulting accord owed much to the unity of the ACP during the 1973–1975 negotiations (and much to the guiding hand of the biggest of the ACP states, Nigeria). Indeed the experience of working together as a bloc helped to forge a sense of identity among the ACP, if not in the more integrationist mold of regional organizations such as ASEAN or the EC itself, then at least as a coordinated grouping with a shared purpose. Today the ACP states try to adopt common positions in international fora such as the World Bank and UNCTAD and not merely in their relations with the EU. They have official observer status at the UN and maintain a general secretariat in Brussels. To this extent, therefore, their relationship to the European Union has served to further not just their economic and development interests vis-à-vis Europe but also their own internal cohesion, enabling them to act as a major international lobby.

The first Lomé convention came into force in April 1976 for a period of five years.[11] Known today as Lomé I, it was followed by Lomé II (1980–1984),[12] Lomé III (1985–1989),[13] and Lomé IV (1990–1999).[14] The EU-ACP relationship has been described variously as being one of "unequal interdependence,"[15] as "a new model for relations between developed and developing states,"[16] "neo-colonialist,"[17] "decolonialist,"[18] or, more prosaically, as "a concrete form of cooperation between a group of countries in the South and a group of States in the North."[19] But if nothing else, it was also an agreed response by some of the world's richest and some of its poorest countries to the unique set of circumstances that followed the post–World War II collapse of empire and the coming together of the former colonial powers in a regional integration organization. In many ways Lomé I was little more than a successor to Part Four association and the Yaoundé conventions; and though it has evolved since the mid-1970s, it is still based on the original notion of promoting development through a combination of trade concessions and financial and technical assistance. What makes it unique, however, is that the development relationship between the EU and the ACP is the result of ongoing *negotiation*, not merely a unilateral policy of aid from rich to poor given on a take-it-or-leave-it basis (as was the case with Part Four association under the EEC Treaty), and in that sense it is indeed part of the new international economic order.

The seventy current members of the ACP range from the poorest LLDCs such as Eritrea, Ethiopia, and Haiti to relatively prosperous LDCs like the Seychelles and many of the Caribbean states. GNP per capita is as low as $80 in Mozambique (and probably even lower in countries like Sudan or Haiti, for which figures are not available) and as high as $11,500 in the Bahamas (putting it well above the poorest EU member states, Greece and Portugal).[20] South Africa finds itself in a special position: although its per capita GNP of just under $3,000 places it comfortably in the midrange of ACP economies, the figures belie its overall economic size and structure. While many of its rural areas suffer from typical Third World development problems, it is highly developed in some sectors. Its total GNP of $118 billion is four times that of the wealthiest ACP state, Nigeria, and on a par with that of other NIEs such as Turkey and Thailand.

The EU proposed that instead of becoming a full member of the ACP, which it could have been expected to dominate, South Africa negotiate a comprehensive trade and development accord with the Union itself (to include an EU–South Africa free trade area). But the precise parameters for such an agreement have not been easy to define, with both sides requiring months of internal discussion on the terms to serve as the basis for negotiation. For the Union, the extent to which agricultural products should feature in the free trade aspects of the agreement was a source of debate. For South Africa, the effects of the agreement's trade arrangements on its relationship with its Southern African Development Community (SADC) neighbors[21] had to be taken into account. For both sides, the impact of any accord on the ACP, and particularly the African members, is crucial: none of the parties wants to see disadvantages for other Lomé states arising from a bilateral EU–South Africa consensus. It is still Pretoria's goal to become a "qualified" member of the Lomé convention. Nevertheless, a bilateral accord of some sort is certain to be agreed with the EU, probably in 1997. In the meantime many of South Africa's products are covered by the GSP and by a number of sectoral trade concessions worked out in 1994 after the country's first free elections. The European Union also intends to negotiate additional sectoral agreements on fisheries, on the labeling of wines and spirits, and on science and technology.

The Structure of the Lomé Convention

Like its Yaoundé predecessor, the Lomé agreement covered two principal areas: trade and aid. The first three conventions ran for a period of five years each. The fourth version of Lomé was negotiated for a ten-year period and expires in 1999. Also like its predecessor, the Lomé agreement was endowed with a formal institutional structure. Still something of a novelty when the convention was first negotiated, the bodies that comprise this structure today find their parallels in many of the other agreements concluded between the European Union and third countries or regional groupings, as earlier chapters of this book have shown. A council of ministers replaces the Yaoundé association council; it consists of the EU's Council and members of the Commission and one member of each ACP government. Because of its size (currently almost ninety members), it meets just once a year under a revolving presidency that alternates between the ACP and the EU. While it is responsible for major political decisions, most of the practical work of implementing the convention is carried out by a committee of ambassadors. The committee in turn is assisted by working groups and other permanent or ad hoc bodies. A general secretariat based in Brussels prepares meetings of both the council and committee. Finally, the ACP-EU joint assembly provides parliamentary oversight. A consultative body, the assembly consists of equal numbers of MEPs and ACP parliamentarians[22] and meets twice a year, alternating between venues in Europe and in ACP countries.

The principle of parity in the joint assembly means that there are currently seventy members of the European Parliament with seats in the body, one for every ACP representative. The EP's Development Committee, with thirty-seven members and another thirty-seven substitutes, adds to the total number of MEPs with an interest in development issues (not every member of the Development Committee is automatically a member of the joint assembly). As a result, the EP follows not only the activities of the EU-ACP relationship extremely closely but also development issues more widely (there are standing EP delegations responsible for relations with Latin America; the Mashreq, Maghreb, and Gulf states; South Asia; and ASEAN and Southeast Asia—all of whose members find themselves dealing with development-related matters on a regular basis). Parliament has thus become something of a lobby for a more generous EU approach to all aspects of development cooperation, arguing forcefully for larger development budgets but also stressing political aspects such as human rights. The EP is also the target for extensive lobbying by outside groups with an interest in development, ranging from specialist NGOs to human rights and environmental organizations.

But it is the Commission that shoulders most of the burden of administering the EU's development efforts. The directorate-general responsible,

DG VIII, is the frontline operational center in Brussels. More recently, a humanitarian aid office (ECHO) was set up to administer food aid and other urgent assistance. In addition to its headquarters staff, DG VIII also deploys delegates in most ACP capitals. Acting as de facto EU ambassadors, the delegates are responsible for overseeing and evaluating EDF-financed projects; in practice, they also fulfill an important symbolic role by underlining the European Union's commitment to its relations with ACP countries. Back in Brussels, this commitment is reinforced by the assignment of a full Commission portfolio to the Lomé convention and relations with the ACP (from 1995 to 2000 held by the Portuguese commissioner João de Deus Pinheiro).

The Lomé Trade Regime

The trade arrangements established under the first Lomé convention have changed little over twenty years, and those arrangements in turn were based largely on the system already established under the earlier Yaoundé agreements. Objectively, they are a model of what richer countries can and should be doing to encourage LDCs and LLDCs to expand their economies through exports. Some 99 percent of all ACP exports enter the EU duty free, yet there is no reciprocal obligation on the partner countries to offer special treatment to the import of European goods (ACP countries are merely required to offer MFN status to and not to discriminate against individual EU member states). The only ACP exports still subject to some import restrictions by the EU are a few agricultural products covered by the CAP, and even they receive preferential treatment compared to similar non-ACP imports. In spite of these apparently favorable conditions, however, the figures fail to reveal any obvious positive impact on the ACP's overall trading position (although the point has been made that without Lomé the situation would be worse still[23]).

Exports from the ACP countries represented 3.4 percent of the EC's total imports in 1975, when Lomé was signed, but had fallen to just 1.5 percent by 1992.[24] This trend was echoed in the ACP's overall trade performance: in 1975 the group accounted for 3.16 percent of total world exports, but by 1992 the proportion had dropped to 1.32 percent.[25] Compared to other developing regions of the world, the ACP has done markedly less well; while EU imports from Asian LDCs increased tenfold from 1976 to 1992 and those from Latin America threefold, imports from the ACP went up by a factor of just 1.7.[26] The reasons for this relative failure of the Lomé trade regime are many. Some of them, such as the impact of the introduction of the GSP to LDCs worldwide and the proliferation of preferential agreements between the EU and many other countries, have been referred to earlier in this chapter. A new and more recent factor is the outcome of the Uruguay Round of GATT negotiations: by further liberalizing trade internationally, which has reduced tariffs worldwide, the round diminishes still more the relative advantage of the EU as a preferential market for ACP exports.

Among the other reasons are the specific nature of the ACP countries themselves and the types of goods they produce. While the EU remains a major importer of raw materials and primary commodities,[27] prices for most of these have fallen in recent years and have, moreover, declined relative to the Union's overall imports. A case in point is crude oil, which typically accounts for 20–25 percent of annual ACP exports to the EU. Oil prices fluctuate from year to year and are lower today than they were in 1975 (Table 8.2 shows the effect of oil exports on overall EU-ACP trade in 1995). The ACP's industrial products enjoy tariff-free entry into the European market, but this advantage has had little impact because the ACP has not made much real headway in expanding its industrial base. This is partly because the rules of origin laid down in the Lomé conventions are complex and restrictive and make it difficult for the ACP countries to capitalize on one of their natural advantages, cheap labor, to produce and export finished products whose content originates outside Lomé. But it is also the result of underdevelopment: production of the types of manufactured goods likely to find markets in the EU require sophisticated production facilities and skills, and these are generally still lacking. Recognizing these shortcomings, the 1995 midterm review[28] of the Lomé IV convention led to a commitment by the EU to place greater emphasis on helping the ACP countries improve their productive capacities.

Another obstacle for the ACP has long been the European Union's Common Agricultural Policy. Many farm products covered by the CAP are not entitled to free entry into the EU market from ACP countries, and although only about 1 percent of ACP exports are affected, the removal of the tariff and quota restrictions could well encourage an expansion of both production and export of a whole range of agricultural items. Even the latest concessions agreed by the EU at the midterm review fall well short of total liberalization. For numerous products that currently do not qualify for any preference, customs duties and levies are reduced by 16 percent across

Table 8.2   EU-ACP Trade, 1995 (in ECU millions)

	Total Trade	Total Trade, Excluding Oil
EU exports to ACP	17,423	16,993
EU imports from ACP	19,831	15,808
Total exports and imports	37,254	32,801
EU balance	−2,408	+ 1,185

Source: Eurostat

the board (the ACP countries sought a 36 percent reduction). Even here, items such as olives, olive products, wine, and lemons (which compete with the same EU products) are excluded. Other improvements are introduced for cereals, meat, and fruit, but some of them are marginal at best; the quota for strawberries, for example, goes up from just 1,500 to 1,600 metric tons.

The most recent updating of the convention, Lomé IV, attempted to address the unsatisfactory position of ACP-EU trade, especially in non-agricultural products. It introduced more generous rules of origin. It placed a new emphasis on trade development, or how to make the most of the op-portunities provided under the convention. A new chapter (Articles 114–116) provided for support for economic development services, such as those required by business, foreign trade, transport, communications, and data-processing services. The parties emphasized the need to stimulate trade promotion and diversification (Articles 135–138) and to make sure that cooperation programs took account of commercial prospects in chan-neling aid to areas such as rural development programs and industrial co-operation. A Trade Development Project, financed by the EDF, was launched in 1993 by the ACP secretariat and has identified new problem areas contributing to poor trade performance. These include the lack of priority accorded by many ACP governments to trade, the transition to market economies from centralized systems in a number of countries, the impact of structural adjustment programs imposed by the Bretton Woods institutions and other lenders (including the EC), lack of management ex-pertise, poor design capability and quality control, inadequate marketing and negotiating skills, and much more.

The 1995 midterm review of the Lomé IV agreement has taken some account of these and other difficulties but not to the extent that any major improvements can be expected in the short term. The review concentrated more on aid issues—for example, a greater emphasis on the programming of financial cooperation—than on trade. Indeed the limits to what is pos-sible under the EU-ACP contract as regards trade have probably been reached. It has become increasingly difficult for the European Union to provide meaningful preferences to the ACP in a world rapidly moving to-ward greater and greater trade liberalization. It seems likely that what im-provements in the trading positions of ACP countries are still possible will come about as the result of aid in the form of financial, economic, and technical cooperation (designed to improve manufacturing and export *po-tential*) rather than through any further fine-tuning of the statutory me-chanics of the trade relationship.

The Aid Dimension Under Lomé

There is one issue that dominates all others in any consideration of the ACP's poor trading performance, and that is the very nature of the ACP countries themselves, in particular in Africa. The African continent (which continues to account for 90 percent of the ACP's population and economic strength) is the most underdeveloped in the world. Many of the African ACP states are classified as LLDCs, the poorest of the developing countries. Africa faces enormous problems, which include its climatic conditions (which lead to drought and desertification), missing infrastructures (transport and telecommunications), political instability and civil war, debt, famine and disease (up to 15 percent of the population of sub-Saharan Africa is now thought to have AIDS), illiteracy and poverty, and much more besides. In these conditions, it is hardly surprising that in spite of some success stories the continent has not made much headway in international trade. As the preceding section made clear, the EU can do little more to encourage further development of ACP trade under the terms of the Lomé convention than it has done already. The problems that remain are largely structural and must be dealt with by a combination of self-help and the generous provision and judicious use of aid.

That is the purpose of EU aid to the ACP states, and aid in turn has been the central plank of all the Lomé conventions. Known for diplomatic reasons as "financial and technical cooperation" (and referred to as such in successive Lomé conventions), it dates back to the days of Part Four association, which was when the European Development Fund was first established. EDF aid (as opposed to bilateral aid from individual EU member states, which continues independently of the Lomé arrangements) comes in two guises. The first, known as "programmable aid," is channeled through the EDF in the form of nonrepayable grants. It is used in national or regional "indicative programs" to finance traditional development cooperation projects. The second, "nonprogrammable aid" is conditional and granted on a case-by-case basis. It includes two schemes until recently unique to the Lomé agreements: Stabex, or stabilization of export earnings, which provides compensation for falls in ACP export earnings resulting from fluctuations in world prices of primary products; and Sysmin, an equivalent scheme to help minerals producers in the event of market collapses. Nonprogrammable aid also includes the provision of reimbursable risk capital for small and medium-size enterprises and emergency and humanitarian aid.

The size of the European Development Fund has grown from ECU 581 million ($726 million) for the first five-year period (1957–1963) of EDF 1 to ECU 14.625 billion ($18.3 billion) for the latest, eighth EDF, which covers the period 1996–2000. On top of EDF funds, the EU's own budget supplies additional financing for a range of specific purposes, principally food aid (worth more than ECU 500 million, or $625 million, annually in recent years) but also for emergency aid and projects related to ecology, forestry, democracy and human rights, combating AIDS, and science and technology. Bilateral aid granted by the EU's various member states to individual African, Caribbean, and Pacific states is independent of the Lomé framework, although efforts are made to coordinate this type of assistance with that provided through the EDF. Bilateral aid still often (though not always) reflects historical links, with member states such as France, Britain, Belgium, or the Netherlands providing a disproportionate part of their ODA to their former possessions.

The European Investment Bank provides funds in the form of low-interest loans from its own resources, that is, money it raises commercially on the capital markets; these are included in the calculation of the total for each EDF (of the ECU 14.625 billion in EDF 8, for example, ECU 1.658 billion is in the form of EIB loans). These funds are used primarily to finance viable projects in economically sounder ACP countries that will be in a position to service and repay the debts. Industrial projects, tourism, mining, energy production, as well as infrastructure projects such as transport, telecommunications, and water are all eligible for EIB financing.

Programmable, or traditional, aid has always constituted the largest share of EDF payments. It is disbursed on the basis of programs drawn up at the level of individual ACP states (national indicative programs) or regions (regional indicative programs). The actual use to which programmable funding is put varies from country to country: rehabilitation of drinking water networks in Equatorial Guinea, hospital construction in Belize, agricultural diversification in Mauritius, trade promotion in Jamaica, primary and professional education in Gabon, forestry management and fisheries in Vanuatu—these are just some examples at the national level under Lomé IV. Regional programs (for example, in southern or Central Africa, the Caribbean, or the Pacific) concentrate on measures with a multilateral regional impact, such as projects in the field of transport, roads, or telecommunications, and specific help is given to encourage moves toward regional cooperation and integration. In recent years there has been a greater emphasis on structural adjustment programs. Structural adjustment in the socioeconomic policies of many LDCs has become a prerequisite before the major international financial institutions such as the IMF and World Bank will make loans: realistic exchange rates, domestic market deregulation and price controls, restructuring of the financial sector, ending government subsidies, improving producer incentives (especially for farmers), improving public-sector efficiency, and other measures have come to be seen as essential if ODA and loans are to be effectively used. Separate finance is now earmarked by the EDF for this purpose and is sometimes supplemented by funds from the national indicative programs.

The cornerstone of nonprogrammable aid has long been the Stabex scheme. Set up by Lomé I in 1975 and often considered to be one of the most innovative aspects of the convention, it was a response to criticism that the Yaoundé model was too inflexible. The system is based on the recognition that economic development in many ACP countries has been hampered by the unpredictability of revenues from key exports of primary products. Countries that are heavily dependent on just one or two major products find themselves at the mercy of fluctuating world market prices. Stabex is designed to provide compensation for loss of earnings from exports to the EU when commodity prices fall below a certain threshold. From twenty-nine products under Lomé I, the scheme now covers forty-nine, ranging from cocoa and coffee to prawns and squid. Compensation becomes payable if a product accounts for at least 5 percent of a country's export earnings and those earnings have fallen by at least 4.5 percent (the thresholds have been progressively reduced from one Lomé convention to the next).[29] Each EDF since 1976 has contained appropriations specifically earmarked for Stabex payments (ECU 1.5 billion under EDF 7, ECU 1.8 billion under EDF 8).

The Stabex scheme covers only agricultural commodities. Lomé II introduced a complementary system to deal with the difficulties encountered by ACP states that relied heavily on exports of minerals, whose prices also tended to fluctuate widely. Called Sysmin, the scheme is designed to provide financial assistance (originally in the form of reimbursable loans) to help ensure that mining facilities are not allowed to deteriorate if export revenue drops. Sysmin covers bauxite, copper, tin, phosphates, manganese, iron, and uranium. Allocations from the scheme (which since Lomé IV have been in the form of grants and totaled ECU 480 million, or $600 million, under EDF 7) may not be simply absorbed into the national budget of the recipient country but require the EU's approval before they can be spent, for example, on the modernization of a mining plant or equipment.

Both the Stabex and Sysmin schemes are handicapped in that they are designed to deal with unpredictable fluctuations. The EDF funds that have been earmarked since the schemes were set up have so far usually underestimated the actual claims made, leaving the Commission to decide which to meet and which to reject. Emergency aid and aid to refugees, or humanitarian aid, are also nonprogrammable because the circumstances in which they may be needed are unpredictable, as the civil war and resulting refugee crisis in Rwanda, Burundi, and Zaire have shown since 1994. Together with other conflicts in Africa, including Sudan, Angola, Liberia, and Sierra Leone, the Rwanda/Burundi crisis left the entire budget for humanitarian aid contained in the seventh EDF exhausted by the end of 1994, well before new funds became available with the entry into force of the eighth EDF. Much of the humanitarian and food aid (some of it financed out of the Community budget) is disbursed through the many specialized NGOs operating in the field.

The EU's assistance to the ACP through the EDF has often been criticized as being too little and the systems for administering and disbursing the aid too complex. Actual payments of programmable aid sometimes lag months or years behind commitments, to the extent that funds from one

EDF often have to be transferred to the next because they remain unspent. At the end of Lomé III, for example, only 42 percent of the sixth EDF had been disbursed.[30] It often takes excessively long for ACP states to submit project proposals on the basis of their national indicative programs and for Brussels to make decisions on them. Completed projects are often under-utilized because no provision has been made for their ongoing upkeep or running costs. Other projects have turned out to be inappropriate or were based on inadequate studies, or their designs were unsuitable for local conditions. A particular criticism often leveled at the EU is the lack of provision for ACP debt write-off in the EDF, particularly that incurred through EIB loans made through the EDF itself.

These shortcomings are due less to any fundamental flaws in the basic design of the Lomé financial and technical cooperation concept than to problems inherent in dealing with developing countries. Implementing projects in rural areas of remote and often backward parts of the world is difficult both for the donor and the beneficiary. Given the slow rate of funds utilization by many of the ACP countries, it is also arguable whether a larger EDF would have much immediate effect on development levels. The EU's own complex institutional structure hardly simplifies matters either. The Commission's DG VIII (Development) is often overburdened and always under-staffed; its delegates on the spot in ACP countries lack support and infrastructure; member state involvement through the EDF Committee complicates decisionmaking; and because the EDF does not form part of the Community's own budget, it escapes the control of the European Parliament and the Court of Auditors and cannot be implemented with the same facility as other de-velopment finance, such as that for Central and Eastern Europe or the Mediterranean. As regards ACP debt, EU member states argue that debt rescheduling is best done on a case-by-case basis, and the EDF does provide some subsidies to ease debt repayments. Nevertheless, the issue still rankles, not least because the cost of meeting the entire annual interest burden on EIB loans would amount to only some ECU 30 million ($37.5 million).[31]

Partly in response to these difficulties, the Lomé IV midterm review has placed a new emphasis on concentrating aid on countries that show themselves best able to use it. Only 70 percent of the eighth EDF will be allocated in the first three years of its lifetime, with the remaining 30 per-cent going to those countries that have shown they can absorb it. The effect will be to reward ACP governments that demonstrate their commit-ment to sustainable development and penalize those more inclined to live from hand to mouth.[32] In the words of Commissioner João de Deus Pin-heiro, speaking at the signing ceremony of the midterm agreement in No-vember 1995, "For the ACP countries, the decisive element will be their ability properly to diagnose their situation and their requirements."[33]

While there is criticism, especially among the ACP, of the increasing international "conditionality" attached to loans and other forms of aid in the form of structural adjustment requirements, the EU has so far been relatively relaxed about the conditions it imposes (though both the seventh and eighth EDFs contain specific amounts for structural adjustment measures). Experience has shown that in the absence of some restructuring within many ACP states, the likelihood that ODA will be used effectively is diminished: certainly, bureaucracy and sometimes corrupt governments have been guilty of mismanaging and occasionally misusing EU and other foreign aid, and macroeconomic reform is increasingly viewed as vital to improving trade prospects and economic performance. More important, for several years now the Bretton Woods institutions, whose members include the EU's member states, have made adherence to structural adjustment policies mandatory for developing countries seeking loans. It would be odd if the same member states were to act otherwise in the framework of their Lomé commitments.

Finally, mention must be made of another kind of conditionality that now applies to the Lomé convention: respect for human rights. In line with the European Union's general insistence that its agreements with third countries contain political conditionality clauses, Article 5 of Lomé IV commits all its signatories to respect the principles of the Universal Declaration of Human Rights. Given the long tradition of the ACP in condemning apartheid in South Africa, the idea of embracing human rights as an ideal is not so far-fetched. But in practice the low levels of development in most ACP countries and their lack of experience with democratic forms and judicial systems acceptable to the West made full compliance unlikely. However, the 1995 midterm review has strengthened the Article 5 provisions by introducing a suspension clause. This states that if any of the essential human rights listed in Article 5 are violated, the partial or total suspension of development aid can follow. This can only happen, however, after prior consultation with ACP nations and the abusing party, other than in particular emergency circumstances defined in a separate declaration.[34]

Lomé as a Model for EU Development Policy

In early 1997 it remained an open question whether there would be a Lomé V or rather a totally new arrangement adapted to the times and better suited to the changing political and development needs of the ACP countries. The lack of convincing progress in improving conditions in many ACP states in spite of almost thirty-five years of Yaoundé and Lomé cooperation is not on the face of it much of a recommendation for the efficacy of the system as it stands. However, it is also not evident that the system has failed completely. There are too many other variables that, taken together, indicate that the lack of progress is not systemic but rooted in a variety of social, economic, and cultural causes that the classic development model is not equipped to address.

At the same time, lack of unity within the EU on the most appropriate policies to pursue (with a recent emphasis on renationalizing aid efforts rather than channeling them through the EDF) has not served to make the Lomé framework more effective. Successive Lomé (and Yaoundé) agreements have attempted to adapt and respond both to changing circumstances and failures and flaws inherent in the model itself. But whatever emerges next, there seems little doubt that the framework established under Lomé will find its reflection in future agreements. It is equally apparent that many of the lessons learned have been applied by the EU to good effect in other development contexts, for example, in Asia and Latin America. The addition at Maastricht of a new article to the EC Treaty (Article 130x) providing for the "Community and the Member States [to] coordinate their policies on development cooperation and [to] consult each other on their aid programs" was also born of the Lomé experience.

It is indicative of the importance of the EU's role in development policy generally that every chapter of this book, with the exception of Chapter 5 on North America, has touched on aspects of development. The EU's relationship with its non-European Mediterranean neighbors, with Central and Eastern Europe, and with most of Asia and Latin America is characterized above all by Europe's role in providing *help*—through trade concessions, technical and economic cooperation, and financial aid—to poorer countries at various stages of development. An expanding world economy has been flanked by a burgeoning global population over the forty years of European involvement in development policy. As a result, poverty and underdevelopment remain widespread. Nevertheless, there have been numerous success stories, led by former LDCs in Southeast Asia and including a number of Latin American countries. These newly industrialized economies are on their way to becoming part of the relatively small but growing community of developed countries.

In recognition of this, the EU has shifted its emphasis from aid to trade in the case of the NIEs and many of the more prosperous LDCs, and from trade to aid for the poorest of the LLDCs. Most of the latter are sub-Saharan members of the ACP, together with a handful of Asian countries, in particular Afghanistan, Cambodia, Myanmar, Bangladesh, Bhutan, the Maldives, Nepal, Laos, and Vietnam. The introduction of the Stabex scheme for Bangladesh and Nepal is one example of the application of a Lomé mechanism to nonassociated LLDCs. But the EU's experience gained in providing assistance to the poorest countries within the ACP is not exclusive. The practical lessons learned in promoting rural development or health care or working with NGOs are usually applicable in much the same way in Asia as they are in Africa. To that extent, the European Union is increasingly approaching the problems of development not merely on the basis of adherence to a particular grouping but on the more objective criterion of need. Development policy is indivisible, in spite of the continued flagship status of the EU-ACP relationship.

The remaining few years of the current Lomé IV convention will provide an opportunity for the European Union and its member states to consider how they wish to pursue their relations with the developing world in the coming century. For all its failings, the EU's development policy is unique, both in terms of the innovative mechanisms it has employed and of the relative generosity of its financial commitment. The provision by the EU and its member states of 0.51 percent of their GNP to ODA may not seem a lot, but it compares well to the 0.15 percent made available by the United States and the 0.32 percent from Japan. Despite growing pressure by national treasuries to reduce spending, there is little doubt that the EU will remain the world's largest aid donor for the immediate future. There is also little doubt that it will continue to seek more effective and cost-efficient ways of implementing its policy.

Notes

1. This article was amended after 1973 to add Denmark and the United Kingdom to this list of member states.

2. See A. Marin, "The Lomé Agreement," in Ali M. El-Agraa (ed.), *The Economics of the European Community* (4th edition) (Hemel Hempstead: Harvester Wheatsheaf, 1994), p. 472.

3. For an account of this and other aspects of Part Four association in the early years of the EEC, see Marjorie Lister, *The European Community and the Developing World: The Role of the Lomé Convention* (Aldershot: Avebury, 1988), pp. 10–31.

4. The text of the first Yaoundé convention can be found in vol. 3 (*Etats Associés hors d'Europe*) of the *Dictionnaire du Marché Commun* (Paris: Dictionnaires André Joly, 1968).

5. Lister, *The European Community*, p. 37.

6. My translation from the French.

7. The Yaoundé convention was not in fact the first EC agreement to feature an institutional structure: the 1961 association agreement with Greece was endowed with an association council and a joint parliamentary committee. The 1963 association with Turkey included similar structures..

8. The NIEO was articulated in May 1974 by UN General Assembly Resolution 3202 (S-VI) ("Programme of Action on the Establishment of a New International Economic Order").

9. Otto Schmuck, "The Lomé Convention: A Model for Partnership," in Geoffrey Edwards and Elfriede Regelsberger (eds.), *Europe's Global Links: The European Community and Inter-regional Cooperation* (New York: St. Martin's Press, 1990), p. 45.

10. Lister, *The European Community*, p. 74.

11. *Official Journal*, L 025, 30 January 1976, p. 2.

12. Ibid., L 347, 22 December 1980, p. 1.

13. Ibid., L 086, 31 March 1986, p. 3.

14. Ibid., L 229, 17 August 1991, p. 3.

15. John Ravenhill, *Collective Clientelism: The Lomé Conventions and North-South Relations* (New York: Columbia University Press, 1985).

16. In the preamble to Lomé I.

17. Lister, *The European Community*, p. 216.

18. I. William Zartman, "Europe and Africa: Decolonization or Dependency," *Foreign Affairs* 54, no. 2, January 1976.

19. C. M. Tibazarwa, "European-African Relations: Challenges in the 1990s," in Stefan Brüne, Joachim Betz, and Winrich Kühne (eds.), *Africa and Europe: Relations of Two Continents in Transition* (Münster: LIT Verlag, 1994), p. 29.

20. This and other figures used here are from the 1995 *World Bank Atlas* (Washington, D.C.: World Bank, 1995) and apply to the year 1993.

21. Angola, Botswana, Lesotho, Malawi, Mozambique, Namibia, Swaziland, and Zimbabwe.

22. Given the absence of a real parliamentary tradition in many ACP countries, many of the ACP seats in the joint assembly have often tended to be filled by ambassadors or others appointed by their governments. The democratic character of the assembly has suffered as a result. The Lomé IV midterm review attempted to address this problem by agreeing that in future, where possible, ACP representatives should be parliamentarians or at least persons appointed by their national parliaments. Others will need to be endorsed by the assembly itself before they can take their seats.

23. Carol Cosgrove, "Has the Lomé Convention Failed ACP Trade?" *Journal of International Affairs* 48, no. 1 (Summer 1994), p. 229.

24. Ibid., p. 223.

25. European Commission, "EU-ACP Cooperation in 1994," special edition of the *Courier,* June 1995, p. 53.

26. Cosgrove, "Has the Lomé Convention Failed ACP Trade?" p. 226.

27. The seven main ACP exports are, in descending order, crude oil, diamonds, cocoa beans, coffee beans, fruit, wood, and refined copper.

28. "Agreement Amending the Fourth ACP-EC Convention of Lomé," *Courier* no. 155, January-February 1996.

29. See Marin, "The Lomé Agreement," pp. 478–481.

30. Joachim Betz, "The New International Environment and EC-ACP Cooperation," in Brüne et al., *Africa and Europe*, p. 133.

31. Ibid., p. 132.

32. Stelios Christopoulos "The Future of European Development Policy," *Courier* no. 154, November-December 1995, p. 76.

33. Quoted in *Courier* no. 155, January-February 1996, p. 20.

34. See Debra Percival, "Successful Conclusion to the Lomé IV Mid-term Review Clinched at Eleventh Hour," *Courier* no. 153, September-October 1995, p. 7.

9

Global Europe: World Power Pro Tem?

If these pages have shown anything, it is that the reach of the European Union is truly global. One way or another, the EU has become ubiquitous, exercising influence, exerting pressure, providing assistance, selling and buying goods and services, making investments all over the world. But central to any assessment of the importance of the EU's international role is clarity about what we mean by "European Union" in the global context. Are we talking about the Union as such or the Union as a collection of member states or both? For that matter, is the distinction relevant?

It is obvious that the EU is more than the sum of its parts. The EU is inclusive rather than exclusive, sheltering its fifteen members within its treaty-built walls and in turn drawing its own strength and authority from their joint will. In some areas it allows its members almost complete freedom of action, with its own role circumscribed by the unwillingness of its subscribers to concede power to it. The Common Foreign and Security Policy is a case in point. Elsewhere, such as in trade policy, the roles are reversed, the member states having ceded to the Union their individual rights to negotiate or determine many of their own trading parameters. Member states are left with little more power than individual states in the Federal Republic of Germany, say, or the United States. In development policy the picture is different again: here the EU as entity acts in some ways like a distinct, sixteenth member, working with but alongside its member states.

At the risk of being repetitive, it is worth recalling that the European *Union* is not the European *Community*. The Union is the Community *plus* two intergovernmental pillars that establish the modalities for cooperation in foreign and security policy and justice and home affairs, respectively. The latter were deliberately designed to give the member states a stronger national voice than they have in the Community institutions. An action of the European Union can therefore be the result of measures taken under the EC Treaty or under the intergovernmental pillars of the Treaty on

European Union (which itself includes the EC Treaty). As the first two chapters of this book have made clear in some detail, commercial policy is the preserve of the EC Treaty, while foreign and security policy is covered by the second pillar of the Maastricht Treaty. Yet both (along with every other policy that impinges on the EU's relationships with the rest of the world) are European Union activities.

To the extent that influence is measured by results, the distinctions between measures attributable to the EC Treaty and those carried out jointly under the second and third pillars by countries that are members of the EU are arguably unimportant. The institutional mechanics of how decisions are reached within the EU are of little interest to the beneficiaries or targets of a given policy. A unanimous decision by the Council on reforming the CAP, a majority Council decision affecting single market legislation, or an intergovernmental decision under the CFSP imposing economic sanctions can all have effects on non-EU countries, yet each policy will have been arrived at on the basis of different decisionmaking procedures. What is important is the outcome. Outcomes tend to be judged on their merits, not on their provenance. Development aid may originate from national EU member states' ODA budgets or may flow from the European Development Fund; but as long as it is coordinated under existing EU mechanisms such as Article 130x of the EC Treaty, its impact can be ascribed to the Union as a whole. A successful joint action under the CFSP, painstakingly agreed by the fifteen foreign affairs ministers acting unanimously, is perceived as (and legally is) an action by the Union, in spite of having been formulated on an intergovernmental basis by sovereign states.

Unsuccessful policies (or failure to agree on any policy) have often been used as illustrations of the EU's inability to take urgent or necessary decisions. Recently, the CFSP has been singled out as one area in need of particular overhaul. It has shown itself to be unsuitable as an effective mechanism for responding to crises and even less adept as a vehicle for formulating medium-term proactive policies, for example, in the field of conflict prevention. The EU's failure to intervene effectively in Yugoslavia has become the bête noire of the CFSP's admittedly brief existence, proof if ever it were needed that fifteen sovereign states have too many diverse interests to be able to act in concert in a complex theater with major security implications. Yet the European Union's shortcomings in the face of one of the more intractable problems of the late twentieth century are no worse than those of numerous other actors. None of the EU's more foreign-policy-conscious member states, France or Britain, say, proved able to use its theoretical sovereignty in foreign affairs to propose or implement a solution to the Yugoslav crisis on its own. Nor did any other legitimate foreign policy actor rush to the rescue. Even the United States was initially unwilling to become involved except in the framework of NATO, in which it participated alongside various EU member states.

The European Union, in other words, is not always a *successful* actor in international affairs, but neither are many traditional protagonists, for all their putative unitary decisionmaking structures. To remain with the Yugoslav example, no one can pretend that in the absence of the European Union and its Common Foreign and Security Policy, the war in Croatia and subsequently Bosnia-Herzegovina would somehow have been dealt with more effectively. The worst that can be said is that the CFSP was no more successful than other available foreign policy instruments (i.e., those of the EU's individual member states or Russia or the United States). The best that can be said is that the EU's joint efforts, which included the provision of emergency relief, the sending of monitors, sanctions on Serbia, the appointment of a mediator, the administration of Mostar, use of the WEU in checks on shipping, and a great deal more besides, were certainly an honest attempt at finding a solution. More than that, in numerous areas they made a substantial contribution to alleviating suffering and to preparing the way for the eventual accord reached at Dayton.

In the area of foreign policy, then, the EU acts together or not, as the case may be; but where it does not, its role is not necessarily assumed by one or more of its member states anxious to fill the vacuum. Instead, no action may be taken at all. Sometimes, however, an individual EU member state may attempt to play a unilateral role (for example, in the spring of 1996, France engaged in a round of national diplomacy in an attempt to bring an end to fighting in southern Lebanon between Israel and Hezbollah guerrillas, somewhat to the irritation of its EU partners). Actions like this demonstrate that the member states do not automatically channel their foreign policy through European Union machinery. Particularly in cases where existing national interest survives, the use of CFSP mechanisms may not even be considered. French interests in Chad, the British relationship with China during the handing back of Hong Kong, and Portuguese concerns in respect of East Timor have all been instances of the primacy of national diplomatic efforts over joint action under the CFSP.

All this remains somewhat confusing at times for third countries, who may find themselves dealing with the European Union on certain issues and with individual members of the EU on others. They negotiate with the Commission on trade agreements but find themselves hosting trade delegations from individual member states seeking to conclude contracts or deals on a bilateral basis. ACP countries relate to the EU in the framework of the Lomé convention but continue to have separate and special relationships with the member state with which they once had colonial links. Political dialogue (between the United States and the European Union under the terms of the Transatlantic Declaration, say) may be in addition to, not instead of, similar dialogues with the leaders of individual EU members. Europe as an entity has thus become an *extra* dimension in an already complex web of international relationships still based primarily on state-to-state contacts but increasingly extending to cooperation in international organizations and with (and between) regional groupings.

The Development of the EU's Role as International Actor

The aim of this book has been to show, in practical rather than theoretical terms, that the European Union is a serious actor in international affairs. It has attempted to do so without prejudice to other states or organizations that might claim a similar role. Yet the evidence amassed in these pages has demonstrated that the sheer collective weight and the institutional structure of the EU puts it not only in a class of its own among other regional and international organizations but also ahead of virtually every major state in the world in terms of its influence and impact (with the one obvious exception of the United States). It may not be a superpower (a term that implies the possession of great military power as well as economic strength), but it is certainly a global power in the sense that its actions—and indeed its very existence—have come to have a significant effect far beyond its borders, both by default and intention.

As we have seen, the European Communities of the 1950s were designed for a regional, European role. An early attempt at creating a defense community not only failed but effectively kept political cooperation (and thus foreign and security policy) off the agenda altogether for many years. But the logic of a Common Commercial Policy, the effects of a Common Agricultural Policy, and the need to grapple with the aftermath of its members' colonial pasts soon combined to force the EC to address its role in the wider world. But when did the European Community transform itself from modest actor on the international scene to global power? And how far was its transformation deliberate and how far the result of external factors?

There is no doubt that part of the growth of the EC's international role was incremental. Certainly, as Chapter 1 made clear, the Community's international trade regime had immediate external policy implications; the same can be said for the EEC Treaty's Part Four, which in an era of rapid decolonization led directly to the formalized development cooperation relationships of Yaoundé and Lomé described in Chapter 8. The Common Agricultural Policy, designed to offer Community consumers secure supplies of food and farmers secure incomes, had a surprisingly heavy impact on agricultural producers worldwide and led to some of the earliest trade disputes between Europe and other producing countries. Other policies and events (ranging from the admission of new members to the Community to rationalization of the steel industry) had similar, often unexpected external effects, sometimes bringing the EC into direct conflict with its international partners and competitors. As time went on, the effects of the EC's policies on the outside world became ever more apparent and the Community's deliberate involvement in foreign relations grew, as successive chapters of this book have shown.

Progress may seem to have been slow at the time, but in historical terms the European Community plunged into its international role at almost breakneck speed. Just twelve years after the EEC Treaty came into force, the concept of political cooperation first surfaced. It did so because between 1958 and 1970 (and with the Community's first enlargement then in prospect), the Six had realized that they could no longer afford the luxury of cooperating economically without at least consulting on the foreign policy implications that resulted. Nothing did more to confirm this view than the oil crisis of 1973 and the Community's need to find an appropriate response. A common position on the Middle East—and one that was not necessarily always in sync with that of the United States—came to be one of the first and longest-lasting examples of political cooperation, and a policy to which all the member states have been able to subscribe with a minimum of disagreement right up to the present.

Political cooperation, even in its later institutionalized incarnations as EPC and CFSP, remained the weak link in the EC's external relations armory. At best it was ersatz foreign policy making. But the spirit of cooperation and joint thinking that it inspired carried over into areas that were not technically regarded as foreign policy issues at all, however political they were in their scope. The growing number of economic agreements covering trade and cooperation with countries around the world were all nominally *Community* operations, negotiated by the Commission under EC Treaty provisions. But every such accord required a mandate not from the foreign ministers meeting in political cooperation (i.e., the intergovernmental, non-Community version of the Council) but the foreign ministers sitting as members of the *Council*, an EC institution. And a Council mandate was always a political green light, a signal that the Council considered the aims of the proposed agreement politically sound. The cooperation agreements concluded with the Maghreb and Mashreq countries in the 1970s, designed as they were to improve relations with the Arab world, were never sold as the outcome of political cooperation. Yet they—and every other agreement signed between the Community and third countries or regional groupings—are ultimately the result of foreign policy considerations, even if their origins do not lie formally in the purview of EPC. It is curious that such eminently political acts as the conclusion of international agreements, many of which contain provisions for political dialogue as well as trade and economic measures, should be dealt with under Community rules rather than through EPC or CFSP procedures. That they are is evidence of how diffuse the distinctions are between the EU's external economic relations and its foreign policy as such.

In terms of the time scale involved, the gradual, incremental pace that characterized the EC's evolution into an international actor continued until the mid- to late 1980s. Until then, internal policy changes had been relatively few, although the growing body of Community law did have some external implications. So, too, did the EC's continued expansion (to twelve members by 1986) and its growing economic strength. A series of international events (the "Prague spring," the Middle East conflict, the Soviet invasion of Afghanistan, the situation in Cambodia, problems in ACP countries like Uganda and the Central African Empire, the imposition of martial law in Poland, the growth of international terrorism, etc.) required responses from the Community and got them, albeit sometimes in modest ways. But there was nothing really precipitous to force the EC into a fundamental reassessment of its role or procedures.

Two things changed this. The first was the Single European Act, which, after ratification delays, came into force in mid-1987; the second was the collapse of communism in Central and Eastern Europe (and the subsequent demise of the Soviet Union). The SEA, of course, saw the quasi-institutionalization of EPC. In fact, this change was less than revolutionary, building as it did on existing political cooperation among the member states. It was the other aspect of the SEA, the creation of the 1992 program for a single market, that had by far the more profound effect on the European Community's place in the world. Decried initially as an attempt to construct a "Fortress Europe," it gave rise to a flurry of diplomatic activity as countries around the world attempted to find out from the Commission in Brussels and member states' embassies and Commission offices abroad what 1992 would mean for them. Between 1986 and 1992, the number of states with separate missions accredited to the European Community in Brussels rose substantially.[1] Only gradually were Europe's partners convinced that the single market would offer traders more opportunities than obstacles. But like nothing previously, 1992 became a symbol for the European Community's coming of age. Whether to their profit or loss, countries everywhere had to reevaluate their economic relationships with the EC.

Precisely at the time that Community Europe was embarking on its bold new path toward a single, integrated market of 340 million consumers, the worn-out Europe of Comecon was starting to fall apart. The implications of this were far-reaching, as Chapter 3 has shown. Not only did the new situation oblige the EC to launch its single biggest foreign policy initiative ever in the shape of a massive program of aid and support (institutional, technical, and practical, as well as financial), it also paved the way for an enlargement of the Community to include the Scandinavian countries and Austria. And in the longer term it opened up the prospect of yet a further expansion to include most of the fledgling market economies of Central and Eastern Europe. Again, it wasn't just Europe that was affected by these events. Apart from the obvious impact of the end of the Cold War on the whole international community, there were new concerns in many countries about what the changed situation would mean for their relations with the Community. Countries and regions all over the world with close ties to the EC saw the Twelve becoming increasingly preoccupied with their Central and Eastern European neighbors.

As 1992 approached and the EC's involvement with its neighbors to the east continued to grow, the next big internal shake-up was on the point of realization: the Maastricht Treaty and the transformation of the EC into the EU, followed closely by an enlargement from twelve to fifteen members. Not only did the new Treaty bring with it the promise of a more coordinated and forceful foreign policy (complete, for the first time, with a security dimension), it also heralded yet another fundamental addition to the new Union's responsibilities: Economic and Monetary Union. From a distance the emerging edifice looked impressive indeed: it was a highly integrated economic and now political colossus soon to have 370 million people and the world's largest GNP, organized as a single, frontier-free area functioning as the planet's biggest trading bloc, equipped with an effective foreign policy machine and soon to have a single currency likely to rival or even replace the dollar as the international currency of choice. Seen in these terms, the impressively titled European Union was surely an international force to be reckoned with. So much so that voices were raised around the world appealing to the EU to widen its horizons, recently constrained by its concentration on Central and Eastern Europe, and to reinvolve itself farther afield, in the Mediterranean, in Latin America, in Asia.

The period from 1993 to 1996 saw a flurry of EU activity directed at precisely these "neglected" areas of the world. A succession of strategy papers from the Commission launched a focused campaign leading to a targeted intensification of relations with the EU's principal non-European partners. This was calculated, proactive policymaking, not a reaction to burgeoning crises or a response to external pressures. The results—among others the New Transatlantic Agenda, the Barcelona Declaration, the EU-Mercosur agreement, the Euro-Asian summit in Bangkok—have shown the European Union to be an international actor as never before. Again, these actions were not carried out in the framework of the CFSP; rather, they involved the EU's *institutions,* often with the Commission taking the lead but with the European Council also providing political direction. To return to the question posed at the beginning of this chapter: if there is a distinction to be drawn between the Union and its member states, its relevance is minimal. Whether policy initiatives come from the institutions or from the member states (in the guise of the European Council or intergovernmental agreement in the CFSP), their impact is likely to be the same.

The Future: Sustaining the Momentum

Ten years, therefore, saw the transformation of the EC's recognizable but modest international position in the context of the certainties of the Cold

War, to a qualitatively new role as a global player in a single-superpower world. From 1986, the year of the signature of the Single European Act, to 1996, when the post-Maastricht intergovernmental conference opened in Turin, the European Community had not only undergone a profound internal metamorphosis unlike any in its history, it had also been forced to acknowledge its responsibilities as a global power. Internally grappling with ratification problems related to two treaty reforms, implementation of the 1992 program, the consequences of one enlargement and negotiations for another, reform of the CAP and its own budget, and a great deal more besides, the EU simultaneously faced a growing external agenda. This included a leading role in meeting the challenge of a disintegrating Central and Eastern Europe; playing a crucial part in the Uruguay Round of GATT negotiations; confronting the political, social, and economic demands of its southern neighbors; attempting to deal with a bloody civil war in the former Yugoslavia; and responding to the expectations of its major industrial partners and allies on the one hand and the developing and newly industrialized world on the other. Despite some failures and setbacks, the Union acquitted itself remarkably well.

Nevertheless, the EU's external role depends more than anything else on its own internal integrity. Its emergence as an internationally recognized power coincided with an increase in its size and a new phase in its integration. Its future as a global power can therefore be expected to go hand in hand with its further development over the coming years. The bigger, stronger, and more unified it is, the greater is likely to be its impact elsewhere in the world.

But as the post-Maastricht IGC opened in March 1996, the European Union was in some disarray. The mood of Euro-optimism that had prevailed in the late 1980s had begun to evaporate by the early 1990s. For all its achievements, the Maastricht Treaty on European Union was a tortuously worded compromise, almost totally lacking in the sort of transparency that might have made it appeal to ordinary Europeans. Its ratification by the member states was a long drawn out and acrimonious affair. The Danish people rejected it in the first of two referenda, threatening a collapse of the whole enterprise and forcing their government to return to the negotiating table to hammer out fresh concessions (including an opt-out from the central plank of the Treaty, Economic and Monetary Union). The British, whose government had already opted out of the Social Chapter of the Treaty and negotiated a caveat on EMU entry, watched a bitterly contested ratification battle take place in parliament. The French electorate endorsed the treaty in a referendum by the narrowest of margins, leaving public opinion split down the middle. Last to ratify was Germany, where a legal challenge to the Treaty had forced the government in Bonn to await a ruling from the constitutional court. The debate that emerged during the

Maastricht ratification process and continued afterward was really about fundamentals: how far should integration go? It was a question that divided both the general population and political elites.

The sour mood in the EU was compounded by the generally less than enthusiastic endorsement of membership by the citizens of the four applicant countries that had applied to join the Union. The Norwegians rejected the accession treaty their government had negotiated, and the Swedes and Finns voted in favor by only modest margins. While the Austrians supported accession by a respectable two-thirds majority, polls taken a year later showed that even there support had dwindled dramatically.

It had become clear by the time the 1996 IGC began that there was no consensus for further dramatic reforms. EMU had already had to be put back from 1997 to 1999, the latest possible date stipulated under the Maastricht Treaty. Rising unemployment and a slower than expected recovery from the recession of the early 1990s left people unconvinced of the value or necessity of further European integration. There was talk of creating a "multispeed" Europe, with some countries moving ahead more rapidly than others. But even in the core countries (Germany, France, and Benelux), public opinion seemed generally cool to the idea of new adventures. Even those already in the pipeline, like the single currency, were supported only reluctantly: polls showed that the majority of Germans, for example, would prefer to keep the deutsche mark than switch to the untested *euro*.

Paradoxically, the intergovernmental conference had been called precisely with a view to addressing shortcomings in the Maastricht Treaty.[2] But at the beginning of 1997 it appeared certain that the IGC would yield few results. Instead of clarifying the murky EU Treaty, increasing the democratic control of the European Parliament, or rationalizing the Council's decisionmaking procedures, the most likely outcome is that things will stay much as they are. Nor do other improvements, such as bringing the two intergovernmental pillars into the Community system, extending the scope of European citizenship, or making the battle against unemployment a formal EU goal—all obvious ways of making the European Union both more effective and people-friendly—have much chance of being accepted.

The Commission, in its February 1996 opinion on the IGC,[3] proposed a number of changes to the CFSP. Recognizing that there would be no support among the governments for "communitarizing" the policy—removing it from its position as a separate, intergovernmental pillar and making it subject to the institutional constraints of the Community in the same way as other common policies—the Commission set forth ways to make the CFSP at least more effective in terms of decisionmaking and more able to respond swiftly to crises. These included making qualified majority voting (QMV) the norm in decisionmaking and allowing a limited number of member states to act on behalf of all, as long as no country actually opposed a planned action. The Union's security capability could be strengthened by giving defense ministers a role in the Council and formally incorporating the Western European Union into the EU.

Yet none of these fairly humble proposals look likely to be enacted. The continuing insistence of a majority of member states that the national veto must survive in foreign policy making is to exclude the notion of leadership and threatens to leave the CFSP hobbled. Indeed the need for unanimity in actually voting through any amendments to the CFSP, or for that matter to other parts of the Treaty, is likely to prevent any meaningful adaptations from being made in this or any other area. And in some senses changing the CFSP is less urgent in terms of the EU's position internationally than modernizing certain more fundamental aspects of the Treaty—above all streamlining the heart of the decisionmaking process itself.

The ability of the European Union to operate in an increasingly complex economic, political, and international environment depends on its facility in taking decisions. As the number of member states has increased and the variety of their viewpoints proliferated, so the difficulty in reaching consensual decisions has similarly grown. While much of the EU's routine legislative work is already dealt with under QMV and is subject to real parliamentary control under the cooperation or co-decision procedures, member states still possess an individual veto in several key areas (under the EC Treaty in areas of transport, competition, and economic and monetary policy, as well as in the non-EC pillars of foreign and security policy and justice and home affairs). But the unanimity rule also applies, for example, to decisions relating to EC Treaty Article 238 on association agreements; it is this article that allowed Greece to hold up progress under the association agreement with Turkey and permitted Spain and Portugal to insist on an economic quid pro quo (in the shape of the cohesion fund) for allowing the Europe agreements to go ahead in the early 1990s.

While a generalized ban on use of the veto in decisionmaking would already be valuable today in promoting more rapid and effective EU action, it will be virtually indispensable in the future. There were in 1997 eleven European countries waiting to join the Union. Current policy is to give fast-track treatment to at least four or five of the applicants,[4] possibly bringing EU membership to twenty by the year 2001 or 2002. This policy has far-reaching internal and external implications. If it is difficult today to reach consensus on legislative decisions, foreign policy actions, joint positions in international organizations or multilateral trade fora, or initiatives to combat terrorism or narcotics trafficking, how much more complex will it become with twenty members around the table, let alone an eventual twenty-five or more? And if the current fifteen governments cannot agree to widen the scope of qualified majority voting, how likely is it that twenty or twenty-five governments will one day be able to do so?

The risk now is that an inability to agree on substantive changes in decisionmaking procedures during the 1996–1997 IGC, coupled with a further enlargement of the Union at the beginning of the twenty-first century, will combine to reduce the EU's role as an international actor, not enhance it. First, an enlarged EU, though constituting an even wider market, will also be a Union less able to offer help to needy third countries, as its new, poorer members absorb budgetary resources that might otherwise have been targeted for external use. Second, in the absence of streamlined decisionmaking procedures, an enlarged EU still working on the basis of unanimity will find it next to impossible to agree on common foreign policy measures except in the most mundane of matters. Third, and ultimately the most grave, enlarging the Union at a time when disaccord on a range of fundamental issues is rife among existing members is likely to hasten the trend, already visible, toward a multispeed, multilayered Europe.

The economic and numerical growth of the European Union has so far gone hand in hand with closer integration. But if a future, enlarged EU breaks up into core, intermediate, and peripheral groups—divided by a "common" currency that not all are economically or politically able to adopt, split between rich and poor, riddled with opt-outs, exemptions, and transitional periods—then the vision of an "ever-closer union" will be dead. The EU will remain important as a set of global statistics (collectively the biggest economy, trader, investor, and so on) for some time to come but is likely to return to being a reactive rather than a proactive force. As Asia consolidates its position as an ascendant region, as China pulls into the first rank of world economic powers, as growth and integration in Latin America turn it into a serious player in the world economy, the European Union risks slipping from global to regional power.

Is there an alternative scenario? Of course. It is that the European Union's member states will continue to build on what they have achieved, both at home and abroad. They will agree to take the tough decisions necessary to improve cooperation among themselves. They will move to the next enlargement only after they have set in place the appropriate institutional machinery and when the economic as well as political factors are right. And they will decide that in an increasingly interdependent world, their collective best bet is to work together on the basis of pooled sovereignty, not separately as minipowers. A Europe able to play an effective international role presupposes an integrated Europe at peace with itself. The world will not have to wait long to find out in which direction the European Union has decided to go.

Notes

1. This was due in part, of course, to the coming into being of a host of new states in the shape of the former Soviet republics and the establishment of diplomatic relations with all the countries of Central and Eastern Europe. But a number of other countries that had formerly had a single embassy in Brussels accredited

to Belgium and the EC jointly (and sometimes to other countries as well) established separate missions accredited to the Community alone.

2. The Maastricht Treaty itself provided for the review conference to take place in 1996 (Article N[2] of the Treaty on European Union).

3. Commission, "Reinforcing Political Union and Preparing for Enlargement," *Official Journal* C 096, 1 April 1996, p. 12.

4. Cyprus, the Czech Republic, Hungary, Poland, and possibly Slovenia.

Appendix 1

Key Trade Provisions of the EC Treaty

Article 110

By establishing a customs union between themselves Member States aim to contribute, in the common interest, to the harmonious development of world trade, the progressive abolition of restrictions on international trade and the lowering of customs barriers.

The common commercial policy shall take into account the favourable effect which the abolition of customs duties between Member States may have on the increase in the competitive strength of undertakings in those States.

Article 113

1. The common commercial policy shall be based on uniform principles, particularly in regard to changes in tariff rates, the conclusion of tariff and trade agreements, the achievement of uniformity in measures of liberalisation, export policy and measures to protect trade such as those to be taken in case of dumping or subsidies.

2. The Commission shall submit proposals to the Council for implementing the common commercial policy.

3. Where agreements with one or more States or international organizations need to be negotiated, the Commission shall make recommendations to the Council, which shall authorize the Commission to open the necessary negotiations.

The Commission shall conduct these negotiations in consultation with a special committee appointed by the Council to assist the Commission in this task and within the framework of such directives as the Council may issue to it.

The relevant provisions of Article 228 shall apply.

4. In exercising the powers conferred upon it by this Article, the Council shall act by a qualified majority.

Article 228

1. Where this Treaty provides for the conclusion of agreements between the Community and one or more States or international organizations, the Commission shall make recommendations to the Council, which shall authorize the Commission to open the necessary negotiations. The Commission shall conduct these negotiations in consultation with special committees appointed by the Council to assist it in this task and within the framework of such directives as the Council may issue to it. In exercising the powers conferred upon it by this paragraph, the Council shall act by a qualified majority, except in the cases provided for in the second sentence of paragraph 2, for which it shall act unanimously.

2. Subject to the powers vested in the Commission in this field, the agreements shall be concluded by the Council, acting by a qualified majority on a proposal from the Commission. The Council shall act unanimously when the agreement covers a field for which unanimity is required for the adoption of internal rules, and for the agreements referred to in Article 238.

3. The Council shall conclude agreements after consulting the European Parliament, except for the agreements referred to in Article 113(3), including cases where the agreement covers a field for which the procedure referred to in Article 189b or that referred to in Article 189c is required for the adoption of internal rules. The European Parliament shall deliver its Opinion within a time limit which the Council may lay down according to the urgency of the matter. In the absence of an Opinion within that time limit, the Council may act.

By way of derogation from the previous subparagraph, agreements referred to in Article 238, other agreements establishing a specific institutional framework by organizing cooperation procedures, agreements having important budgetary implications for the Community and agreements entailing amendment of an act adopted under the procedure referred to in Article 189b shall be concluded after the assent of the European Parliament has been obtained.

The Council and the European Parliament may, in an urgent situation, agree upon a time limit for the assent.

4. When concluding an agreement, the Council may, by way of derogation from paragraph 2, empower the Commission to approve modifications on behalf of the Community where the agreement provides for them to be adopted by a simplified procedure or by a body set up by the agreement; it may attach specific conditions to such empowerment.

5. When the Council envisages concluding an agreement which calls for amendments to this Treaty, the amendments must first be adopted in accordance with the procedure laid down in Article N of the Treaty on European Union.

6. The Council, the Commission or a Member State may obtain the opinion of the Court of Justice as to whether an agreement envisaged is compatible with the provisions of this Treaty. Where the opinion of the Court of Justice is adverse, the agreement may enter into force only in accordance with Article N of the Treaty on European Union.

7. Agreements concluded under the conditions set out in this Article shall be binding on the institutions of the Community and on Member States.

Article 228a

Where it is provided, in a common position or in a joint action adopted according to the provisions of the Treaty on European Union relating to the common foreign and security policy, for an action by the Community to interrupt or to reduce, in part or completely, economic relations with one or more third countries, the Council shall take the necessary urgent measures. The Council shall act by a qualified majority on a proposal from the Commission.

Article 235

If action by the Community should prove necessary to attain, in the course of the operation of the common market, one of the objectives of the Community and this Treaty has not provided the necessary powers, the Council shall, acting unanimously on a proposal from the Commission and after consulting the European Parliament, take the appropriate measures.

Article 238

The Community may conclude with one or more States or international organizations agreements establishing an association involving reciprocal rights and obligations, common action and special procedures.

Appendix 2

Title III, Single European Act

Treaty Provisions on European Cooperation in the Sphere of Foreign Policy

Article 30

1. The High Contracting Parties, being members of the European Communities, shall endeavour jointly to formulate and implement a European foreign policy.

2. (a) The High Contracting Parties undertake to inform and consult each other on any foreign policy matters of general interest so as to ensure that their combined influence is exercised as effectively as possible through coordination, the convergence of their positions and the implementation of joint action.

(b) Consultations shall take place before the High Contracting Parties decide on their final position.

(c) In adopting its positions and in its national measures each High Contracting Party shall take full account of the positions of the other partners and shall give due consideration to the desirability of adopting and implementing common European positions.

In order to increase their capacity for joint action in the foreign policy field, the High Contracting Parties shall ensure that common principles and objectives are gradually developed and defined.

The determination of common positions shall constitute a point of reference for the policies of the High Contracting Parties.

(d) The High Contracting Parties shall endeavour to avoid any action or position which impairs their effectiveness as a cohesive force in international relations or within international organizations.

3. (a) The Ministers for Foreign Affairs and a member of the Commission shall meet at least four times a year within the framework of European Political Cooperation. They may also discuss foreign policy

matters within the framework of Political Cooperation on the occasion of meetings of the Council of the European Communities.

(b) The Commission shall be fully associated with the proceedings of Political Cooperation.

(c) In order to ensure the swift adoption of common positions and the implementation of joint action, the High Contracting Parties shall, as far as possible, refrain from impeding the formation of a consensus and the joint action which this could produce.

4. The High Contracting Parties shall ensure that the European Parliament is closely associated with the European Political Cooperation. To that end the Presidency shall regularly inform the European Parliament of the foreign policy issues which are being examined within the framework of Political Cooperation and shall ensure that the views of the European Parliament are duly taken into consideration.

5. The external policies of the European Community and the policies agreed in European Political Cooperation must be consistent.

The Presidency and the Commission, each within its own sphere of competence, shall have special responsibility for ensuring that such consistency is sought and maintained.

6. (a) The High Contracting Parties consider that closer cooperation on questions of European security would contribute in an essential way to the development of a European identity in external policy matters. They are ready to coordinate their positions more closely on the political and economic aspects of security.

(b) The High Contracting Parties are determined to maintain the technological and industrial conditions necessary for their security. They shall work to that end both at national level and, where appropriate, within the framework of the competent institutions and bodies.

(c) Nothing in this Title shall impede closer cooperation in the field of security between certain of the High Contracting Parties within the framework of the Western European Union or the Atlantic Alliance.

7. (a) In international institutions and at international conferences which they attend, the High Contracting Parties shall endeavour to adopt common positions on the subjects covered by this Title.

(b) In international institutions and at international conferences in which not all the High Contracting Parties participate, those who do participate shall take full account of positions agreed in European Political Cooperation.

8. The High Contracting Parties shall organize a political dialogue with third countries and regional groupings whenever they deem it necessary.

9. The High Contracting Parties and the Commission, through mutual assistance and information, shall intensify cooperation between their representations accredited to third countries and to international organizations.

10. (a) The Presidency of European Political Cooperation shall be held by the High Contracting Party which holds the Presidency of the Council of the European Communities.

(b) The Presidency shall be responsible for initiating action and coordinating and representing the positions of the Member States in relations with third countries in respect of European Political Cooperation activities. It shall also be responsible for the management of Political Cooperation and in particular for drawing up the timetable of meetings and for convening and organizing meetings.

(c) The Political Directors shall meet regularly in the Political Committee in order to give the necessary impetus, maintain the continuity of European Political Cooperation and prepare Ministers' discussions.

(d) The Political Committee or, if necessary, a ministerial meeting shall convene within forty-eight hours at the request of at least three Member States.

(e) The European Correspondents' Group shall be responsible, under the direction of the Political Committee, for monitoring the implementation of European Political Cooperation and for studying general organizational problems.

(f) Working Groups shall meet as directed by the Political Committee.

(g) A Secretariat based in Brussels shall assist the Presidency in preparing and implementing the activities of European Political Cooperation and in administrative matters. It shall carry out its duties under the authority of the Presidency.

11. As regards privileges and immunities, the members of the European Political Cooperation Secretariat shall be treated in the same way as members of the diplomatic missions of the High Contracting Parties based in the same place as the Secretariat.

12. Five years after the entry into force of this Act the High Contracting Parties shall examine whether any revision of Title III is required.

Appendix 3

Title V, Treaty on European Union

Provisions on a Common Foreign and Security Policy

Article J

A common foreign and security policy is hereby established which shall be governed by the following provisions.

Article J.1

1. The Union and its Member States shall define and implement a common foreign and security policy, governed by the provisions of the Title and covering all areas of foreign and security policy.

2. The objectives of the common foreign and security policy shall be:

- to safeguard the common values, fundamental interests and independence of the Union;
- to strengthen the security of the Union and its Member States in all ways;
- to preserve peace and strengthen international security, in accordance with the principles of the United Nations Charter as well as the principles of the Helsinki Final Act and the objectives of the Paris Charter;
- to promote international cooperation;
- to develop and consolidate democracy and the rule of law, and respect for human rights and fundamental freedoms.

3. The Union shall pursue these objectives:

- by establishing systematic cooperation between Member States in the conduct of policy, in accordance with Article J.2;
- by gradually implementing, in accordance with Article J.3, joint action in the areas in which the Member States have important interests in common.

4. The Member States shall support the Union's external and security policy actively and unreservedly in a spirit of loyalty and mutual solidarity. They shall refrain from any action which is contrary to the interests of the Union or likely to impair its effectiveness as a cohesive force in international relations. The Council shall ensure that these principles are complied with.

Article J.2

1. Member States shall inform and consult one another within the Council on any matter of foreign and security policy of general interest in order to ensure that their combined influence is exerted as effectively as possible by means of concerted and convergent action.

2. Whenever it deems it necessary, the Council shall define a common position.

Member States shall ensure that their national policies conform on the common positions.

3. Member States shall coordinate their action in international organizations and at international conferences. They shall uphold the common positions in such fora.

In international organizations and at international conferences where not all the Member States participate, those which do take part shall uphold the common positions.

Article J.3

The procedure for adopting joint action in matters covered by foreign and security policy shall be the following:

1. The Council shall decide, on the basis of general guidelines from the European Council, that a matter should be the subject of joint action.

Whenever the Council decides on the principle of joint action, it shall lay down the specific scope, the Union's general and specific objectives in carrying out such action, if necessary its duration, and the means, procedures and conditions for its implementation.

2. The Council shall, when adopting the joint action and at any stage during its development, define those matters on which decisions are to be taken by a qualified majority.

Where the Council is required to act by a qualified majority pursuant to the preceding subparagraph, the votes of its members shall be weighted in accordance with Article 148(2) of the Treaty establishing the European Community, and for their adoption, acts of the Council shall require at least fifty-four votes in favor, cast by at least eight members.

3. If there is a change in circumstances having a substantial effect on a question subject to joint action, the Council shall review the principles and objectives of that action and take the necessary decisions. As long as the Council has not acted, the joint action shall stand.

4. Joint actions shall commit the Member States in the positions they adopt and in the conduct of their activity.

5. Whenever there is any plan to adopt a national position or take national action pursuant to a joint action, information shall be provided in time to allow, if necessary, for prior consultations within the Council. The obligation to provide prior information shall not apply to measures which are merely a national transposition of Council decisions.

6. In cases of imperative need arising from changes in the situation and failing a Council decision, Member States may take the necessary measures as a matter of urgency having regard to the general objectives of the joint action. The Member State concerned shall inform the Council immediately of any such measures.

7. Should there be any major difficulties in implementing a joint action, a Member State shall refer them to the Council which shall discuss them and seek appropriate solutions. Such solutions shall not run counter to the objectives of the joint action or impair its effectiveness.

Article J.4

1. The common foreign and security policy shall include all questions related to the security of the Union, including the eventual framing of a common defence policy, which might in time lead to a common defence.

2. The Union requests the Western European Union (WEU), which is an integral part of the development of the Union, to elaborate and implement decisions and actions of the Union which have defence implications. The Council shall, in agreement with the institutions of the WEU, adopt the necessary practical arrangements.

3. Issues having defence implications dealt with under this Article shall not be subject to the procedures set out in Article J.3.

4. The policy of the Union in accordance with this Article shall not prejudice the specific character of the security and defence policy of certain Member States and shall respect the obligations of certain Member States under the North Atlantic Treaty and be compatible with the common security and defence policy established within that framework.

5. The provisions of this Article shall not prevent the development of closer cooperation between two or more Member States on a bilateral level, in the framework of the WEU and the Atlantic Alliance, provided such cooperation does not run counter to or impede that provided for in this Title.

6. With a view to furthering the objective of this Treaty, and having in view the date of 1998 in the context of Article XII of the Brussels Treaty, the provisions of this Article may be revised as provided for in Article N(2) on the basis of a report to be presented in 1996 by the Council to the European Council, which shall include an evaluation of the progress made and the experience gained until then.

Article J.5

1. The Presidency shall represent the Union in matters coming within the common foreign and security policy.

2. The Presidency shall be responsible for the implementation of common measures; in that capacity it shall in principle express the position of the Union in international organizations and international conferences.

3. In the tasks referred to in paragraphs 1 and 2, the Presidency shall be assisted if needs be by the previous and next Member States to hold the Presidency. The Commission shall be fully associated in these tasks.

4. Without prejudice to Article J.2(3) and Article J.3(4), Member States represented in international organizations or international conferences where not all the Member States participate shall keep the latter informed of any matter of common interest.

Member States which are also members of the United Nations Security Council will concert and keep the other Member States fully informed. Member States which are permanent members of the Security Council will, in the execution of their functions, ensure the defence of the positions and the interests of the Union, without prejudice to their responsibilities under the provisions of the United Nations Charter.

Article J.6

The diplomatic and consular missions of the Member States and the Commission Delegations in third countries and international conferences, and their representations to international organizations, shall cooperate in ensuring that the common positions and common measures adopted by the Council are complied with and implemented.

They shall step up cooperation by exchanging information, carrying out joint assessments and contributing to the implementation of the provisions referred to in Article 8c of the Treaty establishing the European Community.

Article J.7

The Presidency shall consult the European Parliament on the main aspects and the basic choices of the common foreign and security policy and shall ensure that the views of the European Parliament are duly taken into consideration. The European Parliament shall be kept regularly informed by the Presidency and the Commission of the development of the Union's foreign and security policy.

The European Parliament may ask questions of the Council or make recommendations to it. It shall hold an annual debate on progress in implementing the common foreign and security policy.

Article J.8

1. The European Council shall define the principles of and general guidelines for the common foreign and security policy.

2. The Council shall take the decisions necessary for defining and implementing the common foreign and security policy on the basis of the general guidelines adopted by the European Council. It shall ensure the unity, consistency and effectiveness of action by the Union.

The Council shall act unanimously, except for procedural questions and in the case referred to in Article J.3(2).

3. Any Member State or the Commission may refer to the Council any question relating to the common foreign policy and may submit proposals to the Council.

4. In cases requiring a rapid decision, the Presidency, of its own motion, or at the request of the Commission or a Member State, shall convene an extraordinary Council meeting within forty-eight hours or, in an emergency, within a shorter period.

5. Without prejudice to Article 151 of the Treaty establishing the European Community, a Political Committee consisting of Political Directors shall monitor the international situation in the areas covered by common foreign and security policy and contribute to the definition of policies by delivering opinions to the Council at the request of the Council or on its own initiative. It shall also monitor the implementation of agreed policies, without prejudice to the responsibility of the Presidency and the Commission.

Article J.9

The Commission shall be fully associated with the work carried out in the common foreign and security policy field.

Article J.10

On the occasion of any review of the security provisions under Article J.4, the Conference which is convened to that effect shall also examine whether any other amendments need to be made to provisions relating to the common foreign and security policy.

Article J.11

1. The provisions referred to in Articles 137, 138, 139 to 142, 146, 147, 150 to 153, 157 to 163 and 217 of the Treaty establishing the European Community shall apply to the provisions relating to the areas referred to in this Title.

2. Administrative expenditure which the provisions relating to the areas referred to in this Title entail for the institutions shall be charged to the budget of the European Communities.

The Council may also:

- either decide unanimously that operational expenditure to which the implementation of those provisions gives rise is to be charged to the budget of the European Communities; in that event, the budgetary procedure laid down in the Treaty establishing the European Community shall be applicable;
- or determine that such expenditure shall be charged to the Member States, where appropriate in accordance with a scale to be decided.

Appendix 4

The New Transatlantic Agenda

We, the United States of America and the European Union, affirm our conviction that the ties which bind our people are as strong today as they have been for the past half century. For over fifty years, the transatlantic partnership has been the leading force for peace and prosperity for ourselves and for the world. Together, we helped transform adversaries into allies and dictatorships into democracies. Together, we built institutions and patterns of cooperation that ensured our security and economic strength. These are epic achievements.

Today we face new challenges at home and abroad. To meet them, we must further strengthen and adapt the partnership that has served us so well. Domestic challenges are not an excuse to turn inward; we can learn from each other's experiences and build new transatlantic bridges. We must first of all seize the opportunity presented by Europe's historic transformation to consolidate democracy and free-market economies throughout the continent.

We share a common strategic vision of Europe's future security. Together, we have charted a course for ensuring continuing peace in Europe into the next century. We are committed to the construction of a new European security architecture in which the North Atlantic Treaty Organisation, the European Union, the Western European Union, the Organisation for Security and Cooperation in Europe and the Council of Europe have complementary and mutually reinforcing roles to play.

We reaffirm the indivisibility of transatlantic security. NATO remains, for its members, the centrepiece of transatlantic security, providing the indispensable link between North America and Europe. Further adaptation of the Alliance's political and military structures to reflect both the full spectrum of its roles and the development of the emerging European Security and Defence Identity will strengthen the European pillar of the Alliance.

As to the accession of new members to NATO and to the EU, these processes, autonomous but complementary, should contribute significantly to the extension of security, stability and prosperity in the whole of Europe. Furthering the work of Partnership for Peace and the North Atlantic Cooperation Council and establishing a security partnership between NATO and Russia and between NATO and Ukraine will lead to unprecedented cooperation on security issues.

We are strengthening the OSCE so that it can fulfil its potential to prevent destabilising regional conflicts and advance the prospect of peace, security, prosperity, and democracy for all.

Increasingly, our common security is further enhanced by strengthening and reaffirming the ties between the European Union and the United States within the existing network of relationships which join us together.

Our economic relationship sustains our security and increases our prosperity. We share the largest two-way trade and investment relationship in the world. We bear a special responsibility to lead multilateral efforts toward a more open world system of trade and investment. Our cooperation has made possible every global trade agreement, from the Kennedy Round to the Uruguay Round. Through the G7, we work to stimulate global growth. And at the Organisation for Economic Cooperation and Development, we are developing strategies to overcome structural unemployment and adapt to demographic change.

We are determined to create a New Transatlantic Marketplace, which will expand trade and investment opportunities and multiply jobs on both sides of the Atlantic. This initiative will also contribute to the dynamism of the global economy.

At the threshold of a new century, there is a new world to shape—full of opportunities but with challenges no less critical than those faced by previous generations. These challenges can be met and opportunities fully realised only by the whole international community working together. We will work with others bilaterally, at the United Nations and in other multilateral fora.

We are determined to reinforce our political and economic partnership as a powerful force for good in the world. To this end, we will build on the extensive consultations established by the 1990 Transatlantic Declaration and the conclusions of our June 1995 Summit and move to common action.

Today we adopt a New Transatlantic Agenda based on a Framework for Action with four major goals:

Promoting peace and stability, democracy and development around the world. Together, we will work for an increasingly stable and prosperous Europe; foster democracy and economic reform in Central and Eastern Europe as well as in Russia, Ukraine and other new independent states; secure peace in the Middle East; advance human rights; promote non-proliferation and cooperate on development and humanitarian assistance.

Responding to global challenges. Together, we will fight international crime, drug-trafficking and terrorism; address the needs of refugees and displaced persons; protect the environment and combat disease.

Contributing to the expansion of world trade and closer economic relations. Together, we will strengthen the multilateral trading system and take concrete, practical steps to promote closer economic relations between us.

Building bridges across the Atlantic. Together, we will work with our business people, scientists, educators and others to improve communication and to ensure that future generations remain as committed as we are to developing a full and equal partnership.

Within this Framework, we have developed an extensive Joint EU/U.S. Action Plan. We will give special priority between now and our next Summit to the following actions:

I. Promoting Peace and Stability, Democracy and Development Around the World

We pledge to work boldly and rapidly, together and with other partners, to implement the peace, to assist recovery of the war-ravaged regions of the former Yugoslavia and to support economic and political reform and new democratic institutions. We will cooperate to ensure: (1) respect for human rights, for the rights of minorities and for the rights of refugees and displaced persons, in particular the right of return; (2) respect for the work of the War Crimes Tribunal, established by the United Nations Security Council, in order to ensure international criminal accountability; (3) the establishment of a framework for free and fair elections in Bosnia-Herzegovina as soon as conditions permit; and (4) the implementation of the agreed process for arms control, disarmament and confidence-building measures. While continuing to provide humanitarian assistance, we will contribute to the task of reconstruction, subject to the implementation of the provisions of the peace settlement plan, in the context of the widest possible burden-sharing with other donors and taking advantage of the experience of international institutions, of the European Commission and of all relevant bilateral donors in the coordination mechanism.

We will support the countries of Central and Eastern Europe in their efforts to restructure their economies and strengthen their democratic and market institutions. Their commitment to democratic systems of government, respect for minorities, human rights, market-oriented economies and good relations with neighbors will facilitate their integration into our institutions. We are taking steps to intensify our cooperation aimed at sharing information, coordinating assistance programs and developing common actions, protecting the environment and securing the safety of their nuclear power stations.

We are determined to reinforce our cooperation to consolidate democracy and stability in Russia, Ukraine and other new independent states. We are committed to working with them in strengthening democratic institutions and market reforms, in protecting the environment, in securing the safety of their nuclear power stations and in promoting their integration into the international economy. An enduring and stable security framework for Europe must include these nations. We intend to continue building a close partnership with a democratic Russia. An independent, democratic, stable and nuclear weapons–free Ukraine will contribute to security and stability in Europe; we will cooperate to support Ukraine's democratic and economic reforms.

We will support the Turkish Government's efforts to strengthen democracy and advance economic reforms in order to promote Turkey's further integration into the transatlantic community.

We will work toward a resolution of the Cyprus question, taking into account the prospective accession of Cyprus to the European Union. We will support the UN Secretary General's Mission of Good Offices and encourage dialogue between and with the Cypriot communities.

We reaffirm our commitment to the achievement of a just, lasting and comprehensive peace in the Middle East. We will build on the recent successes in the Peace Process, including the bold steps taken by Jordan and Israel, through concerted efforts to support agreements already concluded and to expand the circle of peace. Noting the important milestone reached with the signing of the Israeli-Palestinian Interim Agreement, we will play an active role at the Conference for Economic Assistance to the Palestinians, will support the Palestinian elections and will work ambitiously to improve the access we both give to products from the West Bank and the Gaza Strip. We will encourage and support the regional parties in implementing the conclusions of the Amman Summit. We will also continue our efforts to promote peace between Israel, Lebanon and Syria. We will actively seek the dismantling of the Arab boycott of Israel.

We pledge to work together more closely in our preventive and crisis diplomacy; to respond effectively to humanitarian emergencies; to promote sustainable development and the building of democratic societies; and to support human rights.

We have agreed to coordinate, cooperate and act jointly in development and humanitarian assistance activities. To this end, we will establish a High-Level Consultative Group to review progress of existing efforts, to assess policies and priorities and to identify projects and regions for the further strengthening of cooperation.

We will increase cooperation in developing a blueprint for UN economic and social reform. We will cooperate to find urgently needed solutions to the financial crisis of the UN system. We are determined to keep our commitments, including our financial obligations. At the same time, the UN must direct its resources to the highest priorities and must reform in order to meet its fundamental goals.

We will provide support to the Korean Peninsula Energy Development Organisation (KEDO), underscoring our shared desire to resolve important proliferation challenges throughout the world.

II. Responding to Global Challenges

We are determined to take new steps in our common battle against the scourges of international crime, drug-trafficking and terrorism. We commit ourselves to active, practical cooperation between the U.S. and the future European Police Office, EUROPOL. We will jointly support and contribute to ongoing training programs and institutions for crime-fighting officials in Central and Eastern Europe, Russia, Ukraine, other new independent states and other parts of the globe.

We will work together to strengthen multilateral efforts to protect the global environment and to develop environmental policy strategies for sustainable world-wide growth. We will coordinate our negotiating positions on major global environmental issues, such as climate change, ozone layer depletion, persistent organic pollutants, desertification and erosion and contaminated soils. We are undertaking coordinated initiatives to disseminate environmental technologies and to reduce the public health risks from hazardous substances, in particular from exposure to lead. We will strengthen our bilateral cooperation on chemicals, biotechnology and air pollution issues.

We are committed to develop and implement an effective global early warning system and response network for new and re-emerging communicable diseases such as AIDS and the Ebola virus, and to increase training and professional exchanges in this area. Together, we call on other nations to join us in more effectively combating such diseases.

III. Contributing to the Expansion of World Trade and Closer Economic Relations

We have a special responsibility to strengthen the multilateral trading system, to support the World Trade Organisation and to lead the way in opening markets to trade and investment.

We will contribute to the expansion of world trade by fully implementing our Uruguay Round commitments, work for the completion of the unfinished business by the agreed timetables and encourage a successful and substantive outcome for the Singapore WTO Ministerial Meeting in December 1996. In this context we will explore the possibility of agreeing on a mutually satisfactory package of tariff reductions on industrial products, and we will consider which, if any, Uruguay Round obligations on tariffs can be implemented on an accelerated basis. In view of the importance of the information society, we are launching a specific exercise in order to attempt to conclude an information technology agreement.

We will work together for the successful conclusion of a Multilateral Agreement on Investment at the OECD that espouses strong principles on international investment liberalisation and protection. Meanwhile, we will work to develop discussion of the issue with our partners at the WTO. We will address in appropriate fora problems where trade intersects with concerns for the environment, internationally recognised labour standards and competition policy. We will cooperate in creating additional trading opportunities, bilaterally and throughout the world, in conformity with our WTO commitments.

Without detracting from our cooperation in multilateral fora, we will create a New Transatlantic Marketplace by progressively reducing or eliminating barriers that hinder the flow of goods, services and capital between us. We will carry out a joint study on ways of facilitating trade in goods and services and further reducing or eliminating tariff and nontariff barriers.

We will strengthen regulatory cooperation, in particular by encouraging regulatory agencies to give a high priority to cooperation with their respective transatlantic counterparts, so as to address technical and nontariff barriers to trade resulting from divergent regulatory processes. We aim to conclude an agreement on mutual recognition of conformity assessment (which includes certification and testing procedures) for certain sectors as soon as possible. We will continue the ongoing work in several sectors and identify others for further work.

We will endeavour to conclude by the end of 1996 a customs cooperation and mutual assistance agreement between the European Community and the U.S.

To allow our people to take full advantage of newly developed information technology and services, we will work toward the realisation of a Transatlantic Information Society.

Given the overarching importance of job creation, we pledge to cooperate in the follow-up to the Detroit Jobs Conference and to the G7 Summit initiative. We look forward to further cooperation in the run up to the G7 Jobs Conference in France, at the next G7 Summit in the Summer of 1996 and in other fora such as the OECD. We will establish a joint working group on employment and labour-related issues.

IV. Building Bridges Across the Atlantic

We recognise the need to strengthen and broaden public support for our partnership. To that end, we will seek to deepen the commercial, social, cultural, scientific and educational ties among our people. We pledge to nurture in present and future generations the mutual understanding and sense of shared purpose that has been the hallmark of the post-war period.

We will not be able to achieve these ambitious goals without the backing of our respective business communities. We will support, and encourage the development of, the transatlantic business relationship, as an integral part of our wider efforts to strengthen our bilateral dialogue. The successful conference of EU and U.S. business leaders which took place in Seville on 10/11 November 1995 was an important step in this direction. A number of its recommendations have already been incorporated into our Action Plan and we will consider concrete follow-up to others.

We will actively work to reach a new comprehensive EC-U.S. science and technology cooperation agreement by 1997.

We believe that the recent EC/U.S. Agreement on Cooperation in Education and Vocational Training can act as a catalyst for a broad spectrum of innovative cooperative activities of direct benefit to students and teachers. We will examine ways to increase private support for educational exchanges, including scholarship and internship programs. We will work to introduce new technologies into classrooms, linking educational establishments in the EU with those in the U.S. and will encourage teaching of each other's languages, history and culture.

Parliamentary links

We attach great importance to enhanced parliamentary links. We will consult parliamentary leaders on both sides of the Atlantic regarding consultative mechanisms, including those building on existing institutions, to discuss matters related to our transatlantic partnership.

Implementing our Agenda

The New Transatlantic Agenda is a comprehensive statement of the many areas for our common action and cooperation. We have entrusted the Senior Level Group to oversee work on this Agenda and particularly the priority actions we have identified. We will use our regular Summits to measure progress and to update and revise our priorities.

For the last fifty years, the transatlantic relationship has been central to the security and prosperity of our people. Our aspirations for the future must surpass our achievements in the past.

Signed in Madrid by
Presidents Clinton, Gonzalez, and Santer,
3 December 1995

Appendix 5

Joint Political Declaration on Canada-EU Relations

Mindful of the ties of history, tradition, culture and kinship that bind us, and of our community of values we, Canada and the European Union, agree to further enhance our co-operation in pursuit of common objectives and on the basis of deeply-held, shared, principles. This joint endeavour is given special meaning by the trading relationship that has characterised the transatlantic region since the age of discovery, and by a commitment to common security and democratic values that have led Canadians and Europeans to join in defence of freedom and democracy in Europe and elsewhere. Our deep attachment to democracy and the rule of law, our shared commitment to the protection of human rights, and our promotion of free market economies, the 1976 Framework Agreement and the 1990 Declaration on Canada-EC Relations, all of these give special meaning to the actions we will undertake together. In this context, we may associate all interested participants, including the Canadian provinces and other subnational entities in their respective areas of competence, in developing transatlantic contacts and in implementing the Joint Action Plan.

The transatlantic community benefits from a long tradition of co-operation in international security and defence. In view of the new security environment on the European continent, we are committed to the construction of a European security architecture in which the North Atlantic Treaty Organisation, the European Union, the Western European Union, the Organisation for Security and Co-operation in Europe and the Council of Europe have complementary and mutually reinforcing roles to play.

We will co-operate actively to give new impetus to democratic development, good governance, the rule of law, and human rights. Preventive diplomacy, peace-keeping and peace-building will receive increased attention in the future. We will co-operate closely on the former Yugoslavia. We will jointly strive to rebuild a viable civil society in this war-torn region and to create the conditions necessary for a lasting peace.

On the basis of our shared experience in assisting the new democracies of Central and Eastern Europe, Russia, Ukraine and other NIS, we will work together seeking to entrench stability, democracy, free markets and economic growth in the region.

We will take new steps to enhance our collaboration in all appropriate fora dealing with arms control and the non-proliferation of weapons of mass destruction. In the area of conventional arms control, including the objective of eliminating anti-personnel land-mines, we have agreed to make a special effort. In response to the challenges posed by the threats to global security, and the transnational impact of global trends, we will enhance co-operation to deal better with issues such as environmental degradation, nuclear safety, uncontrolled migration, terrorism and international crime. We will seek to enlist the support of other members of the UN to promote effective international regimes wherever needed.

Recalling the priority we attach to development aid, notably with respect to the least developed countries, we agree to reinforce our coordination in multilateral fora and cooperate more actively at the bilateral level.

We will promote economic prosperity by adopting measures to strengthen our trading relationship and increase business-to-business contacts and give priority to resolving pending bilateral trade disputes and to enhancing the development of bilateral trade flows. In doing so, we will emphasize co-operation and the rules-based resolution of disputes as guiding principles. Our focus will be on practical results in reducing and removing barriers to trade. We will also work closely in the World Trade Organisation in an effort to open new markets and increase prosperity.

In addition to the common approach between Canada and the European Union in combating secondary embargoes, we will work together under the Action Plan in order to avoid unilateralism and the extraterritorial application of laws.

In order to secure the long-term future of our bilateral relationship we agree to place special emphasis on the people to people links that form a bridge across the Atlantic. In order to renew our ties based on shared culture and values, we will encourage contacts between our citizens at every level, especially among our youth. We will also remove unnecessary barriers between people by making it easier for our respective business men and women to make contact and to identify new commercial opportunities.

In recognition of the impact information technology has had on scientific and academic development, we will take imaginative new steps to enhance collaboration on science and technology. Cognisant of the new realities of globalization and the emerging information society, including the opportunities offered to increase prosperity, we will co-operate to develop information and communication strategies that respect cultural and linguistic diversity.

To ensure that our elected officials remain enganged and sensitive to the new currents of our dynamic relationship, we will actively promote contacts between our Parliamentarians, as well as our young people, and our artists and creators, on issues of common concern.

In order to achieve our common goals we today adopt this Joint Political Declaration and its Joint Action Plan aimed at furthering our bilateral co-operation. These documents do not affect any legal positions of Canada, the European Community, or its Member States, nor do they prejudice the respective legal positions of Canada and the Kingdom of Spain in the Fisheries Jurisdiction Case before the International Court of Justice. The Action Plan is based on our community of values, which is the source of our strength in so many fields. We are committed to sharing these values, and the benefits they bestow, with other countries that may seek our co-operation and support. In this respect, we will consider with the United States, on a case-by-case basis, trilateralisation in specific areas covered by the Joint Action Plan.

As our dynamic relationship continues to evolve we stand ready to respond to new challenges and opportunities by updating and amending our mutual agenda to meet future demands.

Signed in Ottawa by
Prime Minister Chrétien,
Council President Bruton, and
Commission Vice-President Brittan,
17 December 1996

Appendix 6

Principal Commission Delegations Outside the EU

Albania
Tirana
Tel: 355–42–283 20, 428 70/71
Fax: 355–42–427 52

Algeria
Algiers
Tel: 213–2–692170, 691063,
691692
Fax: 213–2–691947

Argentina
Buenos Aires
Tel: 54–1–805 37 59, 805 37 61
Fax: 54–1–801 15 94

Australia
Canberra
Tel: 61–6–271 27 21, 271 27 77
Fax: 61–6–273 44 45, 273 49 44

Bangladesh
Dhaka
Tel: 880–2–88 47 30/31/32
Fax: 880–2–88 31 18

Bolivia
La Paz
Tel: 59–12–43 00 88
Fax: 59–12–43 00 89

Brazil
Brasilia
Tel: 55–61–248 31 22
Fax: 55–61–248 07 00

Bulgaria
Sofia
Tel: 359–2–73 98 41/2/3/4/5
Fax: 359–2–73 83 95

Canada
Ottawa
Tel: 1–613–238 64 64
Fax: 1–613–238 51 91

Chile
Santiago
Tel: 56–2–206 02 67
Fax: 56–2–228 25 71

China
Beijing
Tel: 86–10–532 44 43
Fax: 86–10–532 43 42

Colombia
Bogotá
Tel: 57–1–236 90 40, 256 84 77
Fax: 57–1–610 00 59

Costa Rica
San José
Tel: 506–233 27 55
Fax: 506–221 65 95

Cyprus
Nicosia
Tel: 357–2–36 92 02/03/04
Fax: 357–2–36 89 26

Czech Republic
Prague
Tel: 42–2–32 50 51, 32 48 30
Fax: 42–2–311 08 60

Egypt
Cairo
Tel: 20–2–341 93 93, 340 83 88
Fax: 20–2–340 03 85

Georgia
Tbilisi
Tel: 995–8832 99 96 02, 93 55 82
Fax: 995–8832 99 08 33

Hong Kong
Tel: 852–25 37 60 83
Fax: 852–25 22 13 02

Hungary
Budapest
Tel: 36–1–166 44 87
Fax: 36–1–166 42 21

India
New Delhi
Tel: 91–11–462 92 37/38
Fax: 91–11–462 92 06

Indonesia
Jakarta
Tel: 62–21–570 60 76, 570 60 68
Fax: 62–21–570 6075

Israel
Tel Aviv
Tel: 972–3–696 41 66
Fax: 972–3–695 19 83

Japan
Tokyo
Tel: 81–3–32 39 04 61
Fax: 81–3–32 61 51 94

Jordan
Amman
Tel: 962–6–66 81 91/92
Fax: 962–6 68 67 46

Kazakhstan
Almaty
Tel: 7–3272–63 65 55, 63 78 65
Fax: 7–3272–63 06 84, 63 09 94

Korea
Seoul
Tel: 82–2–271 07 81/82
Fax: 82–2–271 07 86

Lebanon
Beirut
Tel: 961–9–93 71 47
Fax: 961–9–93 71 54

Malta
Tel: 356–34 51 11, 34 48 91
Fax: 356–34 48 97

Mexico
Mexico City
Tel: 52–5–540 33 45/46/47
Fax: 52–5–540 65 64

Morocco
Rabat
Tel: 212–7 761217, 761246
Fax: 212–7 76 11 56

Norway
Oslo
Tel: 47–22 83 35 83
Fax: 47–22 83 40 55

Pakistan
Islamabad
Tel: 92–51–21 18 28, 21 24 15
Fax: 92–51–82 26 04

Palestinian Authority
East Jerusalem
Tel: 972–2–28 16 17
Fax: 972–2–28 16 20

Peru
Lima
Tel: 51–1–221 72 02, 221 64 62
Fax: 51–1–422 87 78

Philippines
Manila
Tel: 63–2–812 64 21
Fax: 63–2–812 66 86

Poland
Warsaw
Tel: 48–2–621 64 01/02
Fax: 48–2–625 04 30

Romania
Bucharest
Tel: 40–1–211 18 02, 211 18 04
Fax: 40–1–211 18 09

Russia
Moscow
Tel: 7–502–220 46 58, 220 46 55
Fax: 7–502–220 46 54

Slovenia
Ljubljana
Tel: 386–61–125 13 03
Fax: 386–61–125 20 85

South Africa
Pretoria
Tel: 27–12–46 43 19
Fax: 27–12–46 99 23

Syria
Damascus
Tel: 963–11–32 76 40/41
Fax: 963–11–42 06 83

Thailand
Bangkok
Tel: 66–2–255 91 00
Fax: 66–2–255 91 14

Tunisia
Tunis
Tel: 216–1–78 86 00
Fax: 216–1–78 82 01

Turkey
Ankara
Tel: 90–312–437 68 40/41/42/43
Fax: 90–312–437 79 40

Ukraine
Kiev
Tel: 70–44–291 89 63
Fax: 70–44–291 89 92

United States
Washington
Tel: 1–202–862 95 00/01/02
Fax: 1–202–429 17 66

Uruguay
Montevideo
Tel: 598–2–40 75 80
Fax: 598–2–41 20 08

Venezuela
Caracas
Tel: 58–2–91 51 33, 91 53 98
Fax: 58–2–91 88 76

Yugoslavia
Belgrade
Tel: 381–11–64 86 66
Fax: 381–11–65 14 58

Delegations accredited to international organizations:

Switzerland (United Nations and other international organizations)
Geneva
Tel: 41–22–918 22 11
Fax: 41–22–734 22 36

France (OECD and UNESCO)
Paris
Tel: 33–1–44 05 31 60
Fax: 33–1–44 05 31 79

United States (United Nations)
New York
Tel: 1–212–371 38 04
Fax: 1–212–758 27 18

Italy (FAO)
Rome
Tel: 39–6–678 26 72, 679 37 55
Fax: 39–6–679 78 30

Austria (IAEA)
Vienna
Tel: 43–1–505 8411/12
Fax: 43–1–505 8411

(List does not include Commission offices in the ACP countries)

Appendix 7

List of Abbreviations

AAMS	Association of African and Malagasy States
ACP	African, Caribbean, and Pacific (states)
AIPO	ASEAN Interparliamentary Organization
APEC	Asia-Pacific Economic Cooperation
ASEAN	Association of Southeast Asian Nations
ASEM	Asia-Europe (summit) meetings
Benelux	Belgium-Netherlands-Luxembourg economic union
CACM	Central American Common Market
CAP	Common Agricultural Policy
CCT	Common Customs Tariff
CFSP	Common Foreign and Security Policy
CIS	Commonwealth of Independent States
CMEA	Council for Mutual Economic Assistance
Comecon	Council for Mutual Economic Assistance
Coreper	Committee of Permanent Representatives
CSCE	Conference on Security and Cooperation in Europe (now OSCE)
EAEC	European Atomic Energy Community
EAGGF	European Agricultural Guidance and Guarantee Fund
EBRD	European Bank for Reconstruction and Development
EC	European Community
ECHO	European Community Humanitarian Office
ECIP	European Community Investment Partners
ECSC	European Coal and Steel Community
ECU	European currency unit
EDC	European Defence Community
EDF	European Development Fund
EEA	European Economic Area
EEC	European Economic Community
EFTA	European Free Trade Association

EES	European Economic Space
EIB	European Investment Bank
EMU	Economic and Monetary Union
EP	European Parliament
EPC	European Political Cooperation
ERDF	European Regional Development Fund
ETP	Executive Training Programme
EU	European Union
FAO	Food and Agricultural Organization
FDI	foreign direct investment
GATT	General Agreement on Tariffs and Trade
GCC	Gulf Cooperation Council
GRULA	group of Latin American ambassadors (Brussels)
GSP	generalized system of preferences
IAEA	International Atomic Energy Agency
IBRD	International Bank for Reconstruction and Development (World Bank)
IGC	intergovernmental conference
ILO	International Labour Organisation
IMF	International Monetary Fund
IRELA	Institute for European–Latin American Relations (Madrid)
JCC	joint cooperation committee
LDC	less-developed country
LLDC	least-developed country
MEP	member of the European Parliament
Mercosur	Southern Cone Common Market
MFA	Multifiber Arrangement
MITI	Ministry of International Trade and Industry (Japan)
NAFTA	North American Free Trade Agreement
NATO	North Atlantic Treaty Organization
NAFO	Northwest Atlantic Fisheries Organization
NGO	nongovernmental organization
NIE	newly industrialized economy
NIEO	new international economic order
NIS	Newly Independent States (of the former Soviet Union)
NTA	New Transatlantic Agenda
NTB	nontariff barrier
OAS	Organization of American States
ODA	official development assistance
OECD	Organization for Economic Cooperation and Development
OEEC	Organization for European Economic Cooperation
PHARE	Poland and Hungary: Aid for Reconstruction of the Economy
PLO	Palestine Liberation Organization

SAARC	South Asian Association for Regional Cooperation
SADC	Southern African Development Community
SEA	Single European Act
SICA	Central American Integration System
TAC	total allowable catch
TACIS	Technical Assistance to the Commonwealth of Independent States
UNCTAD	United Nations Conference on Trade and Development
WEU	Western European Union
WHO	World Health Organization
WTO	World Trade Organization

Selected Bibliography

Allen, David, and Alfred Pijpers (eds.), *European Foreign Policy Making and the Arab-Israeli Conflict* (The Hague: Martinus Nijhoff, 1984).

Allen, David, Reinhardt Rummel, and Wolfgang Wessels, *European Political Cooperation: Towards a Foreign Policy for Western Europe?* (London: Butterworths, 1982).

Al-Mani', Saleh A., *The Euro-Arab Dialogue: A Study in Associative Diplomacy* (London: Pinter Publishers, 1983).

Andersson, Thomas, *Managing Trade Relations in the New World Economy* (London: Routledge, 1993).

Angarita, C., and P. Coffey, *Europe and the Andean Countries: A Comparison of Economic Policies and Institutions* (London: Pinter Publishers, 1988).

Baldwin, Robert E., C. B. Hamilton, and Andre Sapir (eds.), *Issues in US-EC Trade Relations* (Chicago, IL: University of Chicago Press, 1988).

Barfield, Claude E., and Mark Perlman, *Industry, Services, and Agriculture in the 1990s: The United States Faces a New Europe* (Washington, DC: American Enterprise Institute, 1992).

Bethlen, Steven, and Ivan Volgyes (eds.), *Europe and the Superpowers: Political, Economic, and Military Policies in the 1980s* (Boulder, CO: Westview, 1985).

Bhargava, Kant K., and Ross Masood Husain, *SAARC and European Union: Learning and Cooperation* (New Delhi: Har-Anand Publications, 1994).

Blinken, Antony J., *Ally Versus Ally: America, Europe and the Siberian Pipeline Crisis* (New York: Praeger, 1987).

Bloed, Arie, and Ramses A. Wessel, *The Changing Functions of the Western European Union (WEU): Introduction and Basic Documents* (Dordrecht: Martinus Nijhoff, 1994).

Booth, Ken, and Steve Smith, *International Relations Theory Today* (University Park: Pennsylvania State University Press, 1995).

Brandon, Henry (ed.), *In Search of a New World Order: The Future of U.S.-European Relations* (Washington, DC: Brookings Institution, 1992).

Brüne, Stefan, Joachim Betz, and Winrich Kühne (eds.), *Africa and Europe: Relations of Two Continents in Transition* (Münster: LIT Verlag, 1994).

Bulmer, Simon, and Wolfgang Wessels, *The European Council: Decision-Making in European Politics* (London: Macmillan, 1987).

Burgess, Michael, *Federalism and European Union: Political Ideas, Influences and Strategies in the European Community, 1972–1978* (London: Routledge, 1989).

Burlingame, Scott, *North American Integration and the Lessons from Europe* (Copenhagen: Jurist- og Okonomforbundets Forlag/DJOF Pub., 1994).

Burstein, Daniel, *Euroquake: Europe's Explosive Economic Challenge Will Change the World* (New York: Simon & Schuster, 1991).

Cahan, Alfred, *The WEU and NATO: Strengthening the Second Pillar of the Alliance* (Washington, DC: Atlantic Council, 1990).

Calingaert, Michael, *European Integration Revisited* (Boulder, CO: Westview, 1996).

Corbett, Richard, Francis Jacobs, and Michael Shackleton, *The European Parliament* (3rd edition) (London: Cartermill, 1995).

Cromwell, William C., *The United States and the European Pillar* (Basingstoke, England: Macmillan, 1992).

De Ruyt, Jean, *European Political Cooperation: Toward a Unified European Foreign Policy* (Washington, DC: Atlantic Council, 1989).

Demaret, P., J. Bourgeois, and I. van Bael, *Trade Laws of the European Community and the United States in a Comparative Perspective: Conference Organized with the Support of the Commission of the EC, 14–15–16 September 1989* (Brussels: E. Story-Scientia, 1992).

Dinan, Desmond, *Ever Closer Union: An Introduction to the European Community* (Boulder, CO: Lynne Rienner, 1994).

Douglas, Gordon K., *The New Interdependence: The European Community and the United States* (Lexington, MA: Lexington Books, 1979).

Edwards, Geoffrey, and David Spence (eds.), *The European Commission* (Harlow: Longman, 1994).

Edwards, Geoffrey, and Elfriede Regelsberger, *Europe's Global Links: The European Community and Inter-regional Cooperation* (New York: St. Martin's Press, 1990).

El-Agraa, Ali M. (ed.), *The Economics of the European Community* (4th edition) (Hemel Hempstead: Harvester Wheatsheaf, 1994).

Faber, G. J., *The European Community and Development Cooperation: Integration in the Light of Development Policies of the Community and Its Member States* (Assen, Netherlands: Van Gorcum, 1982).

Faini, Ricardo, and Richard Portes, *European Union Trade with Eastern Europe: Adjustment and Opportunities* (London: Centre for Economic Policy Research, 1995).

Featherstone, Kevin, and Roy H. Ginsberg, *The United States and the European Community in the 1990s: Partners in Transition* (New York: St. Martin's Press, 1993).

Federal Trust and Study Group, *The EC and the Developing Countries: A Policy for the Future* (London: Federal Trust, 1988).

Feld, Werner, *The Future of European Security and Defense Policy* (Boulder, CO: Lynne Rienner, 1993).

Frey-Wouters, Ellen, *The European Community and the Third World: The Lomé Convention and Its Impact* (New York: Praeger, 1980).

Fukuyama, Francis, *The US-Japan Security Relationship After the Cold War* (Santa Monica, CA: Rand, 1993).

Fursdon, Edward, *The European Defence Community: A History* (London: Macmillan, 1980).

Gianaris, Nicholas V., *The European Community, Eastern Europe, and Russia: Economic and Political Changes* (Westport, CT: Praeger, 1994).

——, *The European Community and the United States: Economic Relations* (New York: Praeger, 1991).

Ginsberg, Roy H., *Foreign Policy Actions of the European Community: The Politics of Scale* (Boulder, CO: Lynne Rienner, 1989).

Grant Richard L., *The European Union and China: A European Strategy for the Twenty-first Century* (London: Royal Institute of International Affairs, Asia-Pacific Programme, 1995).

Grilli, Enzo R., *The European Community and the Developing Countries* (Cambridge: Cambridge University Press, 1993).

Groom, A., and P. Taylor, *Functionalism: Theory and Practice in International Relations* (New York: Crane, Roussak, 1975).

Haas, Ernst B., *The Uniting of Europe* (Stanford, CA: Stanford University Press, 1958).

Hanrieder, Wolfram F., *Germany, America, Europe* (New Haven, CT: Yale University Press, 1989).

Harrisson, Martin M., *The Reluctant Ally: France and Atlantic Security* (Baltimore, MD: Johns Hopkins University Press, 1981).

Hill, Christopher (ed.), *National Foreign Policies and EPC* (London: Allen & Unwin, 1983).

Hine, R. C., *The Political Economy of European Trade: An Introduction to the Trade Policies of the EEC* (New York: St. Martin's Press, 1985).

Holland, Martin, *The European Community and South Africa: European Political Cooperation Under Strain* (London: Pinter Publishers, 1988).

———— (ed.), *The Future of European Political Cooperation* (New York: St. Martin's Press, 1991).

Hufbauer, Gary Clyde, *The New Europe in the World Economy* (Washington, DC: Institute for International Economics, 1993).

Ikenberry, J., D. A. Lake, and M. Mastanduno (eds.), *The State and American Foreign Economic Policy* (Ithaca, NY: Cornell University Press, 1988).

Ismael, Tareq Y., *International Relations of the Contemporary Middle East* (Syracuse, NY: Syracuse University Press, 1986).

Joffe, Josef, *The Limited Partnership: Europe, the United States and the Burdens of Alliance* (Cambridge, MA: Ballinger, 1987).

Jovanovic, Miroslav N., *International Economic Integration* (New York: Routledge, 1992).

Kaiser, Manfred, and H. Werner, *ASEAN and the EC: Labour Costs and Structural Change in the European Community* (Singapore: ASEAN Economic Research Unit, Institute of Southeast Asian Studies, 1989).

Kegley, Charles W., Jr., *Controversies in International Relations Theory: Realism and the Neoliberal Challenge* (New York: St. Martin's Press, 1995).

Keohane, Robert O., *After Hegemony: Cooperation and Discord in the World Political Economy* (Princeton: Princeton University Press, 1984).

Keohane, Robert O., and Stanley Hoffmann (eds.), *The New European Community: Decision-making and Institutional Change* (Boulder, CO: Westview, 1991).

Kirby, Stephen, Terry McNeill, and Sally Harris, *Europe After the Gulf War: Re-assessing Security Options* (Cheltenham: Edward Elgar, 1992).

Kolodziej, Edward A., and Roger E. Kanet, *Coping with Conflict After the Cold War* (Baltimore, MD: Johns Hopkins University Press, 1996).

Langhammer, Rolf J., and Hans Christoph Rieger, *ASEAN and the EC: Trade in Tropical Agricultural Products* (Singapore: ASEAN Economic Research Unit, Institute of Southeast Asian Studies, 1988).

Lebow, Richard Ned, and Thomas Risse-Kappen, *International Relations Theory and the End of the Cold War* (New York: Columbia University Press, 1995).

Lepgold, Joseph, *The Declining Hegemon: The United States and European Defense, 1960–1990* (New York: Greenwood, 1990).

Levine, Michael K., *Inside International Trade Policy Formulation: A History of the 1982 US-EC Steel Arrangements* (New York: Praeger, 1985).

Lister, Marjorie, *The European Community and the Developing World: The Role of the Lomé Convention* (Aldershot: Avebury, 1988).

Lodge, Juliet, *The European Community and New Zealand* (London: Pinter Publishers, 1982).

—— (ed.), *The European Community and the Challenge of the Future* (London: Pinter Publishers, 1989).

Ludlow, Peter, *Beyond 1992: Europe and Its World Partners* (Brussels: Centre for European Policy Studies, 1989).

Mason, T. David, and Abdul M. Turay (eds.), *Japan, NAFTA, and Europe: Trilateral Cooperation or Confrontation?* (New York: St. Martin's Press, 1994).

Matthews, Jacqueline D., *Association System of the European Community* (New York: Praeger, 1977).

Mayes, David G. (ed.), *The External Implications of European Integration* (Hemel Hempstead: Harvester Wheatsheaf, 1993).

McAleese, Dermot (ed.), *Africa and the European Community After 1992* (Washington, DC: Economic Development Institute, 1993).

McGovern, Edward, *International Trade Regulation: GATT, the United States, and the European Community* (Exeter: Globefield Press, 1982).

Mennes, L. B. M., and Jacob Kil, *European Trade Policies and the Developing World* (London: Croom Helm, 1988).

Merritt, Giles, *Eastern Europe and the USSR: The Challenge of Freedom* (London: Kogan Page; Luxembourg: Distributed by the Office for Official Publications of the European Community, 1991).

Michalski, Anna, and Helen Wallace, *The European Community: The Challenge of Enlargement* (London: RIIA, 1993).

Milward, Alan S., *The Reconstruction of Western Europe, 1945–51* (Berkeley: University of California Press).

Mitrany, David, *A Working Peace System* (Chicago, IL: Quadrangle Books, 1966).

Morgan, Roger, *The United States and West Germany, 1945–1973: A Study in Alliance Politics* (London: Oxford University Press, 1974).

Morgenthau, Hans J., *Politics Among Nations* (5th edition) (New York: Knopf, 1978).

Mower, Alfred Glenn, *The European Community and Latin America: A Case Study in Global Role Expansion* (Westport, CT: Greenwood Press, 1982).

Neuwahl, Nanette A., *European Union and Human Rights* (Dordrecht: Martinus Nijhoff, 1995).

Nicholson, Frances, and Roger East, *From the Six to the Twelve: The Enlargement of the European Communities* (Harlow: Longman, 1987).

Nicolaides, Phedon, *The Trade Policy of the European Community: Legal Basis, Instruments, Commercial Relations* (Maastricht: European Institute of Public Administration, 1993).

Nugent, Neill, *The Government and Politics of the EC* (2nd edition) (Durham, NC: Duke University Press, 1992).

Nuttall, Simon, *European Political Cooperation* (Oxford: Clarendon Press, 1992).

Paemen, Hugo, and Alexandra Bensch, *GATT to WTO: The European Community in the Uruguay Round* (Leuven, Belgium: Leuven University Press, 1995).

Palankai, Tibor, *The EC and Central European Integration: The Hungarian Case* (Boulder, CO: Westview, 1991).

Palmer, John, *Europe Without America? The Crisis in Atlantic Relations* (Oxford: Oxford University Press, 1987).

Perle, Richard, *Reshaping Western Security: The United States Faces a United Europe* (Lanham, MD: University Press of America, 1991).

Peterson, John, *Europe and America in the 1990s: Prospects for Partnership* (Brookfield, VT: Edward Elgar, 1992).

Pijpers, Alfred, Elfriede Regelsberger, and Wolfgang Wessels (eds.), *European Political Cooperation in the 1980s: A Common Foreign Policy for Western Europe?* (Dordrecht: Martinus Nijhoff, 1989).

Pinder, John, *The European Community and Eastern Europe* (New York: Council on Foreign Relations Press, 1991).

Pomfret, Richard W. T., *Mediterranean Policy of the European Community: A Study of Discrimination in Trade* (New York: St. Martin's Press, 1986).

Portes, Richard, *The EC and Eastern Europe After 1992* (London: Centre for European Policy Research, 1990).

Purcell, Susan K., and Françoise Simon (eds.), *Europe and Latin America in the World Economy* (Boulder, CO: Lynne Rienner, 1995).

Redmond, John, *Prospective Europeans: New Members for the European Union* (New York: Harvester Wheatsheaf, 1994).

———, *The Next Mediterranean Enlargement of the EC: Turkey, Cyprus and Malta?* (Aldershot: Dartmouth, 1993).

——— (ed.), *The External Relations of the European Community: The International Response to 1992* (London: Macmillan, 1992).

Rogers, J. Philip, *The Future of European Security: The Pursuit of Peace in an Era of Revolutionary Change* (New York: St. Martin's Press, 1993).

Rosenau, James N., *The Study of Global Interdependence: Essays on the Transnationalism of World Affairs* (New York: Nichols, 1980).

Rothacher, Albrecht, *Economic Diplomacy Between the European Community and Japan 1959–1981* (London: Gower, 1983).

Rummel, Reinhardt (ed.), *Toward Political Union: Planning a Common Foreign and Security Policy* (Boulder, CO: Westview, 1992).

———, *The Evolution of an International Actor: Western Europe's New Assertiveness* (Boulder, CO: Westview, 1990).

———, *Western European Security Policy: Asserting European Priorities* (Boulder, CO: Westview, 1989).

Schaetzel, J. Robert, *The Unhinged Alliance: America and the European Community* (New York: Harper & Row, 1975).

Schmitt-Rink, Gerhard, *EC-ASEAN: Trade Among the European Community and the Association of South-East-Asian Nations 1974–80: Trends and Structures* (Bochum: Studienverlag Dr. N. Brockmeyer, 1982).

Schwok, Rene, *U.S.-EC Relations in the Post–Cold War Era: Conflict or Partnership?* (Boulder, CO: Westview, 1991).

Secondo, Tarditi (ed.), et al., *Agricultural Trade Liberalization and the European Community* (New York: Oxford University Press, 1989).

Shanti, Jagannathan, *EC and India in the 1990s, Towards Corporate Synergy* (New Delhi: Indus, 1993).

Smith, Hazel, *European Union Foreign Policy and Central America* (London: Macmillian, 1995).

Smith, Michael, and Stephen Woolcock, *Redefining the U.S.-E.C. Relationship* (London: RIIA, 1993).

Snyder, Richard C., H. W. Bruck, and Burton Sapin, *Foreign Policy Decision Making* (New York: Free Press, 1962).

Steinberg, James, *An Ever Closer Union: European Integration and Its Implications for the Future of U.S.-European Relations* (Santa Monica, CA: Rand, 1993).

Taylor, Robert, *China, Japan, and the European Community* (London: Athlone Press, 1990).

Tovias, Alfred, *Foreign Economic Relations of the European Community: The Impact of Spain and Portugal* (Boulder, CO: Lynne Rienner, 1990).

Tsoukalis, Loukas, *Europe, America and the World Economy* (Oxford: Basil Blackwell, 1986).

———, *The European Community and Its Mediterranean Enlargement* (London: Allen & Unwin, 1981).

van Ham, Peter, *The EC, Eastern Europe and European Unity: Discord, Collaboration and Integration Since 1947* (London: Pinter Publishers, 1993).

Viotti, Paul R., and Mark V. Kauppi, *International Relations Theory* (2nd edition) (New York: Macmillan, 1993).

Wallace, Helen (ed.), *The Wider Western Europe: Reshaping the EC/EFTA Relationship* (London: Pinter Publishers, for the RIIA, 1991).

Wallace, Helen, William Wallace, and Carol Webb (eds.), *Policy-making in the European Communities* (New York: Praeger, 1981).

Winand, Pascaline, *Eisenhower, Kennedy and the United States of Europe* (New York: St. Martin's Press, 1993).

Woolcock, Stephen, *Trading Partners or Trading Blows? Market Access in EC-US Relations* (New York: Council on Foreign Relations, 1991).

Yannopoulos, George, *Customs Unions and Trade Conflicts: The Enlargement of the European Community* (London: Routledge, 1988).

——— (ed.), *Europe and America: 1992* (New York: Manchester University Press, 1991).

Young, Soogil, and Moonsoo Kang (eds.), *The Single European Market and Its Implications for Korea as an NIE* (Seoul: Korea Development Institute/Friedrich Ebert Stiftung, 1991).

Zartman, William (ed.), *Europe and Africa: The New Phase* (Boulder, CO: Lynne Rienner, 1992).

Ziring, Lawrence (ed.), *The New Europe and the World* (Kalamazoo, MI: New Issues Press, 1993).

Index

African, Caribbean, and Pacific states (ACP): aid to, 183–188; economies of, 179; EU relations with, 9, 178–179; exclusions from, 160, 179; formation of, 178. *See also* Lomé convention; Yaoundé convention
Agreements, 3–4, 5–9, 101; assent procedure and, 27–28; association, 17–19, 27, 57–60; cooperation, 19; environmental, 43–44; legal bases for, 15–20; mixed, 58; types of, 17–20. *See also specific country*
Agriculture: Stabex scheme and, 185–186; U.S.-EU disputes and, 106, 107–108. *See also* Common Agricultural Policy
Airbus dispute, 107
Albania, EU relations with, 63–64
Andean Pact, 7, 12n.5, 134–135
Arab-Israeli conflict, 74, 75, 85, 99–100
Arab League, 75, 77, 78
Arafat, Yasser, 85
ASEAN. *See* Association of Southeast Asian Nations
Asia-EU relations, 139–165; aid component of, 144–145; background of, 139–140; bilateral basis of, 139, 140, 142; centrality of trade in, 140–142; cooperation agreement of 1980 with, 146–147, 148; Euro-Asian summit and, 6, 45, 140, 144; framework of, 142–145; GSP and, 149, 161, 162; political dimension of, 140. *See also* Association of Southeast Asian Nations (ASEAN);

South Asia; South Asian Association for Regional Cooperation (SAARC)
Associated countries, rights and responsibilities of, 170
Association agreements, 3, 17–19, 27, 57–60. *See also specific country*
Association of African and Malagasy States (AAMS), Yaoundé convention and, 171–174, 177
Association of Caribbean States, 136
Association of Southeast Asian Nations (ASEAN): East Timor and Myanmar issues in, 148–149; EU relations with, 146–148; EU trade with, 141–142, 149; nations and economies of, 145–146; security issues and, 147
Australia: interparliamentary links with, 165; major trading partners of, 163; proposed framework agreement with, 19, 29n.5, 165; regional orientation of, 6; trade relations with, 163–165
Austria, EC membership and, 50, 54

Baker, James, 108
Bangladesh, EU relations with, 161, 162
Barcelona Declaration, 81–84
Bosnia-Herzegovina: joint peace efforts in, 62–63; recognition of, 61
Britain, EC accession of, 48–50, 95, 173, 177
Brittan, Leon, 115
Bush, George, 108

245

About the Book

The European Union (EU), though comprised of fifteen separate, sovereign states, is constrained by treaty to act "as one" in key areas. And as trader, investor, aid donor, and most recently, foreign policy maker, it has come to play, in a very short time, a pivotal role on the world stage. This book offers a succinct summary of all of the EU's external activities and of the impact European integration has come to have far beyond the EU's borders.

Piening traces how the EU's external relations have grown over the forty-odd years of its existence to become what they are today. Discussions of trade policy, emerging foreign and security policy, the role the Union plays in the developing countries and in its own "near abroad," and the kinds of influence it exerts internationally all demonstrate the complex web of formal and informal ties that now link it with all but half a dozen of the world's countries.

Global Europe provides a unique, and uniquely engaging, overview of an increasingly important international actor.

Christopher Piening heads the European Parliament's interparliamentary relations division for non-European countries. Before joining the EP in the 1970s, he wrote for the *Financial Times* and *Der Spiegel*. He pursued postgraduate research in European Community politics at the University of Kent at Canterbury (UK) and in 1995–1996 was European Union Fellow and visiting professor at the University of Washington's Jackson School of International Studies.